Transcultural Psychiatry

Ari Kiev

Transcultural
Psychiatry

THE FREE PRESS
A Division of Macmillan Publishing Co., Inc.
NEW YORK

The Free Press
A Division of Macmillan Publishing Co., Inc.
866 Third Avenue, New York, New York 10022

Collier–Macmillan Canada Ltd., Toronto, Ontario

Library of Congress Catalog Card Number: 73–163235

First Free Press Paperback Edition 1973

Printed in the United States of America

case bound printing number
1 2 3 4 5 6 7 8 9 10

paperback printing number
1 2 3 4 5 6 7 8 9 10

For my father—
whose love of books and knowledge
has been a continual source
of inspiration to me

CONTENTS

PREFACE

CULTURE DETERMINES THE SPECIFIC WAYS in which individuals perceive and conceive of the environment and strongly influences the forms of conflict, behavior, and psychopathology that occur in members of the culture. These issues are most clearly documented by the study of other cultures in varying degrees of social, economic, and cultural development. Such studies are of value in delineating the boundaries between cultural and biological phenomena. They provide opportunity to extend the clinical picture of psychiatric conditions with special emphasis on the relationship between environmental factors and psychiatric disorders.

Social and cultural phenomena influence disorders which, in turn, have a significant effect on the social system. Conflicting social values may intensify social and group conflict and a variety of responses which determine whether an individual will be able to function in a particular culture.

Ultimately, the initiation, perpetuation, and consequences of development turn on the behavior of people, acting individually and as members of sociocultural systems. Knowledge of specific factors that facilitate adjustment, deviance, maladjustment and social crisis in specific sociocultural contexts can thus significantly affect the process of development. Data on exotic disorders can be of immediate value to those planning services by pointing to specific cultural stress points and the the most vulnerable groups in the population. Similarly, data on the prevalence of disorders may be of great value in underlining stress areas in the culture which might benefit from special reinforcement through special treatment, rehabilitative or supportive programs.

This book then is an attempt to formulate the boundaries of transcultural psychiatry, to assess the current state of knowledge in the field, to outline feasible areas for further research, and to specify priorities and needs in the developing world. The urgency of these considerations cannot be minimized. The population explosion and the problems of urbanization, industrialization, and modernization in the third or developing world which embraces some two thirds of the world's population and much of the world's resources, make it imperative that data hitherto collected for other purposes be examined in terms of their implications for developing services.

This book draws heavily on my own studies over the past decade in various aspects of transcultural psychiatry. During this time, I have been influenced by many different people representing a number of disciplines and approaches; and this I believe accounts for my own particular eclecticism. I am especially indebted to Talcott Parsons, John W. M. Whiting, the late Harold G. Wolff, George Devereux, Oskar Diethelm, Jerome Frank, John C. Whitehorn, Aubrey Lewis, Michael Shepherd, Ernest Gruenberg, and Nathan S. Kline whose intellectual stimulus and unique perspectives have been especially significant for me. I am grateful to Dr. William Lhamon, Chairman of the Department of Psychiatry, Cornell University Medical College, who has provided the most ideal kind of academic setting in which to work on this book during the past several years.

As before, I am deeply indebted to my wife, Phylliseve Kiev, a constant source of support who has shared the travel, reflections, and efforts that led to this book.

I am most appreciative for the editorial assistance of Helen Richardson who helped me with several drafts of the manuscript. Finally, special thanks are due Joan Leyden who patiently and skillfully typed draft after draft of the manuscript.

Transcultural Psychiatry

CHAPTER 1

THEORETICAL CONSIDERATIONS

THE NATURE OF PSYCHIATRIC DISORDERS

PSYCHIATRY DEALS WITH A WIDE RANGE of clinically recognizable disorders of mood, thought, and behavior. These disorders are so far distinguishable from each other only in terms of descriptive criteria. Firm etiological knowledge, of the sort that would permit more certain classification and diagnosis, is still a hope for the future. It is therefore essential to define certain basic assumptions about psychiatric disorders that will serve to delimit the kinds of inferences that can be drawn from the material considered in this book, and at the same time to emphasize the distinction that needs to be made between sociocultural and psychological phenomena.

Psychiatric disorders as a whole can be divided into two main groups: biological disorders of memory, perception and feeling; and secondary or compensatory processes of rationalization and action, which are influenced by social and cultural factors. This division of psychological functioning into an organic substratum and a superimposed, culturally conditioned layer of response and behavior enables us to understand why the *form* of psychiatric disorders remains essentially constant throughout the world, irrespective of the cultural context within which the disorders appear. In this view, the schizophrenic and manic-depressive psychotic disorders are fixed in form by the biological nature of man. The secondary features of

Notes for Chapter 1 will be found on page 197.

psychiatric illness, such as the *content* of the delusions and hallucinations, are determined by the pathoplastic or compensatory effects of particular cultures; as such, they differ from culture to culture. Cultural factors also determine which psychological defenses or adaptive patterns are likely to be most prominent in members of a given society. It is probable that these patterns of defense and adaptation are initiated during the individual's early socialization experiences.

The psychophysiological patterns of response have been subject to much theoretical consideration by various workers, even though the fundamental neurophysiological and neuroanatomical basis of psychopathological behavior patterns has not yet been determined. It is quite clear that there are fundamental distinctions among the response patterns of individuals with different constitutional predispositions. Pavlov[1] suggested a useful scheme for differentiating temperamental types in accordance with their responses to stress or conflict. His studies indicated that a *choleric* or strong excitatory temperamental type responds with marked excitement or aggression; a *sanguine* or lively type responds in a purposeful and controlled way; a calm, imperturbable or *phlegmatic* type does not respond at all; and the *melancholic* or weak inhibitory type responds with passivity and tension avoidance, while to really powerful stresses it responds with brain inhibition and fear paralysis. Moreover, in these weak inhibitory types, the protective or transmarginal brain inhibition that generally takes place in response to lighter stresses develops much more rapidly than it does in the other temperamental types.

Transmarginal inhibition occurs in stages. In the first or *equivalent* phase of cortical activity, all stimuli lead to the same response, although discrimination is possible between important and less important stimuli. When stronger stresses are introduced in the next or *paradoxical* phase, weak stimuli produce livelier responses than do stronger stimuli, presumably because the latter produce a protective inhibition at a time when the former are still producing positive responses. The final or *ultraparadoxical* stage appears when positive conditioned responses become negative and negative ones become positive. Behavior is then the *reverse* of previous conditioning.

Etiological theories of psychiatric disorder, whether they are biological (genetic, biochemical, constitutional) or psychological, have generally focused on something that is going on *within* the patient. Most of these theories have not concerned themselves with *external* sociological or environmental stress, as a factor producing psychiatric disorder. One result of this is that no clearcut environmental etiologies have yet been established. The presence of an environmental stress can be assessed only by observation of pathological responses to it; where the conditions produce no effect, the inclination is to note that these factors were not stressful.

My own view is that non-specific stresses produce biological responses in the individual, and that, once they are set in motion, these responses operate independently of the original stresses. Biological responses occur at the cellular and biochemical levels and it is from there that they exert an influence on the individual's psychological process. The clinical manifestations of the resultant symptoms, on the other hand, are colored by socio-cultural factors.

Sociological theorists tend to view psychiatric illness as one form of social deviation, thereby placing their stress on the phenomenon of social labeling. In this model, the patient is regarded as mentally ill primarily because he has broken the local code of social conduct or norms. Implicit here is a conception of psychiatric disorders as motivated acts of norm-breaking, rather than as products of underlying biological reactions, which remain outside the individual's control. The violation of social codes is certainly one aspect of many disorders, but it is not a *sine qua non* for their existence. What these theories promulgate is a static view of patient-environment interaction, which has little relevance to reality, except insofar as it pertains to the emergence of secondary patterns of disability or to the cultural coloration of symptomatology. It is true that cultural responses to the disorder—for example, the assignment of the patient to sickness or to deviancy—can significantly influence whether the patient improves or worsens. The social symptom and the patterns of labeling are clearly important in this context, but mainly to the secondary symptomatology and to the pattern of disability of disorders that have been caused by other factors.

A more reasonable view would seem to be that biological or constitutional factors determine the basic diathesis, or the individual's proneness to develop one or another type of psychological disorder. Just as some individuals are prone to hypertension and peptic ulcer, so others are prone to schizophrenia or depressive disorders. What environmental factors contribute to the development of the disorder is their stressful impact on the individual. Thus, whether or not an individual develops a clinically indentifiable disorder will depend on the interaction of his susceptibility with non-specific environmental stress, to the extent that the latter is present. Those who are highly susceptible may develop a specific disorder at an early age, even though they have experienced no more than the usual stresses of daily life; less susceptible individuals, on the other hand, may require exposure to severe and enduring stress before they manifest any disorder.

SOCIAL AND CULTURAL STRESS

The feature that is unique to human beings, by contrast with members of the animal world, is that they live in social groups, whose activities, sentiments and interactions are to a great extent determined by cultural patterns handed down from generation to generation. Like tuberculosis, psychiatric illness is multifactorially determined. Unlike the tubercle bacillus, however, which is a necessary but not a sufficient cause of tuberculosis, cultural factors are not necessary to mental disorder, but they may be sufficient causes of it.

Cultural factors interact with a number of variables in the development and natural history of psychiatric disorders. They may, for example, perpetuate the environmental conditions for the breeding of infectious agents, or they may contribute to the reduction of resistance in the human host. The incidence of paresis, syphilis, yaws, malaria, nutritional deficiency, sleeping sickness and other organic disorders is affected by such conditions as the technology of water use; the availability of labor supply for brush-clearing; the awareness of the value of chemical treatment, and economic pressures affecting migration and political boundaries.

It is useful to note that most studies fail to give adequate consideration to the temporal relationship between stress and disease, so that at times it is difficult to know for certain which came first. The usual inclination is to view stress as a precursor of illness; indeed, if the patient himself relates his history along those lines, no effort is generally made to search further. Stressful experiences are in effect acceptable as rationalizations of most psychiatric illnesses: to the extent that most disorders go unrecognized in their insidious early phases, and are then intensified by stress, they often do appear first as the result of stress.

It is likely that the visible stresses and conflicts that precede a full-blown illness have developed out of the failure of an already disturbed but still covertly ill individual to cope adequately with ordinary life stresses; indeed, it is the individual's deficiency in coping ability, resulting from some as yet unexplained changes in the basic chemistry of his being, that initiates the whole cycle, which thereafter accelerates. In other words, while life experience may influence the nature of psychological conflict, clinical manifestations of psychiatric disorder are most likely the product of an individual's constitutional predisposition. The symptoms of the disorder may not have any special psychodynamic significance (despite much elaborate theorizing to the contrary), and the patient's own theories about the origins of his illness cannot be taken as valid bases upon which to construct psychodynamic explanations of it. Rather, the interaction of patient and environment may set in motion self-cycling spirals of behavior that further increase distress, so that attempts to cope with stress only serve to increase it.

To the individual's basic biological patterns are added characteristic personality factors, which strengthen or weaken his ability to withstand various stresses. It is thus possible to visualize the development of conditioned responses to specific culture-bound stimuli but not to others; these additional dimensions must be weighed in assessing patterns of response to stress. "Adaptive" reactions may induce responses in others, which then feed back to the individual, further complicating his mental state. It is here that culture plays a crucial role, for it is culture that influences both the nature and the perception of stress, as well as the kinds of responses that have been developed for coping with it by members of the particular culture.

Thus, the specific objective character of the stress is less important than the fact that it is experienced as stressful by the individual. Whether the stress be fortuitous, as in a natural disaster, intentional as in a concentration camp, or simply inherent in the life cycle, it may set in motion in the individual, a series of emotional reactions of biological origin, and these may in turn undermine his confidence in his habitual ways of doing things, making him dependent on new situational and interpersonal stimuli, and increasing his susceptibility to environmental influences. Stress may induce fear, guilt, jealousy, anger or other emotions, and efforts to control these may lead in susceptible or ill-prepared individuals to maladaptive patterns. The flooding of consciousness with strong emotions that are unmanageable can alter alertness, acuity, awareness, mood or consciousness, producing clinical abnormalities in mood, thought and behavior that further impede attempts at adaptation. These abnormalities may not come to a halt when cessation of stress takes place. Indeed, it may be that persistent stress sets in motion chemical or neurohumoral changes in the individual's highest integrative centers, much as happens in psychosomatic conditions, such as peptic ulcer. These then continue to function pathologically, independent of whether the stress persists or not.

Unforeseen and unexplained changes in the behavior of others, for example, can unsettle the individual's perception of the world, challenge his sense of identity, disrupt his orientation and produce a state of cognitive dissonance. Attempts to correct this by altering behavior in accordance with the needs and expectations of the group may appear to the individual to be irrational or abnormal and may place a further strain on him. On the other hand, strong drives to reduce uncertainty may be more intolerable than the task of meeting the expectations of others, so that individuals may rely on regressive or self-defeating techniques in order to elicit responses from others. While these responses may in fact be deleterious to the individual, they may nevertheless be familiar to him; to the extent that they are, they produce in him a certain sense of security.

While specific stresses may be more characteristic of one culture than of another, it is the non-specific aspect of stress, or the conflicts inherent in the culture, that may precipitate psychiatric disorder in a vulnerable individual. Which particular disorder develops depends on the individual's constitutional predisposition, as well as his early experience and family history. By distinguishing among stress systems and specific disorders, one can study the extent to which different disorders occur under the impact of different kinds of stress. It is possible for an individual to be exposed to stress without being conscious of it, and that alone may be sufficient to produce a manifest disturbance; most often, however, it is the individual's perception of stress that leads to the maladaptive behaviors constituting the epiphenomena of illness. Whether stress then leads to maladaptive responses depends on the individual's general vulnerability, as well as his ability to adapt to a particular kind of stress. Psychological defenses and/or cultural defenses—e.g. belief systems—may succeed in preventing the stress from impinging upon the individual's psychological or psychosomatic integrity.

This view differentiates among psychological disturbance, social stress, cultural support systems, and individual vulnerabilities. Culture is quite obviously not simply a system for the satisfaction of biological needs; it is rather a system of psychological defenses related to ego functioning. Indeed, cultural factors set limits on human behavior to a greater extent than do biological needs. The environment and the individual are reciprocally related, in that shifts in one tend to be accompanied by corresponding changes in the other. Perception of the environment may be altered by physical injury and abnormal psychological stress; conversely, changes in the environment may alter the individual's responses. Human beings must define the nature of their immediate environment in order to be able to define their own place in it.

The availability of beliefs and rituals for the reduction of tensions is an important factor in determining how stressful cultural pressures will be. According to Montagu,[2] conflicting values are minimal in those cultures that provide institutionally sanctioned means of expressing aggression, reducing anxiety, and supporting dependency needs. The cultural context determines in large measure which patterns of expression will become institutionalized and which will become labeled as deviant. For example, cooperation, kindness, religious outlets for hostility, and the benevolence of the chiefs contribute to healthy behavior in the Caroline Islands, while witchcraft techniques and ill-will, among the Dobuans in Melanesia, encourage paranoia as a useful trait for adaptation. This is particularly striking since the same behavior may be decidedly maladaptive in another culture. Emotional withdrawal is encouraged in Bali, for example, but it does not limit adaptation there.

It is quite clear that different cultures support or reinforce different psychopathological patterns, and also provide acceptable roles for their expression. This does not mean that such patterns are not psychopathological, for they are likely to be rooted in the same inherited biological matrix. More to the point is the fact that, to the extent that different cultures respond differently to different symptoms, one will see varying kinds of secondary elaborations of these symptoms, as well as varying degress of disability displayed by individuals. Where symptoms are tolerated, encouraged or reinforced, individuals appear not to suffer from them, and they are not labeled as "sick." Such support may be crucial for preventing the development of disability and recognizable disorder.

THE PRODUCTION OF PSYCHIATRIC DISORDERS

The actual mechanism by which sociocultural factors produce psychiatric disorders is difficult to specify. Leighton[3] has noted that sociocultural events may interfere with conscious sentiments or they may fail to provide a necessary component for the functioning of a sentiment.* Thus, if individuals are striving for mutually incompatible objects, or if the objects that are requisite for achieving essential sentiments are vague, multiple or few in the culture, individuals will be unable to obtain the necessary components for the maintenance of sentiments. They may also be unable to perceive or to obtain the necessary objects in the environment as the result of certain inherited or acquired deficiencies of character or intelligence. Thus, difficulties in the individual, his goals, or the process of arriving at these goals may all contribute to an inadequate homeostasis of normal sentiment and normal emotional well-being. This view, which recognizes the existence of specific inadequacies in the environment, is an advance over previous theories, which have placed almost exclusive emphasis on intrapsychic phenomena.

A related formulation is that by Hughes:

Social patterns become accepted and perpetuated only by being internalized as motivational elements in the personality system of people involved on the scene; in order to become thus accepted, they must at some level address themselves more comprehensively and satisfactorily to the need dispositions of human beings confronted by these alternatives; for such a change and substitution, there must be a lessening of the hold of pre-existing culturally defined goal objects; decisions must therefore be made by the individual among usually legitimate alternative decisions which are based on the manipulation of information and the reconciliation, repression or compartmentalization of conflict or "dissonance," decisions which are in no sense based entirely (nor even perhaps predominantly) on "cognitive information."[4]

The formulations put forward by Leighton and Hughes are perhaps best illustrated by situations of social change, where the visibility of cultural stresses and the need for methods of reducing anxiety are both increased, by virtue of the strain that is being put on the culture and the social system. Social change is

* Sentiment, as used by Leighton, refers to the emotionally meaningful beliefs and feelings used by people to structure psychologically the sociocultural environment.

accompanied by the intensification of social and cultural sources of psychological conflict, by new stresses and new adaptation requirements in new milieus, and by the loss of the stabilizing effect of old cultural patterns. Even the improvement of living conditions may not be without its deleterious effects: the environment may still be stressful, even though visible economic indicators of poverty and crowding are no longer present. In the United States, revolutions in automation, communication and transportation are highly valued and even equated with progress, and yet they are all clearly associated with discontent and turmoil.

Little has been written on the specifically noxious factors that are present in different types of social change, and little attempt has been made to characterize social variables objectively, although numerous heuristic concepts—such as "object loss," "separation anxiety," and "disorientation"—have been used to explain the psychological response to social change. The study of such a complex phenomenon as change requires that various factors be controlled. Unrest and dissatisfaction are often attributed to oppression, poverty, malnutrition, urbanization and industrialization, but they are rarely attributed to change itself.

SOCIAL CHANGE AS STRESS

Loss of Old Culture

It is important to distinguish among different types of social and cultural change and the stress that results from them. Particularly stressful, for example, is the loss of culture that is experienced by the educated yet still semi-primitive marginal African, who has become a member of a partially urbanized and Westernized society. Having renounced his old culture, yet so far having failed to assimilate the new, he is particularly prone to malignant anxiety. According to Lambo:

In many parts of Africa, changes, physical and otherwise, are being introduced, thereby producing changes in the structure and function of the traditional African family . . . Such changes in our experience are, in many cases, leading to altered social habits, to economic pressures and to the general relaxation of traditional authority. Consequently, in many areas concerned there has been a higher incidence of behavior disturbances. In four new industrial areas surveyed by us, we found a higher incidence of drug addiction, abnormal sexuality, delinquent and other anti-social behavior, than in the entire population of the region . . . It is evident that psychiatric disorders would increase steadily in the populations of Africa consequent upon the great social and economic changes.[5]

The African's life has always been highly organized and regulated by his tribal group. Indeed, he derives his sense of identity from the group. Multiple parent figures in childhood; the absence of any opportunity to establish a lasting or intense bond with one parent; and economic, religious and ritualistic group activities—all these contribute to this sense of merging with the group. There also is a strong continuity with the dead, who, in the form of ancestral spirits, influence matters on earth through the medium of the chief. Such tremendous support from both a living group and a spirit group fades fast in the urbanizing world. According to Amara:

The African child is brought up in an atmosphere which does not freely sanction individuality but emphasizes group activity. This is observed early in the child's life when he is greatly influenced by maternal "uncles" and "classificatory fathers," that is, father's brothers who, like the father, are called "father." Identification with a father-figure or mother-figure, which normally forms the matrix for individuality in Western culture, is lost in the vast anonymity of the extended family circle. The child learns to identify and integrate with groups. Aggression, love, hate, identification normally directed towards parents are therefore displaced to the group.[6]

Later training, such as initiation rites and participation in secret societies, which are essentially group activities, reinforces this group solidarity. The African thus tends to regard personal problems as group problems and feels protected thereby.

With the increasing sophistication, new opportunities for education, easier communication, and exodus from the villages to the city, the family, which used to be the socioeconomic unit, is being disrupted. There is marked diminution in the "ancestral authority" invested in the fathers and elders, and consequent diminution in the protective powers of such authority. The migration to the city removes the group protection, the psychological "prop" of the African; he therefore finds himself psychologically isolated and vulnerable. The symptoms of anxiety that ensue can be relieved only by traditional methods.

Urbanization

Another major source of psychiatric difficulties in developing societies is the marked conflict between the norms of the traditional culture and those of the modernizing society. These norms place different and often conflicting demands on individuals. Patterns of behavior and expectations learned in the home or village, which emphasize community and family ties and obligations, often conflict with the realities of the marketplace, factory or urban area, which instead emphasize individual self-interest and self-reliance. Those who fail to learn the appropriate strategies for dealing with the modern world may experience marked psychological and value conflicts. This is particularly true of those with severe disorders, who might nevertheless be able to function in sociocultural situations of less stress.

Schizophrenic illnesses, which are characterized by disorders of perception, thought processes, and feeling, make functioning difficult in situations that emphasize competitiveness, achievement and universal criteria. Insofar as the schizophrenic individual, by virtue of his weaknesses, has to pay close attention to details of his inner life and to the subtle cues of interpersonal relationships, he may not have the capacity for competing or for coping with the variety of shifts that are so necessary for adaptation in the complex urbanizing community. Situations that make little allowance for his tendency to misperception, and situations that pay little heed to his inner anxieties, are stressful for him and generate an even greater anxiety. He may strive for acceptance in terms of what he perceives to be the group's standards. Because of his excessive sensitivity to subtle, often unconscious cues and his inability to discriminate between the latent and manifest demands of the situation, the schizophrenic may experience feelings of failure sooner and more deeply than normal individuals do. This is likely to lead to rapid retreats from the scene, in order to recoup strength. Following such a retreat, however, he must again generate sufficient confidence to be able to overcome his fears and inhibitions, as well as anxiety about doing something. In an individualistically oriented urbanizing and industrializing society, such psychological retreats are more difficult to find than are others in traditional societies, where the need for them is less. Pressures build up to inordinate levels more often in the urban setting.

Passive and dependent individuals also seem to suffer a great deal in urban society, where emotional and family supports are not as readily available. Depression and anger may be their responses to the system's failure to meet individual needs for support.

Women, old people, and adolescents experience particular difficulty in urbanizing societies. New economic demands and employment opportunities conflict with traditional values, which require women to remain at home. The rural-urban shift reduces respect for the authority of the elderly, and there emerges a concomitant loss of feelings of obedience toward them. Ill-equipped to obtain the economic resources that are so necessary for the maintenance of status and power, they are often neglected or rejected by their families in this new situation. Adolescents encounter special problems. In Africa, for example, where socialization is distinguished by multiple parental surrogates and strong peer groups, with less emphasis placed on individualism and self-interest, inner standards never develop. An orientation to the present, and constant efforts to reduce anxiety by gaining acceptance, remain the dominant personality traits, and the development of an orientation to the future, which is essential for adaptation to urban living, lags behind. The result is conflict and maladaptation.

The Stress of Change Itself

Sudden change is itself a source of stress. The interplay of culture and psychiatric illness is most dramatically illustrated in natural or man-made disasters, forced migration, and war—all of which expose individuals to new, strange and sometimes hostile environments. Reusch[7] noted, for example, that older responses are no longer appropriate for dealing effectively with present realities during the transition period that follows migration, and that the necessity of changing one's values and rearranging one's behavior can have disastrous consequences. Overwhelmed by his immediate problems, the migrant may become frustrated, angry, insecure, isolated and helpless. Mead[8] has suggested that the migrant is a culturally disoriented person, subject to special strains that intensify conflicts, and at the same time bereft of the cultural means for reducing tensions. Seguin[9] outlined a disadaptation syndrome among Peruvian Indians in Lima who had migrated from the mountains to the coast. As a result of the higher oxygen content in the coastal air, as well as of the numerous social, economic and cultural problems of adjustment, this syndrome appeared during the first year; it was characterized by depression and anxiety and by a number of circulatory, respiratory, neurological, and gastrointestinal symptoms.

Tyhurst[10] in 1951 described two stages of adjustment among eastern European immigrants in Montreal, Canada. During the first two months, a subjective sense of well-being appeared, which was associated with increased psychomotor activity and appreciation of the social situation; this was then followed by a sense of alienation, linked with language difficulties and value differences. Clinical psychiatric reactions appeared within six months. Three clinical trends were particularly prominent: suspiciousness and paranoia; anxiety and depression; and somatic complaints of fatigue, muscle and joint pains, nausea, anorexia, trembling, peptic ulcer, ulcerative colitis, and asthma.

Increased hospitalization in acculturating groups, as the result of an increased incidence of illness or of changed criteria for entry into the sick role, is usually a reflection of sudden social change.

Cultural Responses to Social Change

Cultural responses to the stress of social change include a variety of attempts to maintain, reestablish or create systems of anxiety-reduction, in order to assist the process of adaptation. In the less developed societies, folk psychiatry plays an important psychotherapeutic role in situations of social change.

In some areas, new tribal associations and religious sects have emerged to assist in the adaptation of immigrants. In Great Britain, pentecostal sects developed among the West Indians when they began to realize that many British institutions were not open to them. The resurgence of folk practices, as well as their continued use among various groups throughout the world, may account for the low reported rates of psychiatric disorder among these groups. Many disturbed people are able to adjust while remaining outside hospitals, because of their involvement in a sect or movement. In such cases, personal problems mesh with sectarian ideologies and with group behavior patterns or rituals, which are often indistinguishable from idiosyncratic behavior patterns.

Messianic religious cults, such as the nineteenth-century ghost dance religion of the American Prairie Indians and the cargo cults of the Southwest Pacific Islands, provide psychological support for oppressed peoples in disintegrating cultures. Prairie tribes have sought salvation in beliefs about the regeneration of the earth, reunion with the dead, and a life of aboriginal happiness without disease, misery or white men. The ghost dance ceremony, with its associated purificatory sweat, bath, ceremonial painting and trance induction, brings anticipation of the blessed state and visions of those already deceased. In the same vein, the cargo cults believed that, at the millenium, the spirits of the dead would return with cargoes of modern goods sufficient for all native needs, thus rendering work unnecessary and freeing the natives from their previous subjection to white control.

Some groups remain insulated and avoid new situations, while continuing their traditional folk practices. Mexican customs remain the predominant focus of the values and attitudes of Mexican-Americans, many of whom have been in the United States for as much as six generations. The geographic proximity of Mexico permits these people to maintain close enough ties with relatives and friends to prevent any abrupt break with the past. At the same time, discrimination and prejudice in the southwestern United States has prevented acculturation and thus encouraged a continuing identification with traditional practices. The continued use of a folk psychiatry (curanderismo) probably accounts for the lower recorded rates of mental illness among Mexican-Americans than among Anglo-Americans in the same area. Those who try but fail to acculturate can be reintegrated into the Mexican-American culture, by redefining their alienation from the group as evidence of illness in need of folk treatment.[11]

Folk therapies thus contain many elements for conflict resolution, corrective emotional experience, and the prevention of emotional illness. They provide sufficient social support for chronic schizophrenics to enable them to function outside hospitals; they also furnish opportunities for catharsis; the sharing of feelings, attitudes and ideas; group acceptance, and the development of new ideologies and belief systems. Having developed in response to broad social stresses and needs, folk therapies persist because of their success in meeting these needs. They also develop in response to different culture-specific personality patterns and conflicts, succeeding when they serve the particular needs and conflicts of these patients, which have been intensified to the extreme by the stress of social change. Folk therapies may be viewed as culture-specific techniques and strategies for assisting troubled individuals to cope with conflict and stress. Since these strategies ideally have to fit the needs of patients, the criteria as to who needs treatment or what constitutes a case must be generally known to members of the culture, so as to facilitate the entry into folk therapy systems of those who are most likely to benefit from them. This indeed is generally the case in less developed cultures, where there is an extraordinary sharing of beliefs by the members of the culture, along with a general sensitivity about who needs help and who does not.

There are, of course, considerable differences in these criteria of what constitutes a case. The concepts of normal and abnormal are, however, intrinsically related to the cultural beliefs and practices in each culture, as well as to the broader issue of how the culture also delimits the behavior of its members and contributes to the development and perpetuation of psychiatric disorders. These questions are dealt with in the next chapter.

CHAPTER 2   THE PROBLEM OF NORMAL AND ABNORMAL

IN ADDITION TO DEALING WITH THE HEALING practices of primitive people, the body of information that has comprised the second largest area of transcultural psychiatry has had to do with studies and reports of the effects of culture on different personality and psychopathological patterns. These studies have given rise to much theorizing and interesting speculation; they are particularly important insofar as they point to a significant area of cultural impact.

CULTURE-PERSONALITY STUDIES

Freud first examined the relationship of cultural factors to personality in *The Ego and the Id;* in particular, he formalized the notion that tension between actual attainments and the ego ideal is experienced as a sense of guilt. From his viewpoint, social feelings derive from identification with others on the basis of shared ego ideals—i.e. cultural values. In 1918, Freud had already postulated in *Totem and Taboo* that society originated from the need of the tribal horde, who had overcome the father, to establish a social structure in order to protect the members from one another. He emphasized the parallels between the magical rituals of primitive people and the repetition-compulsion and primary-process thinking of neurotics and psychotics. Jung

Notes for Chapter 2 will be found on pages 197–199.

16

also relied heavily on primitive myth and symbolism for his theory of the "collective unconscious," as did Rank for his theory of "birth trauma."

While ethnographers like Codrington, Taylor and Morgan in the nineteenth century, and Frazer in the early twentieth century, were concerned primarily with describing and cataloguing primitive practices and beliefs, later twentieth-century anthropologists sought to relate their observations to more general theories of human behavior. They formulated the concept of culture as those shared beliefs, attitudes, and behaviors that constitute a group's view of the world and style of life. Their studies of primitive cultures were immeasurably influenced by psychoanalytic theory and by the functionalist schools of anthropology, associated with Radcliffe-Brown, Evans-Pritchard, and Malinowski, which held that cultures were social units kept stable by sets of complementary institutions. Religion and primitive medicine, for example, not only satisfied spiritual and physical needs and helped to integrate individuals into society; they also contributed to the equilibrium of the society. Institutionalized rituals and beliefs strengthened the meaning of the group's symbols and reinforced the values of the group.

Culture-personality studies have been plentiful and have stimulated an interest in anthropological materials among psychiatrists. While basic personality patterns have been usefully related to cultural experiences in particular societies, there has been a tendency to use psychological labels to describe what are characteristically normal behavior patterns for certain societies. For example, the institutionalized patterns of suspicion, witchcraft, and grandiose behavior noted among the Kwakiutl, in British Columbia, have been described as "paranoid," without regard for the fact that that term does not have the same meaning in this native context as it has in Western society.[1] The culture-personality approach has also led to the production of psychodynamic formulations of social processes, despite the fact that psychodynamic concepts, being derived from a different level of analysis, are essentially inapplicable to the examination of social forces. It has also been difficult to determine in these studies whether, in fact, data have been collected selectively so as to fit a specific predetermined theoretical model, or whether the data have simply been collected and a theory or a set of hypotheses then constructed out of them.

Because of the complexity of the issues and the limitations imposed by field conditions, most of these studies have failed to adhere to scientific models of investigation and have instead shown a tendency toward theoretical speculation. The data collected have generally been of a different order of magnitude from the theories expounded, making the relationships that have been established less than fully meaningful. However, despite their limitations, such studies have usefully emphasized the importance of cultural factors in the patterning of the inner lives of group members and in the development of maladjusted and disturbed personalities.

CONCEPTS OF DISEASE

To the extent that different cultures are similar in certain respects, it is not surprising to find that supernatural and unscientific concepts of disease etiology and treatment contain a number of elements that are also found in the medical concept of contagion. In the same sense, the Freudian model, which attributes behavior primarily to internal, psychic motivations, derives as much from Western culture as it does from the objective study of behavior. It does not pay as much attention, however, to the social determinants of behavior as the pre-scientific model does in certain traditional cultures, in which the individual is believed to act in relationship to his ancestors, the community and the opinions and expectations of others. In most cultures, psychiatric disorder is usually conceptualized in terms of culture-bound concepts of role performance and normality.

Much of the confusion encountered in the literature originates with the field worker who observes strange customs that upset him, and who therefore feels required to formulate some explanation. A case in point is the potlatch ceremony of American Indians of the Northern Pacific Coast, especially the Kwakiutl. This ceremony—an Indian version of "oneupmanship" —is the recognized way of settling disputes, and a competitive means for establishing new titles on the basis of wealth. At potlatch festivals, a chief demonstrates his power by presenting his rivals with more gifts and property than could be returned with the required interest, thereby destroying his own property in a show of wealth that the guests could not surpass. The main destruction involved is usually of valuable candlefish oil—by burning it or feeding it lavishly to the guests. The host must also exhibit complete indifference to the destruction of his house. If the oil feast surpasses anything the guest has ever given, he is expected to leave the house and to begin preparations for a return feast that will outstrip that of his rival. If he believes that it has not equaled a feast he previously gave, he heaps insults upon his host, who then takes some further way of establishing his greatness, such as killing a slave, or breaking canoes into pieces and throwing them on the fire.

Benedict[2] has taken the irrational and grandiose behavior of the potlatch contestants to be evidence of paranoid and megalomaniacal trends in their culture. Similarly, she has attributed the widespread fear, suspicion and taboos among the Dobuan Islanders in Melanesia to their basic paranoid personality.

There are several errors in such attempts to diagnose whole cultures psychiatrically. The first is the error of characterizing cultures by means of concepts that were developed for studying phenomena at an individual level. The second is the assumption that one can adequately assess an abnormal mental state simply by observing the individual's behavior in socially defined situations. Psychiatric diagnosis can be made only on the basis of mental state, not in terms of social behavior. This is a particularly important distinction to make, if one is to understand the relationship between social behavior and psychiatric disorder. A relationship between psychiatric disorder and social behavior patterns can be determined only by studying diagnosed or known cases of psychiatric disorder that manifest particular social behavior patterns and comparing them with non-cases that exhibit the same behavior. The third error is to assume that one can assess the characteristics of psychiatric disorders, in terms of incidence and prevalence, by making an assessment of the quality of life in a given sociocultural milieu. While the two are clearly related, the relationship is not predictable on the basis of those measures of sociocultural variables that are currently available.

As we indicated in Chapter 1, an individual who has been exposed to stress is likely to become less able, as a result, to rely on automatic, habitual ways of responding, and thus increasingly dependent on immediate environmental cues as a way of reorienting himself. Under such circumstances, it is cultural factors that provide the cues for appropriate behavior, and assist the individual in making judgments about reality. Where such cues are ambiguous or uncertain, however, reorientation and reintegration become more difficult. Similarly, cultural attitudes toward particular symptoms, patterns of behavior and modes of functioning will influence whether the environment labels the individual as ill, dangerous, hospitalizable, or unfit for maintaining ordinary social roles. This cultural response may impair a patient's own confidence and judgment, and thereby increase his dependency on the environment. The sociocultural environment and the patient interact continually and predictably within cultural contexts. Western culture is quick to favor the sick role for paranoid ideation, hallucinations and depressive states, while traditional societies are equally quick to set up sanctions against behavior patterns, such as adolescent rebellion and lack of respect for elders, that threaten the status quo. These selective cultural reactions set in motion other processes in the patient and in the social system; these result in various culture-bound symptom states and therapeutic responses.

A positive response to mental illness is most dramatically seen in the case of paranoid schizophrenics, who make no effort to find out how their hallucinations were produced, or why they have occurred, in those cultures in which such phenomena are not regarded as unnatural. Indeed, they are often seen as an indication of something especially worthwhile—as, for example, in Puerto Rico, where spiritualist healers are selected on the basis of their hallucinatory experiences. The Puerto Rican with hallucinations who becomes a spiritualist healer incorporates his symptoms into the role and thereby reduces the likelihood that secondary symptoms or complicating patterns will develop.[3]

It is this tolerance for what is considered to be abnormal behavior that has led in our own society to the relativist view—namely, that abnormality is dependent solely on labeling or social definition, rather than on a set of universally observable and measurable clinical phenomena. This view ignores much clinical evidence that psychiatric conditions may arise *de novo* in developing societies, albeit without some of the secondary complications that are to be seen in our own society. Acceptance by one group of what another group regards as symptoms does not mean that the individual does not have a psychiatric disorder; it means only that individuals with similar disorders are permitted to function differently in different settings. This is of value in enabling us to learn more about the range of function and dysfunction that is possible with different disorders. It is also useful in helping us to separate and study the interaction of social and clinical phenomena, and to differentiate between the primary and secondary symptoms of psychiatric illness.

SYMPTOMATOLOGY

What then does account for differences among patients in different cultures? Differences in the symptoms shown by patients with the same diagnosis may be due to actual differences in the basic underlying disorders, even though the presence of certain shared symptoms suggests the same diagnosis; or else they may arise from variations of the same disorder, produced by genetic, personality or sociocultural factors. Weaknesses in diagnostic methods can account for the relative ease with which certain diagnoses are made in a given culture: what leads to admission in one culture may not do so in another culture. There are also considerable differences in the training of the psychiatrists who make the diagnoses, and this too can account for differences in the diagnoses made.

Symptoms may be exaggerations of normal behavior. They may have a large social component: as Devereux has suggested, they may conform to cultural expectations of how symptoms *should* appear.[4] To the extent that the emotionally ill are all expected to fit the behavior patterns of the "insane" role, there will be a certain amount of similar behavior on the part of patients in the same culture who may in fact be suffering from different disorders. Behavioral patterns and symptoms, having been learned in a particular culture, are then grafted onto the underlying disorder. According to Devereux, models of psychiatric illness are known to the laity and condition the individual's expression of his abnormal emotions. For example, patients seeking help usually describe their difficulties in a way that will "make sense" to the healer. Devereux maintains that the malingering of insanity stems from a conscious attempt to display those singularities of behavior that are explicitly recognized by the group as fitting certain diagnostic models. He has also suggested that there are signal symptoms, by which the incipient neurotic or psychotic informs others that he is about to change his status from normal to insane. This presents a form of cooperation between patient and diagnostician.

Sometimes the early outbreak of psychosis is signalled in a conventional way: the Crow "crazy dog wishes to die" talks backwards; the Moro who is about to run amok often asks the permission of his parents.[5] Sometimes the incipient psychotic acquires certain regalia or objects needed for the proper enactment of the psychotic role. According to Devereux, the psychotic puts his behavior into a cultural pattern; Linton[6] calls this a "pattern of misconduct." By becoming insane, the individual opts out: he both accepts and attains certain advantages of the sick role. There is a tremendous increase in what Devereux has called "social mass," or the ability to get attention. This provides the individual with the opportunity to obtain the support he needs. A diagnosis is made when the patient conforms to the model of psychotic or neurotic behavior in the particular culture.

Implicit in Devereux's formulation is the notion that the individual is motivated, consciously or unconsciously, to behave in an abnormal way. It is more likely that, while culturally conditioned responses and methods of adapting to the symptoms may indeed be motivated by psychological factors, the primary symptoms remain unaffected. Indeed, there are clearly certain basic or pathogenic psychiatric processes that are invariant. Loosening of associations, diurnal variation of mood, and clouding of consciousness, for example, do not appear to be influenced by culture or by individual motivation. As we have seen, pathoplastic or culturally compensatory determined symptoms do, of course, vary from culture to culture, and entry into the sick role is determined in large measure by them. While the historical accounts or etiological "hypotheses" of events leading to the symptoms are no doubt *ex post facto* explanations, it is not so easy to assert that behavior is similarly motivated. Different behavioral patterns may be the result of particular personality responses to the stress of the psychiatric disorder itself. Insofar as culture determines many aspects of personality, certain responses to illness are likely to occur with greater frequency in certain cultures. This no doubt accounts for the compatibility of certain behavioral patterns with the criteria for entry into the sick role.

The availability of alternative models for explaining deviant behavior may diminish the kind of intolerance that leads to suicide in depressed patients, and to passivity, atrophy of skills and the development of chronicity in schizophrenic patients. A balance must be found between tolerance of symptoms and encouragement of treatment, so as to stimulate the restoration of functioning without causing the patient any stress. The rarity of deterioration in schizophrenia and the rarity of suicide in depression are perhaps the most striking features of these disorders in the less developed societies. This was first observed by Kraepelin,[7] in his cross-cultural studies in Java; he found that dementia praecox cases rarely manifested preliminary depression, catatonia, hallucinations, coherent delusions, or terminal dementia. Chronic confusional states were the most common outcome. Pure depressive states, guilt feelings and suicide were also extremely rare among manic-depressives.

Cultural factors, as determinants of certain patterns of behavior that are labeled abnormal and treated as such, are especially significant in the psychosocial disorders, such as alcoholism, homosexuality, and delinquency, in that these disorders derive from a combination of personality and socioenvironmental factors.

While *alcohol* is used around the world, for example, the problems associated with it vary from culture to culture, irrespective of the extent of its use. Alcohol serves to relieve depression, reduce tension and release inhibitions; it may indeed prevent the outbreak of a serious psychiatric disturbance, when it is used in moderation and in the appropriate fashion. Alcoholism develops only when the users have other problems, which alcohol cannot help. Many American Indians who have lost their identity on the restrictive reservations can no longer benefit from the institutional and ritualistic restraints that normally operate to prevent the development of alcoholism among those who begin by using alcohol for its sedative and therapeutic benefits.[8]

Alcohol is particularly interesting to study, because of the various physical and neurological complications that are associated with excess use of it. These evolve independently of the basic symptoms for which the alcohol has been taken; to some extent, they develop because of the failure to treat the underlying disorder adequately. The study of alcohol use is also complicated by its role in religious and sacramental contexts, and by its medicinal properties, which make it popular among those in search of relaxation or surcease from difficulties. It is especially difficult to differentiate conventional alcohol use from the abnormal addictive use that is defined as alcoholism. This has led many to define alcoholism in terms of physical symptoms and signs of impaired function or damage. While this approach enables one to be definite about what cases are to be included, there are many whose drinking is already out of control, but who have not as yet manifested signs of damage or disability. To exclude them is to be left with a limited picture. In addition, one must learn to deal with those subliminal phenomena that exist yet may be denied by the informant, thereby necessitating the utilization of additional procedures for getting below the surface of the informant's account. This is also true of homosexuality and delinquency.

Homosexual disorders are even less well defined, and there is considerable difference of opinion as to whether this behavior pattern does in fact constitute a disorder. There is quite clearly a wide range of attitudes toward homosexual behavior in different cultures. Carstairs reports that homosexual behavior was more or less proscribed, and therefore clandestine, in 27 out of the 76 societies whose customs are well-documented in the Yale Human Relations Area files, while in 49 of these societies such behavior was regarded as normal and socially acceptable for certain members of the community.[9] The patterns of homosexuality also vary considerably from society to society. Among the Keraki and Kiwai of New Guinea and the Siwans of North Africa, all male members of the tribe were expected to practice pederasty prior to their entry into adult heterosexual life. In New Guinea, mutual masturbation was a recognized form of male homosexual activity among certain groups; among some Indian groups in the American Southwest, ritualized transvestitism was often practiced. Female homosexuality occurs much less often throughout the world. There is fairly good evidence that the inclination toward homosexual behavior originates in childhood; what remains to be determined is how social approbation or disapproval influence whether or not the individual becomes disturbed. Where it is not approved, the individual is likely to develop conflicts about its expression, or those secondary complications that are generally associated with stigmatized behavior.

In the United States we are inclined to attribute *delinquency* to social conditions, to unresolved childhood conflicts (psychoanalytic model), or to basic flaws in a psychopathic personality (constitutional and behaviorist model). In each of these instances, delinquent behavior is viewed from a moralistic perspective, which regards such behavior as bad. In certain instances delinquency may be simply a behavioral complication, or a secondary symptom of a psychiatric disorder. Culture determines what individuals will behave in what ways; it also conditions the form of the behavior. Rising delinquency rates in Africa have been attributed to the scattering of the extended family, changing attitudes toward industrialization, polygamy (with its partiality toward the children of favored wives and the resultant neglect of other children), displacement of families by tribal conflict and political instability, the novelty of city life, child labor, unstable families, alcoholism and cruelty. Indeed, it has been blamed at one time or another on all the social and cultural changes that are so characteristic of the developing countries. There is obviously a need for a more detailed analysis of the mechanism involved in particular behavior patterns, since these derive from different drive patterns, personality traits, and experimental patterns in different individuals. Closer study of individuals should reveal much about the way these patterns are learned, their meaning in terms of the whole person, and what part cultural factors have played in their development.

Perhaps the most extreme form of anti-social behavior is *homicide,* studies of which have shown that it results from mental illness as well as from social stresses. The major study of homicide in pre-literate cultures was carried out by Bohannon;[10] it revealed, unexpectedly, that obvious mental disorder was never a major factor in causing homicide, while witchcraft beliefs, which frequently provoked anxiety, did contribute to it. My own view is that, in every culture, witchcraft beliefs are most often *ex post facto* rationalizations of inexplicable behavior, serving to label the murderer, and to exclude him from the group, thereby maintaining the stability of the group. These same beliefs may on occasion trigger homicidal behavior in paranoid individuals.

Study of the characteristics of both the murderer and the victim, and of their relationship to each other, is of interest to students of particular social systems. Knowledge of these culturally determined factors should point to loci of stress in the system, as well as to those people who show a high risk of behaving in these particular ways. Homicide takes place most often in situations in which the individual who is provoked into murder has been threatened psychologically by individuals who have overstepped certain social boundaries through a too intimate personal contact with him. This pattern is particularly common in Latin-American culture. A similar pattern has been described for the Philippines by Sechrest,[11] who has noted that homicide frequently involves strangers or acquaintances on a drinking spree, who are offended when an "outsider" refuses to join them for a drink. This phenomenon may be explained in part by recent experiments, which suggest that individuals tend to surround themselves with various invisible layers of psychological space or territory, which can be entered to varying degrees by others. According to Augustus Kinzel, violent individuals have a wider space into which others cannot enter safely; whoever invades it can induce a panic that swiftly expands into irrational assault.[12] He has tested his theory on a group of federal prisoners —some known to be violent, others more tractable. On the average, the violent subjects stopped him at a distance of three feet, and showed markedly increasing tension and hostility as the circle shrank; the nonviolent subjects, on the other hand, let him approach to within half that distance. Moreover, the two areas of insulating space differed radically in shape. That of the violent prisoners bulged to the rear—an avenue of approach that they regarded as unusually menacing—where the nonviolent subject's personal zones were nearly elliptical.

Kinzel's study is further proof of a contemporary psychological premise (advanced by such theorists as Edward T. Hall of Northwestern University and Mardi J. Horowitz of the Medical Center of Mount Zion)—namely, that man unconsciously projects a sphere of "personal space" that admits no trespass by strangers. Whenever this zone is penetrated without permission, the occupant responds by defending it, often with violence. Kinzel himself believes that the dimensions of the zone may provide a clue to the violence potential of its inhabitant: the larger the zone, the more intolerant its inhabitant will be to invasion of his personal space. A rapidly expanding zone may signal that dangerous moment when the panic that has been evoked by intrusion is about to escalate into destructive action.

Customs governing expressions of hostility, as well as patterns of repression of aggression, obviously play a part in accounting for the differences that are seen from one culture to another. They undoubtedly influence some of the constitutional or personality factors described above. Where aggression is repressed, it takes a very intense emotional pressure to generate the kind of explosive violence that is so frequently associated with homicide. This sort of pressure is more often generated in intense personal or family relationships than in impersonal relationships with strangers—which may mean that close relationships permit individuals to enter into those psychological spaces that are otherwise protected against such contacts. Families may thus be more likely to overstep the psychologically safe boundaries of inner space, and in that way to trigger unexpectedly these violent reactions. This is well illustrated by Driver,[13] who found that, of 144 cases of homicide in India, there were only 8 instances in which the murderer and the victim were not of the same religion. In 70 of the 144 cases, the victim was a relative of the criminal; in only 6 instances was he neither a kinsman, a close associate nor a representative of the law. The most frequent victim was either a neighbor of the same caste, or a wife who had been unfaithful or shameful in her behavior; the next most common victim was a brother or uncle who had been involved with the murderer in a property right dispute. Homicide in this culture thus emerges when special strains are superimposed on close relationships.

Homicide regularly occurs in association with alcohol consumption—which suggests that alcohol may affect impulsivity and the perception of threat, in such a way as to reduce the size of the psychological space surrounding the individual.

The high valuation that is placed on aggressive behavior in a particular subculture may also be associated with high homicide rates. Wolfgang and Feracutti found, for example, that in the American Negro subculture violence was evaluated highly and its avoidance adversely criticized.[14] The rate of homicide was thus found to be directly related to the degree of integration of violence within the individual's subculture. Knowing whether there is indeed such a high value placed on violence is especially important in assessing the nature of homicidal behavior, since the behavior may indicate adherence to cultural norms rather than the existence of an underlying psychopathology.

UNUSUAL MENTAL STATES 7

Much of the conceptual confusion with regard to "normal" and "abnormal" comes from the employment of different criteria in different cultures. In some cultures, failure to conform to a certain model of behavior is deemed sufficient evidence for making a diagnosis of that sort. In other cultures, as we have already noted, in order for an individual to be able to enter into the culturally prescribed "sick role" and to obtain available treatment, he has to explain the origins of his difficulty in terms of historical events that are culturally acceptable; in addition, he must respond to these and express his fears in appropriate ways, behaving according to the cultural norms for the particular disturbance.

Deciding on what constitutes psychopathology is most difficult when one is studying people from other cultures. This has led to the view that illness or abnormality can be defined operationally, rather than judged against an absolute standard, insofar as the patient's symptoms can be viewed as distressing either to him or to the group. According to this view, it is not the idea or belief, but rather the way in which the idea or belief is distorted by the individual, in relation to the standards of the group, that is the crucial determinant of a psychopathological label.

Such a relativist approach, while of immediate practical value, obscures the fact that certain behavioral phenomena are universally judged to be abnormal, and that there are some features of psychiatric disorders that are completely independent of the processes of social labeling. A more appropriate and valuable step than merely deciding on what is normal and abnormal from one culture to another, would be to distinguish between the essential nuclear elements of specific psychiatric disorders and the culturally conditioned aspects of these same disorders. Cross-cultural psychiatric studies can be of particular value in helping to make these distinctions. One approach to this problem is to be found in the study of unusual mental states; depending on the context in which they occur, these are variously defined as religious, deviant, or sick role behavior. Such a study can serve to differentiate between the nuclear features of illness and the effects of culture on it.

Trance

One mental state that has been frequently encountered and studied is that of trance or possession; this usually refers to a relationship between spirits and humans, manifested as the spirit's entering the human being and taking control of his behavior. In ancient Greece, an oracle who could enter a trance was held in the highest regard; the Bible also records many instances of seizures, trances, and visions that were thought to be of divine origin. Similarly, unusual forms of behavior, particularly glossolalia and dissociative states, were associated with the Wesleyan revival in eighteenth-century England and with the nineteenth-century American revivalist sects. To this day, such behavior remains a cardinal focus of pentecostal sects throughout the world. There are also many ethnologic references to ecstatic states among primitive peoples and, similarly, accounts of unusual mental states among contemporary religious groups. In various cultures, unusual mental conditions, such as hallucinations, hysterical seizures, and trance states, have held a central role in religious beliefs and practices. Repeated illness, hysterical fits, or trance behavior have been regarded as prerequisite experiences for aspiring priests in a number of North American Indian tribes, as well as in African and Asiatic tribes; and group rituals, breathing exercises, dancing, torture, fasting, or such stimulants as alcohol, Indian hemp, peyote, and mescaline have often been employed in order to induce such states.

Yuji Sasaki[15] has described a fairly typical path of mystical states taken by one aspiring shaman in Japan, who at age 23 climbed the sacred mountain to begin self training (shygyo).

Meditation, fasting, prayer, postural exercises, and repeated climbs up the mountain at length produced a state of emotional tranquility. In his third year, during the last night of the annual two-week meditation, he hallucinated and entered a state of ecstasy. Several nights later, while meditating he felt his hands being pulled up and something rushing from his chest to his throat. His mouth tightened and he could not speak; he began to murmur in a fragmentary way, and heard a voice commanding him to save others by becoming a shaman. As a shaman, he began regularly to enter *uranai* (possession states), during which time he was presumed to be in touch with God's will. With increasing experience, he was able to enter into such states with little alteration of consciousness.

The techniques of trance induction described here involve repetitive bodily movements, reduced sensory stimulation, exhaustion, hypoglycemia, and physical stress—all of which together diminish consciousness and ego activities. Alteration of consciousness enhances suggestibility, as well as the ecstatic or meaningful quality of the experience.

It is useful to study the conditions in which altered states of consciousness develop, the degree to which those who experience such states are suffering from psychiatric disorder, and the extent to which they derive social benefit from entering these states. The altered state of consciousness may very well be a final common behavioral pathway for different cultural patterns. The psychophysiological aspect of the altered states of consciousness may themselves be the same, however, despite its different routes and meanings in different cultures.

Unusual mental states include: soporific states, produced by alcohol and opium; excited states, produced by stimulants such as tea, kat* and benzedrine; delirious states, produced by "loco weed" and nutmeg; and hallucinatory states, produced by LSD, mescaline and ayahuasca. Depending upon the contexts in which these pharmacologically active substances are ingested, they may be used for withdrawal from daily stresses, for meaningful religious experiences, for psychotherapeutic purposes, or for improved functioning in the presence of starvation or oppression.

Various non-pharmacological methods have also been used to induce dissociative states. The Egyptians relied upon sensory deprivation, fasting and social isolation to induce religious states

---

* Kat or *Cathaedulis*, an evergreen shrub found in East Africa or South Arabia, contains the central nervous system stimulant cathine (d-nor iso-ephedrine).

of dissociation. In Delphi in Graeco-Roman times, trance was induced in the Pythoness by carbon dioxide, which emanated from rock fissures. The Sun Ritual of the Sioux placed its emphasis on the physical stress of heat and thirst. Yoga rituals in India rely on physical contortions and breathing exercises, while the religious activities of the Sufi Fraternal Order in Iraq depend on vigils, breath retention and dancing for the performance of "miraculous" feats, such as swallowing glowing embers and passing knives through their bodies.

The symbolic value of induction procedures sometimes makes it difficult to recognize their physiological and psychological impact in the production of altered states of consciousness. The use of directed fantasy, abandonment to trance, body postures, music, body-rocking, fixation on lighted candles, concentration on God, and fasting may act as a form of self-hypnosis. In Indonesia, for example, trance is induced by the monotonous and rhythmic music of drums, gongs, bamboo instruments, and songs, as well as by complete seclusion, fumigation, fire-gazing, dancing, and body rotation.

It is important to note that there are sometimes an epileptic-like aura, convulsions, and retrograde amnesia in trance states; unlike convulsions, however, trance rarely produces any of the aftereffects of fits, such as tongue-biting, bladder incontinence or prolonged feelings of exhaustion.

Techniques such as the employment of psychopharmacological agents, intensive psychoanalytic therapy and brainwashing procedures have the effect of physiologically inducing regressive or altered states of consciousness, through either a reduction or an increase of external stimuli; this either overstimulates and taxes the central nervous sytsem, or understimulates and deprives it of its necessary input.

A number of different factors thus appear to be capable of producing possession or trance states, ranging from the hypnotic-like effects that are produced by the reduction in sensory stimuli which accompanies yoga exercise, to the driving effect that may be produced in the temporal complex by the incessant sensory stimuli of voodoo drum rhythms. Alcohol, fatigue, hallucinogenic plant substances increase individual susceptibility in different settings. The contagiousness of excitement, along with the variety of emotions generated at religious ceremonies, ranging from anger, confusion and fear to exaltation, may also lead to a breakdown of the higher integrative functions of the central nervous system, thereby producing the possession state. The puzzling feature of possession is the appearance of partial functioning. The individual appears to be at one and the same time in contact in some spheres and out of contact in others; it is difficult to tell whether he is simulating, game-playing and manipulating, or is psychotic and/or under the influence of outside forces.

The Pavlovian theory of transmarginal stimulation and inhibition explains different possession experiences as different types of responses of the central nervous system to excessive stimulation, which leads at first to a state of hysteria. Further transmarginal inhibition produces excitement, inhibition of judgment and various degrees of stupor and tremors. In some, what occurs is a total inhibitory collapse—the complete disruption of previous conditioning, or of recently acquired abnormal patterns; with recovery, however, there is a natural return of healthier patterns. This theoretical explanation has the merit of helping us to formulate the phenomenon in terms that are compatible with our scientific system. More data, however, are needed for an adequate understanding of the mechanisms, the specific stimuli, and the individual factors in these processes. In particular, we need to know what effect sensory deprivation has on the mechanisms of transmarginal inhibition. Losing one's self-awareness and self-consciousness in a spirited assembly that reaches its zenith in the possession experience, where all ego defenses and morbid dissatisfactions are transmarginally inhibited, would seem to contribute to the therapeutic efficacy of possession and treatment ceremonies; but it is difficult to say how and why this occurs.

It is easier to see how the possession experience prepares the individual to accept a healer's assurances of improvement, as well as his directions with regard to ways of making more satisfactory adjustments. The anxiety and panic that are associated with loss of the usual defenses induces the individual to try to understand the experience, which cannot readily be understood in commonsense terms. The cognitive dissonance that is engendered in the possessed, and in those who witness them genuinely behaving as if in the control of outside forces, cannot fail to impress everyone involved with the validity of whatever theory is immediately at hand to explain the phenomenon, and with the abilities of the healer who has sponsored this visit from these particular spirits.

Behavioral patterns that have been institutionalized in group rituals or ceremonies are usually sufficiently broad to provide suitable channels for the expression of a variety of needs and personality traits. For the depressed and guilt-ridden, a comprehensive ideology or theology and a group ritual together furnish a useful guilt-reducing device; to the hysteric, they offer a socially acceptable model for acting out; and for the obsessional, they provide encouragement in the form of a reduction of inhibitions and an increase in emotionality. For such accompaniments of neurotic and real suffering as feelings of inferiority, self-consciousness, suspiciousness and anxiety, the social aspects of the ceremonies would also seem to be of value. Most groups that employ altered states of consciousness in their practices agree on the efficacy of these methods for those individuals who believe in their value; what they emphasize is the fact that belief in the ritual and its symbolic trappings is crucial for the achievement of successful results, although casual seekers after help often find relief as well. Where possession states are part of the ritual behavior, the highly emotional and supportive setting is inextricably intertwined with those themes and activities that promote religious conversion and participation in the particular group. Having seen or heard of the workings of the spirits, in previous meetings, individuals are likely to have both faith in the healer and an expectant attitude toward the chances of his producing positive results.

The manifestations of spirit possession range from faints, trances, glossolalia, and rigid postures to violent dancing, with the latter often ending in states of exhaustion. Upon being "touched" by a spirit, an individual may do no more than twitch, tremble or make hand-fluttering motions. Some may perform feats of agility, such as climbing down tree-trunks, head first; others may hold hot irons in their hands, chew broken glass, or walk barefooted over hot coals. What the act is appears to be culturally determined. After the termination of possession states, most people are amnesic with regard to the preceding events.

The quality of possession varies from one individual to another. Some enter into possession states with relative ease, by way of prayers and symbolic offerings; this usually applies to healers, mediums and leaders. Save for the changed voice, posture and facial expression, most of the "possessed" maintain a keen awareness of the ongoing situation and their role in it. In others, possession states are often marked by a loss of self-control and consciousness. The range of spirits is so great that a great number of patterns of behavior appear to be acceptable as possession states; this accounts for the labeling of certain behavior patterns as possession, in non-participants and non-believers as well as within ceremonial contexts.

Toxic psychoses stemming from drugs that have been used to produce dissociative states can be severe and dangerous. The trance itself, particularly if it is associated with regression, hallucinations, and the loss of ego boundaries, may be quite traumatic. A panic state is likely to ensue if the individual enters the dissociative state outside of a socially defined context of support.

The form of possession also varies from culture to culture. Ritual trance occurs only among the young in Bali, while in voodoo settings in Haiti it is more common among adults. In other cultures, trance is associated with theatrical occasions, clubs, trance dancers, séances, mediums or other circumstances in which the alteration of personality and behavior patterns is rewarded and given special meaning. Numerous studies have sought to establish the underlying characteristics of possession-prone individuals. Sargant[16] has suggested that while depressed or obsessional patients lack the requisite flexibility to become possessed, they can do so after a course of treatment.

Douyon[17] found that the possession-prone in Haiti were less rigid and defensive on Rorschach tests than his controls; yet they evidenced much anxiety and infantilism; deficiencies of ego control mechanisms; a family history of possession; a history of childhood and adolescent trance; strong maternal and weak paternal attachments; feelings of self-depreciation; fear of sexuality, ridicule and betrayal; and strong inclinations to passivity. They also gave evidence of an inclination to escape from unpleasant reality. Sixty-four percent of them reported loss of consciousness after a quarrel, deception, the death of a parent, a friend or even a neighbor; loss of consciousness was in fact never provoked voluntarily, but always followed the impact of external stimuli. Observation of others in public or ritual possession states often precipitated similar states in the onlookers; this suggested to Douyon that possession was an infantile reaction in a pathological personality.

Douyon also noted that possession had a positive effect as a defense against deeper mental illness. This has been frequently reported in the literature on possession; it derives in part from the view that mental illness can be prevented only by cathartic strategies, which release the dammed-up emotion that produces it. The cathartic model may be applicable to the prevention of psychoneurotic disorders; it is likely, however, that a model of anxiety reduction and support is more appropriate for the prevention of schizophrenic disorders, while what is indicated for the psychopathic personality is control strategies. Dissociative states can provide emotional catharsis, a sense of renewal and an improved capacity for dealing with reality; they reinforce group values and group integration.

In the early stages of psychiatric illness, individuals frequently seek out dissociative experiences, in the hope that beliefs and rituals will provide solutions and a sense of psychological integration. The stress of participation may, however, lead to an increase of emotional disturbance, although when this occurs it is difficult to establish the presence of a pre-existing illness.

This kind of help-seeking is common; it reflects the inclination of people to interpret the subjective distress of their psychological symptoms as manifestations of difficulties in their life situation, rather than as manifestations of illness calling for treatment. Paranoid symptoms of depressive illness, for example, may not distress the patient: he may merely express vague discomfort and uncertainty about values, the world, and particular people, while acting against others or participating in some religious, social or political group whose belief system serves his needs.

Even hallucinations and delusions may be ignored as symptoms, despite the fact that they are influencing the individual's perception of, and his response to, the environment, and propelling him into potentially deleterious social movements and activities. It is particularly difficult to differentiate between culturally acceptable behavior and serious psychiatric disorders, when such disorders are clinically resolved by the adoption of a shamanistic or other culturally prescribed role.[18] Training for a shamanistic role is often psychotherapeutic, enabling the individual to incorporate idiosyncratic and disturbed behavior and thoughts into a culturally acceptable role. In South Africa, Laubscher[19] examined cases of *thwasa,* a condition marked by limb pains, nausea, loss of appetite, hallucinations, excitability, and elaborate dreams, and resembling the catatonic or depressive phase in schizophrenic, manic-depressive or epileptic psychoses. A diviner handles the treatment; it culminates in an initiation ceremony, in which the patient's dreams are symbolically interpreted as communications from the guiding ancestral spirits. If a person is thus "called," he must undergo further training to become a diviner; failure to do so can result in insanity. Identification of the early stages of illness with "religious calling" occurred to Laurent Mellon, a voodoo priestess or mambo in Haiti; she then resolved a paranoid illness by becoming a priestess, successfully filling this role until her old age, when her power declined and her paranoid symptoms returned.

The ill effects of revivalist conversion procedure were recognized by the New England preacher, Jonathan Edwards. According to Sargant, he made a practice of inducing guilt and acute apprehension as the first step toward conversion, keeping up the pressure until the sinner broke down and indicated complete submission to the will of God.[20] In instances of individuals who were already suffering from religious melancholia, the possibility of suicide or insanity was always recognized; it was usually "put down to the debit side of the conversion ledger."

The difficulties of distinguishing unusual but culturally acceptable behavior from morbid states have been considerable, as suggested by the vast theologic, psychiatric, and anthropoligic literature on the subject. They have been further complicated by the acceptance of morbid states within a religious context.

Participation in an esoteric group is often thought to cause mental illness. Such groups seem to attract many individuals who are in distress; they usually offer a philosophy that answers ultimate questions and provides goals toward which the individual can direct his life, especially since these goals seem more readily attainable than those of the everyday materialist world. Sects are usually small; they can therefore provide a sense of exclusiveness, together with a feeling of belonging to a true community, in which the individual remains all-important. Thus, for many unhappy and dissatisfied individuals, who are socially isolated, membership in a religious sect fulfills a variety of needs. Further, a technique is usually offered that promises to lead to self-improvement.

The urge to change, however, seems to be capable of promoting anxiety in those who feel that they are not making the necessary progress. In addition, the unfamiliar situation of group exercises or rituals may enhance anxiety. The behavior of the older members may disturb newcomers, who realize that they too may in time behave in the same strange manner. At the same time, the excitement of entering a new world of experience is likely to drive them on when they themselves begin to show loss of control. If they feel guilt, embarrassment, and anxiety about their behavior in the exercises, they will be all the more likely to accept the interpretations that are offered by the sect, which relieve these discomforts. What determines the individual's pattern of behavior in the ceremony seems to vary from person to person. Suggestion and imitation, particularly when they are enhanced by the reduced or magnified sensory stimuli that are available in the setting in which the ritual is performed, are bound to play an important role. Furthermore before joining one particular sect, many people have already been steeped in a variety of other movements, so that they are already familiar with such things as symbols and rituals. The absence of any recognized leader in some groups would seem to reduce the effectiveness of the exercise in producing change; this is by contrast with the active role taken, for example, by a Zen master. But since a leader can arouse resistance, and since the decision to participate in the group is made by the individual, he may be willing to commit himself even more deeply to the exercises, because he always feels that the decision to proceed rests in his own hands alone.

Although the content of the thoughts and the explanations that are offered by patients for their behavior shows the influence of sectarian theory, it seems likely that what they have borrowed from the sect soon becomes inextricably intertwined with their own personal fantasies and needs. There is little doubt that many individuals manifest symptoms of psychological disturbance prior to their entry into a sect; in fact, conscious dissatisfaction with themselves is often their main motive for joining a sect. A reduction of distress and a marked feeling of calmness after participation in the sect's exercises take place from the start, these inner changes are not apparent to independent observers, who view membership in the sect as being itself indicative of mental abnormality. In most spiritual sects, people find a close community with an ideology that emphasizes inner faith and the capacity for spiritual progression, and offers a philosophy that explains and sets a value on many of the psychologic changes they are experiencing. In that regard, religious sects may well have an ameliorative effect on the course of illness in patients.

Most people experience an inclination, in the setting of certain spiritual activities, to review past events in their lives that have at some time aroused feelings of guilt, fear, and depression. With increasing participation, they experience a heightened emotional intensity, and feel correspondingly less restrained and inhibited. Gradually, they become more interested in the sect, and begin to devote much of their energies to solving the problems that are posed during the exercises. More and more of their lives center about the sect, until they become totally immersed in its practices and beliefs. Occupied with problems of self-knowledge and spiritual attainment, they lose interest in old ties and old interests, and realistic issues become less significant for them. However, the progressive tension associated with feelings of guilt, repentance, and little spiritual advancement may have undesirable effects on some individuals. In the absence of an acknowledged leader, there is no one to recognize progressing symptoms and to discourage their participation. Those who are unable to cope with the stresses of the sect's spiritual exercises, or to approach them with moderation, participate more and more fully, thereby potentiating their anxiety and distress, and enmeshing themselves in a vicious cycle. The tolerance and acknowledgement of traits that are ordinarily suppressed in Western societies may lead to an accentuated expression of them in individuals whose defenses are not sufficiently flexible to keep them under control.

Thus, many methods of religious and political conversion that are designed to promote intense emotional experiences may sometimes, in predisposed individuals, set in motion underlying pathologic processes. The question then naturally arises whether such participants are experiencing genuine religious ecstasies or suffering from severe psychiatric illnesses.

Bleuler[21] described ecstasy as a state of rapture in which "association with the outer world is so completely interrupted that an absolute analgesia exists. The patients see the heavens open, associate with the saints, hear heavenly music, experience wonderful odours and tastes, and an indescribable delight of distinct sexual coloring that pervades the entire body." James[22] emphasized the transiency of these states, their ineffability, the passivity of the mystic who "feels as if his own will were in abeyance," and the noetic quality whereby individuals find new significance in the familiar. In a comprehensive review of the literature, Anderson[23] noted the rarity of states of ecstasy, the existence of different types of ecstasy and the frequent observation that they are common to schizophrenia, epilepsy, and hysteria. He noted that psychopathologically these states were characterized by a "peculiar feeling of joy" or *Glucksgefuhl,* consisting of a remarkable blend of feeling with knowledge. He recorded four cases in which "a special feeling of joy, a component of which was a sense of calmness, was experienced, associated with an alteration of consciousness. This change involved an altered experience of the ego, described as a feeling of merging with the cosmos or with God, although the personal identity did not become lost."

Janet[24] noted in a patient the complete suppression of motor activity, the feeling of "a sort of possession," the sense of certitude of internal peace and power, and the feeling of being able to solve all problems and answer all questions. In a study[25] of patients who had become ill while participating in Subud, an Indonesian spiritualist sect, it was found that they all described experiences that resembled religious ecstasies:

P. S., prior to admission, reported a sense of heightened awareness and a feeling of being influenced by external force; V. S. described moments in the *Latihan* (spiritual exercises) when he felt detached, purified, and peaceful and, when he was admitted, he was convinced that he had a messianic role; F. P. suddenly stopped "suffering," felt "freed of the Cross" and experienced an inner calm and peacefulness. However, the three men continued to feel "different" for much longer than the brief periods usually described in ecstatic states. Most important, their experiences lacked the quality of ineffability cited by James, and were always related to Subud. In addition, the absence of sustained joy, and the presence of marked hyperactivity, instead of quietude and submissiveness, were not in keeping with genuine religious ecstasy.

In addition, P. S.'s heightened sensibility and feelings of influence were associated with hyperactivity, a flight of ideas, and delusions of grandeur, and were thus more likely concomitant features of a manic state than elements of genuine religious ecstasy; V. S.'s certainty of a messianic role, of having been chosen, coupled as it was with ideas of influence and reference and persecutory delusions, was more likely an elaborate delusion in an acute schizophrenic reaction than the expression of a heightened religious acuity; F. P.'s sense of spiritual freedom, combined as it was with much exhibitionistic acting-out, grandiosity, and hysterical manipulating seems more to have been an expression of hypomania in a person naturally recovering from a depression than a sense of merging with divinity so characteristic of ecstatic states.

In conclusion, it seems likely that these individuals were suffering from psychologic conflicts prior to their participation in Subud, and that these latent processes were exacerbated by their participation in the sect. Although Subud may have temporarily slowed the course of illness in these patients and provided some relief for their distress, it seems most likely that it ultimately contributed to the development of their illnesses through the excessive anxiety and conflict it aroused.

Possession may also play a formalized role in native systems of psychotherapy. Psychiatric illnesses in members of the North African Zar cult are believed to be due to possession by unfriendly Zar spirits, who must be placated or replaced by benevolent spirits in order to resolve the illness. In treatment, the healer, himself a former patient, calls upon the Zar spirit to identify itself and the sacrifice it requires, so as to protect the patient. The patient studies trance techniques, learning the behavior that accords with popular notions of the personality of his Zar. Zar possession is most common among women; it is the only way they can obtain influence over others.[26]

Abnormal mental states, or states that are deemed unusual by participants in a religious or esoteric sect, may occur during the course of religious activities. Occasionally, the group may itself recognize the need for special treatment of these states. These considerations are of some importance in contemporary theological discussions. Thomas Merton and others have argued that there are differences between the levels reached in regressive trance states and those attained in religious mystical experiences. According to Merton, genuine ecstatic religious experiences go beyond manic excitements, in that they involve mystical union and are religiously valid; regressive and narcissistic experiences, by contrast, involve no self-transcendence but only immersion in the self. This is normal in the transitional and early phases of mystical development. Regression here enables the individual to rest and return to the "root," to establish a deep continuity with the past and experience the profound rupture of going over into the future. In the state of sublimation beyond the mystical state, the perfect integration of personality creates harmony both within and with the world outside. The individual is free from desires, attachments, prejudices and prepossessions. This higher state does not bring on mental disorders and it cannot be obtained by the use of psychedelic or narcotic drugs. "In Indian mystic discipline, adept gurus guarded the disciple's progress from sublimation to the higher state of complete integration. There are some techniques which bypass altogether the borderlines of blind faith, superstition, ecstasies and mental disorder, which techniques of sublimation bring so close to the mind of man."[27]

Development to maturity in the mystical life is rare because of the difficulty of relinquishing regressive attachments to narcissistic stages. According to Merton, one must undergo "death" in order to "live again." This may be among the reasons why the Cartesian or pragmatic scientific viewpoint minimizes the significance of the intuitive and direct apprehension of reality, and views mystical experiences in terms of psychopathology.

Unusual mental states, such as trance, possession, and other forms of dissociation, generally occur in ritualistic contexts, or make their appearance prior to the assumption of special roles. They can be distinguished from psychiatric disorders by exploring the content of beliefs; the duration of the particular episode; the context in which they occur; the individual's ability to control his entry into the state; the outcome in terms of the rewards the role offers, and the extent to which behavior is idiosyncratic or conforms to the culturally prescribed patterns of the role.

Dreams

Many of the cultures in the developing world place great emphasis on non-verbal communication; they have therefore ritualized certain non-verbal phenomena, such as trance and also dreams. To the extent that dreams are the mental productions of the altered state of consciousness of sleep, and to the extent that both the process and the content of dreaming are invested with conscious ritual institutionalization, they may reasonably be regarded as an unusual mental state, differentially treated from culture to culture.

For many groups dreams are links to their ancestors. The Zulu believe that it is through dreams that the ancestral spirits communicate their approval or disapproval of individual behavior. The Zulu diviner, who functions as diagnostician, interpreter and healer in one, is believed to have a "soft head," or to be a "house of dreams" or "new home of the ancestors"—which is what gives him his healing powers.[28]

Many preliterate groups do not differentiate between waking and dreaming, and therefore incorporate highly stereotyped dream experiences into their daily routine. Such standardized, culturally patterned dream sequences are influenced by direction, suggestion and example. The most notable examples of this phenomenon are the "vision quests" of the Plains and Northwest Coast Indians, the "healing herb" dreams of the Bantu, the shamanistic dreams of the Australians and Formosans, and the temple dreams of the Greeks and Chinese. Among the Negritos of Luzon (Philippines), dying men instruct their sons to have a series of dreams, in which they will receive instruction and advice after the father's death.

Stewart[29] has examined the relationship between dream patterns and psychological test results among the Yami of Botel Tobage,* the Negritos of Luzon, and the Senoi of Malaya. The Negrito and the Yami sacrifice and pray to their children's dream

* This small island southeast of Taiwan, which is inhabited by aborigines, is now known as Hung-T'ou Island

characters, thus encouraging an increase of dreams about specific characters, who seek attention and demand to be placated by the dreamer. According to Stewart, the institutionalization of specific dream sequences may make the dream less adequate as a release, the result being psychosomatic and mental illness. The Yami pray to the good gods to protect their children from the bad dream characters, but they give no directive dream interpretation. When illness occurs among the Negritos, the dreamer is directed to face up to and kill off the offending dream characters. A Shaman may appear in the dream to destroy the dream enemies. The Senoi use the dream therapeutically, preventively, and constructively. They routinely analyze the dreams of the children in the family, and the dreams of men and older children in council, believing that all men, with the aid of others, can master and utilize all beings and forces in the dream universe. Senoi adolescents are initiated into manhood by learning, from specially trained dream teachers, certain inventions, poems, music, color-line designs and original dances; indeed, the dream process is a crucial aspect of leadership selection. The social integration effects of group dream interpretations are apparent.*

The Mohave believe that snamans and singers acquire their special knowledge in dreams. What in fact actually happens, according to Devereux,[30] is that knowledge learned subliminally in waking life is condensed into dream form and then reported by the potential shaman to have been learned in the dream. The power of the songs does not depend on whether they are letter-perfect reproductions of the existent Mohave knowledge, but rather on whether they are acceptable condensations and equivalents of the myth. It is knowledge of the culturally stereotyped dream patterns that confers shamanistic power on individuals. Each shaman overvalues his own version of the myth or song, as a way of satisfying his own idiosyncratic needs and implementing his social negativism; he does not acknowledge the cultural foundations of the dream experience.

---

* Stewart developed a system of dream direction for psychotic and psychosomatic patients on the basis of his studies of dream patterns in other cultures, and on the assumption that dreams can be influenced by interested physicians. He also assumed that direction of the dreaming process is beneficial to patients and more useful therapeutically than if the process is allowed to operate uninfluenced. The amenability of dreams to suggestion and to cultural influence is further supported by experiences with LSD and other mind-expanding drugs, which have been shown to be significantly influenced by group processes and are thus suitable vehicles for the reinforcement of various belief systems.

According to Devereux,[31] the borderline psychotic in our own society acquires "magical powers" by way of psychological processes that are identical to those by which the shaman acquires *his* socially sanctioned and accepted powers. The psychotic condenses various misperceptions of daily life into stereotyped dreams and condensation experiences, which he thinks are unique and superior to those of others; non-acceptance of his views only strengthens his convictions. This in turn may lead to negative or rejecting responses by others, which further reinforces the psychotic's idiosyncratic beliefs. Special beliefs and experiences thus create a special relationship between the individual and the community, such as fosters paranoid thinking. At the same time, it provides a certain stability and a kind of consensual validation, albeit a negative one, so that the patient is not totally isolated because of his misperceptions. One may even conjecture that the paranoid and the shaman have a need for generating some disagreement and discord with their fellows; this enables them to maintain contacts with others, while still remaining different from them. In some societies this is reinforced by such special roles as those of shaman, healer, and medium. In these cultures, the compensatory patterns are acceptable and tolerated; they help the disturbed individual to adapt without being identified as mentally ill. In more reality-oriented societies, these individuals are likely to be labeled as mentally ill and treated accordingly.

The central role of dreams in Iroquois life was well described by Father Freman, a Jesuit father who visited with the Seneca tribe of the Iroquois nation during the late seventeenth century:

The Iroquois have, properly speaking, only a single Divinity—the dream. To it they render their submission, and follow all its orders with the utmost exactness. The Tsonnontouens (Seneca) are more attached to this superstition than any of the others; their religion in this respect becomes even a matter of scruple; whatever it be that they think they have done in their dreams, they believe themselves absolutely obliged to execute at the earliest moment. The other nations content themselves with observing those of their dreams which are the most important; but this people, which has the reputation of living more religiously than its neighbors, would think itself guilty of a great crime if it failed in its observance of a single dream. [They] think only of that, they talk about nothing else, and all their cabins are filled with their dreams. They spare no pains, no industry, to show their attachment thereto and their folly in this particular goes to such an excess as would be hard to imagine. He who has dreamed during the night that he was bathing, runs immediately, as soon as he rises, all naked, to several cabins, in each of which he has a kettleful of water thrown over his body, however cold the weather may be. Another who has dreamed that he was taken prisoner and burned alive, has found himself bound and burned like a captive on the next day, being persuaded that by thus satisfying his dream, this fidelity will avert from him the pain and infamy of captivity and death, which according to what he has learned from his Divinity, he is otherwise bound to suffer among his enemies. Some have been known to go as far as Quebec, traveling a hundred and fifty leagues, for the sake of getting a dog, that they had dreamed of buying there . . .[32]

Culture can be seen to affect personality traits, the labeling and the reinforcement of certain psychological mechanisms that can then become institutionalized patterns; these are differently labeled and rewarded in different societies. In some instances, psychopathological phenomena may become the criteria for certain institutionalized patterns. It is of value to recognize these limits in making determinations as to what is pathological and what is the normal range of human behavior. Such distinctions are examined in the next two chapters.

CHAPTER 3   THE EFFECT OF
CULTURE ON
PSYCHIATRIC
DISORDERS

PSYCHIATRISTS HAVE LONG BEEN PAYING
attention to mental illness in different communities and cultures.
Kraepelin[1] noted that, in Java, melancholia and mania were rare
and that depressive reactions rarely contained any elements of a
sense of "sinfulness." Later, Bleuler[2] commented upon the differences between English and Irish patients, as well as between
Bavarian and Saxon patients. Others[3] have described various
"culture-bound" syndromes, such as *amok,* the *windigo* psychosis
of the Cree, Salteaux and Ojibwa, *latah* and Arctic hysteria. More
recently Tooth[4] has described a special category of "delusional"
states in West Africans, while Carothers[5] has reported on "ill
defined" states and "primitive" psychoses among West Africans.

Other writers have stressed the significance of cultural factors
in the *distribution* of mental illness. Seligman[6] noted in 1929 that
confusional states were more common than systematized insani-
ties among the Papuans of New Guinea, and that he could not
find any cases there of manic-depressive illness. Berne[7] observed
that toxic confusional psychoses rather than the schizophrenias
were predominant among hospitalized Malaysians. Carothers[8] related Westernization to an increase in manifest paranoid behavior among patients in Kenya. Similarly, Spiro[9] took note of
the fact that the Ifaluk in the Carolines had violent paranoid
outbursts only after the Japanese occupation, while Slotkin[10]
emphasized the presence of phenomena of paranoid schizophre-

Notes for Chapter 3 will be found on pages 199–201.

nia among acculturated Menomini. Opler[11] found that lower-class Filipinos had a high proportion of the affective disorders and catatonic confusional states that were present among the Hawaiian hospitalized, while Carothers[12] and Tooth[13] both found in Africa statistically low incidences of depression and suicidal states, side by side with relatively high rates of confusional states among African natives.

The finding of significant differences in the content of the delusions of disturbed individuals in different cultures has contributed to an emphasis on the pathogenic effects of cultural factors. Careful examination of these delusional systems, however, has frequently revealed their close relationship to the belief system that is prevalent in the culture, others highlighting the functional and restitutive significance of delusions, rather than their pathological significance. Laubscher[14] found that schizophrenic symptoms among Africans in Queensland included auditory and visual hallucinations, with mythological content, as well as delusions of grandeur (becoming a chief or doctor), and of being poisoned and bewitched; the delusions of Europeans, by contrast, included influences operating from a distance, through electricity, telepathy and hypnotism. Similarly, Tooth[15] found that the delusional content of "bush" people in the north of Ghana was associated with the ramifications of the fetish system, whereas among the sophisticated people of the south of Ghana and, in particular, Accra, it included ideas of influence and control by electricity and wireless, along with messianic delusions and delusions of grandeur. Stainbrook[16] has noted that lower-class Bahians in Brazil, when they are schizophrenic, suffer from anxieties and fears of retribution relating to African or Catholic deities, while the delusions of middle-class Brazilians are expressed in terms of economic and class conceptions of power, along with such impersonal influences as that of electricity and physical waves. Lambo[17] found that delusions among rural nonliterate Yorubans related to supernatural concepts and ancestral cults, while in literate Africans hypochondriacal delusions were prominent. These considerations take on special significance when one is attempting to establish the relationship between cultural factors and psychiatric disorder.

The view that cultural factors condition the basic form and structure of psychiatric symptoms and illness has been in large part derived from reports of special transient forms of schizophrenia, along with a high frequency of hysterical disorders, and a low frequency of depressive disorders, in the developing societies. While it is relatively easy to see how culture can contribute to patterns of psychological defense, criteria for entry into the sick role, and attitudes towards specific symptoms, it is more difficult to understand how culture is able to affect the basic structure of psychiatric disorder. An examination of the data will serve to clarify some of these issues. At the outset, however, it should be noted that these studies do not prove that cultural factors produce illness, nor even that some psychiatric entities occur only in specific cultures. Their importance is in demonstrating how culture may influence both the manifestations and the treatment of psychiatric illness, and how it determines the content and the symbols that are associated with such illness.

SPECIAL TRANSIENT FORMS
OF SCHIZOPHRENIA

Characteristics

The view that culture can exercise an influence on the basic structure of the major psychotic disorders has derived its most explicit support from reports of certain atypical forms of schizophrenia that are found among tribal Africans. Lambo[18] in 1955 reported that schizophrenia in non-literate Africans is manifested in anxiety, depression, alteration of time and space perception, hypochondriasis, magicomythical projection symptoms, episodic twilight or confusional states, depersonalization, emotional lability, retrospective falsification of reality by transitory and ill-defined hallucinatory experiences, and transient delusions, which lack tenacity of conviction. The twilight state, the dominant feature of this illness, is sometimes characterized by frenzy and homicidal excitement. In addition, this atypical form of schizophrenia differs from the schizophrenic-like psychosis that is precipitated by organic illness, in that bizarre symptoms appear acutely, while disturbances in association and affect are not prominent; on the other hand, pathoplastic features are very much in evidence.

Carothers[19] in 1959 characterized the manifestations of confusional states as general excitability, impaired sleep, excessive speech, visual hallucinations, singing, dancing, wandering aimlessly, and talking to oneself. The same syndrome has been described among Filipinos,[20] Mexican-Americans[21] and Formosan[22] aborigines. Confusional states are often preceded by fever, agitation and violence; unlike toxic delirium in Western patients, however, which disappears when the underlying physical illness is checked, delirium and confusion among Africans comes about with the mildest toxic agent or infection. In Africans, delirium is often the predominant symptom of general paresis, schizophrenia and trypanosomiasis. Initially, it may mask the underlying psychiatric disorder, while the delirious frenzy may be so severe as to persist until death intervenes. This frenzy, which is similar to Malayan amok, may be precipitated by acute mania, epilepsy, cerebral malaria or psychopathy. It has been described by Carothers[23] as follows:

The African is evidently prone to develop a kind of twilight or confusional state—sometimes brief (a matter of an hour), sometimes more prolonged (a matter of weeks)—but always tending to spontaneous recovery within a matter of time. These states occur in many backgrounds of physical disease, underlying psychosis or neurosis or even of apparent normality, and are precipitated by a variety of physical and mental traumata. It may be surmised that physical or psychotic factors play a larger part in the more lasting phases, and emotional factors are larger in the transient. Anxiety, with or without depression, precedes the onset of acute cases, but is not sustained for long. It is always related by the patient to bewitchment, and he is fully cognizant of the latter's origin and object. Premonitory symptoms of a Ganser-syndrome type, with childish unaccountable behavior, may precede the onset of the major episode. The key note of the episode itself is a confusion and dominance of action by emotion. The emotional state is usually one of fear (which may be panic), or of hostility; and activity may reach the height of violence directed to the subject or more often those around him. Reality is distorted on lines of parallel mood and there may or may not be an hallucinosis. Recovery when this occurs is usually remarkably complete, or followed by Ganser's syndrome or various symptoms.

Thereafter amnesia for the episode appears to be the rule; care is cast aside; and unless the cause of the trouble continues in an active form, or some new one arises, the subject may pass for normal once again and the episode will not be repeated.

According to Amara:[24]

The most common form of schizophrenic presentation in the African is catatonia or acute excitement. Catatonia is usually manifested in posturing, mutism, facial grimaces and mannerisms. When the patient is brought in with acute excitement, a mistaken diagnosis of hypomania is quite possible. There are associated delusions of grandeur, loquacity and hyperactivity. Very often the patient has been bound, and hands and feet show deep abrasions where the ropes have bitten through the skin. Under observation, the patient can be seen alternating between catatonia and excitement within a few days. This fluctuation in symptoms was also observed by Tewfik in the records of his patients.

Primary delusions are at best difficult to elicit; from the African patient, it is almost impossible to do so. Secondary delusions of grandeur, religion, nihilism, passivity and persecution are the most common; ideas of reference are also quite common. Auditory hallucinations which are usually attributed to voices of God or to the devil are prevalent. Tactile hallucinations—ascribed to witches gnawing at the patient's skin and bones, or to poisonous objects or dangerous insects that are being thrown at or implanted in the patient—may be the only initial symptom described.

According to Amara, the loosening of ideas is common in African schizophrenics; but thought-blocking is difficult to demonstrate, because of the African's customary difficulties with expression and verbalization. Disorders of volition, such as lack of initiative, denial, obstinacy and weakness, are quite common; they seem to be more evident than in the European counterpart. Emotional disorders, with incongruity, shallow affect and apathy, are very prominent symptoms.

Differential Diagnosis

Pharmacologically active stimulants, hypnotics, and hallucinogens produce problems of abuse and addiction, toxic psychoses, and withdrawal syndromes that may at times take schizophrenic-like forms.* Patterns of drug use must therefore be considered in any attempt to make a differential diagnosis. Visual hallucinations, unsystematized delusions, agitation, insomnia and hyperirritability are more compatible with the toxic confusional syndromes that are secondary to systematic infection (such as a mild encephalomeningitis), than they are with a functional disorder.

Hypoproteinemia, anemia, parasitic infestation, and avitaminosis increase vulnerability to the functional psychiatric disorders, as well as producing debilitating psychological syndromes, such as pellagra, which is widespread throughout Africa, especially in Egypt, Nyasaland, South Africa, Sierra Leone, Sudan and Nigeria. Tooth[25] found that 80% of the hospital cases of trypanosomiasis had mental symptoms; trypanasomiasis also ac-

---

* These transient schizophrenic illnesses nave also been attributed to the limited development of the African brain, physical and nutritional factors; and the pathoplastic effects of culture.

counted for the majority of patients who were brought in "raving mad" to the Accra Mental Hospital.

That physical disability can increase susceptibility to psychological disorders is certainly demonstrated in Collis'[26] report on physical health and psychiatric disorders in Nigeria. A series of therapeutic diagnostic tests were given, over a period of three months, to 33 people with functional psychiatric illness and to a group of 20 who had previously been rated by the Cornell-Aro study group as mentally normal. The purpose of these tests was to compare the results of treatment; using placebos for controls, treatment was directed toward the resolution of functional symptoms and the achievement of good physical health.

The cases were divided into three treatment groups. The first received "total push" physical therapy for hookworm and malaria, as well as for vitamin, iron and calcium deficiencies; the second group received placebos, and the third psychopharmaceuticals. The third group as a whole evidenced a greater rate of improvement than the first; but when thin and weak patients were compared with well-nourished patients, the superiority of the results obtained by psychiatric treatment was found to be confined to the well-nourished: in the 14 "thin and weak" patients, there was no significant difference between the results achieved by physical treatment and those achieved by psychiatric treatment. These and other results led the authors to conclude that many factors must be at work, in combination with one another, in producing psychiatric illness, and that difficulties are encountered when efforts are made to attach etiological primacy to the physical segment alone.

The schizophrenic process is fundamentally a state of disordered cognitive function; this is the common final manifestation of a variety of processes, some constitutional and some acquired. One highly susceptible group includes those with weak egos, like the African villager who has been placed in an unfamiliar situation without his customary group supports. Anxiety is poorly tolerated by pre-literate Africans; indeed, for many of them, it constitutes a threat to life. The disorder of cognitive function is generally interpreted in terms of bewitchment and other such culturally frightening conceptions. These generate much anxiety, especially among those who are dependent on their peer groups for a sense of psychological integrity.

According to Lambo,[27] African culture is characterized by belief in supernatural forces; faith in the magic of symbols; expectations of supernatural punishment; orally preserved tribal legends and mythological concepts, with an emphasis on animism; full play of affective activity in daily life; complete identification with the group; lowering of ego boundaries and thought processes; ancestor worship; belief in the existence of idealized good objects; a tendency to regard dream life as objective reality; a simple, restricted, ill-defined and rudimentary usage of symbols, and strong religious belief. These characteristics suggest fixation at the oral level of development, and seem to be suitable to a society in which ego boundaries do not have to be clearly maintained, because of heavy individual reliance on the support of the community. It is quite likely that such undifferentiated ego patterns are related to the high frequency with which hysteriform and schizophrenic-form illnesses occur among Africans, when they experience the social change of urbanization.

Similarly, the frequency of confusional excitement and the low incidence of depression and suicidal behavior in developing countries have been attributed to the outward rather than inner expression of hostility among the people. In fact, they appear to be similar to those catastrophic reactions, characterized by acute psychotic and confusional symptoms, that are seen in disaster situations and which promptly remit. These acute confusional psychoses occur most often among unstable emotional types, who are stimulus-dependent and therefore have little in the way of habitual patterns for dealing with acute stresses.

These are not classical schizophrenic reactions, in which primary thought disorders progress to states of deterioration. Catastrophic anxiety is generally associated with inability to cope with the severe, life-threatening stresses of nature, sickness and death, as these are daily experienced in the developing countries, quite by contrast with the situation in industrial societies, where people are protected from them. Increasing urbanization in the developing countries, with its accompaniment of new living patterns and new adaptive skills, may lead to lower rates of acute confusional states, as people come to be increasingly protected from acute stresses. Self-restraint, emotional inhibition and compliance are essential for adaptation to the urban setting: since the work schedule provides less time for group rituals and fewer opportunities to depend on group supports, there is a great need for internal controls—for example, conscience—to help the individual to adapt to complex situations. This should make for new patterns of socialization, and these in turn should have a profound effect on the adaptive patterns that are the behavioral manifestation of the unconscious foundations of personality. The

African does not suffer from a "weak" superego; he is simply demonstrating a pattern of adjustment that is suitable to a world in which there is opportunity to express drives with little delay.

The highly stylized nature of these acute confusional episodes suggests that some role-playing may be taking place—that is, that patients are behaving in accordance with the cultural cues that distinguish between sickness behavior and sick-role behavior. Confusional manifestations result from the interaction between non-specific external or physiological stresses and the specific psychological defense systems of the rural African. Acute physical illness, or constitutional vulnerability, may predispose the patient to react in this way. An important role in producing this constitutional vulnerability is played by the high incidence of asphyxial events at birth, as the result of poor obstetrical care, and by chronic malnutrition from dietary deficiencies and endemic parasitism. Better control of nutritional parasitic-infectious illnesses should lead to reduced rates of these conditions.

It seems likely from the study of atypical schizophrenia that culture does affect the content of the symptoms, as well as the basic course of the illness. The ideas and beliefs that are distorted and exaggerated in delusional formation derive, in the first place, from the culture. In fact, it is sometimes possible to detect stress points in the social system by assessing the frequency with which certain individuals are felt to be the source of persecution, in persecutory delusions. Rather than taking the delusional belief as evidence of illness, it may make more sense to take it as evidence of, or at least as a clue to, an understanding of the social system. In traditional societies such as India[28] and Mexico,[29] for example, persecutory ideas commonly center around mothers-in-law, members of the extended family, and the spirits of the dead. Examination of the sociocultural system does indeed reveal that these constitute stress points for everyone.

According to Wittkower,[30] social and emotional withdrawal, which is common among schizophrenics in Asia, may be related to the Hindu and Buddhist teaching of withdrawal as an acceptable mode of reacting to difficulty. The high frequency of catatonic rigidity, negativism and stereotypy among Indian schizophrenics has similarly been related to the traditional Indian passive-aggressive response to a threatening world. In the same way, persecutory ideas occur more frequently in Europeans than in Asiatics; this may be due to a lower tolerance of aggressive impulses among Europeans. While it is extremely difficult to ascertain the relationship between culture and psychiatric symptomatology, without knowing the distribution of symptom patterns in all schizophrenic patients, both in and out of treatment, these preliminary reports have added support to the clinical impressions of a number of investigators.

What accounts for the different effects of culture on the manifestations of psychiatric disorder? Lenz[31] of Austria has suggested an interesting view—namely, that the paranoid form of schizophrenia is more common in differentiated cultures throughout the world; that catatonic and hebephrenic subforms prevail elsewhere; that aggressive behavior is common in primitive cultures, while auditory hallucinations are common in cultures in which verbal expression and abstract thinking are highly developed. Where abstract thinking is common, he believes, systematic delusions are also common. Lenz explained differences in psychopathological pictures by the fact that primitive man has no conscience, and is therefore inherently incapable of experiencing feelings of guilt. According to this view, rapport with the deity is for the primitive what rapport with self or conscience is for the Westerner. Wittkower has similarly noted that feelings of guilt, depression, and schizophrenia are related not only to the Christian religion, but also to certain degrees of emotional and intellectual differentiation and personality development.

This view is consistent with the clinical observation that the patient's character or basic personality, as well as his adaptive skills, influence the way he copes with psychotic illness. The manner of coping will manifest itself in terms of various secondary symptoms that give the illness its characteristic local flavor. A schizoid individual who develops schizophrenia is likely to show exaggerated evidence of autism; a more aggressive personality would probably be more prone to hyperactivity and violent behavior; an obsessional would characteristically show thought disorder and delusion formation. Characterological patterns are likely to affect the depressive disorders in similar fashion.

FREQUENCY OF HYSTERICAL DISORDERS

It is generally believed that hysterial disorders are more common among less educated and less sophisticated individuals, in both the developed and the developing societies. This has been deduced from the characterological patterns that are commonly found in primitive societies, as well as in persons with hysterical character structures or with personality traits of suggestibility, emotional liability, poor frustration tolerance and hyperreactivity —all of which have been seen as favoring the various symptoms of hysterical disorders. In India hysterical convulsions, numbness, paralysis, blindness, deafness, vomiting, aphonia and association reactions were found to be common symptoms of hysteria among the lower classes, the less educated, and women. According to Vahia,[32] the joint family system and the lack of emancipation contributed to the pathogensis of hysteria in women. Insofar as marriages are arranged, a woman is virtually in bondage for life; to improve her lot, her only recourse is illness. Hysterical fits attributed to supernatural forces are socially acceptable ways for the oppressed wife to gain sympathy and attention, as well as relief from her duties.

While hysterical symptomatology does lead to conflict avoidance, it is not necessary to assert, as Vahia and others have done, that it is the secondary gain that is the motivation for the development of such symptoms. Hysterical phenomena may actually derive from weaknesses of the central nervous system or of the personality, rather than from unconscious motivational patterns; they may indeed develop simply as a non-specific result of the stress that has been imposed on the individual.

Parker[33] has suggested that hysteria may prevail in groups in which there is a greater degree of dependency-need satisfaction and less stress on early independence and individual achievement. In such situations, emotional expression is quickly recognized and rewarded. This formulation does to some extent account for the high frequency of hysterical disorders in pre-literate societies, females, ethnic minorities, members of groups of any sort, and the lower classes. The achievement-oriented middle class stress frustration tolerance and postponement of gratification; these enable the individual to get along without much dependency frustration in his early life, as a result of the ready satisfaction of the needs of the young. The individual is not forever fixated at an infantile level, where he needs, yet finds it hard to obtain emotional support. The constellation of early support and subsequent preparation for independence and mastery is lacking in those groups that show a high frequency of hysterical reactions. The preliterate tribesman, who has a number of parental surrogates, a diffuse system of supports for his dependency needs, and a great dependency on his peer groups, never develops the inner confidence that comes from total initial satisfaction of dependency needs. While the peer group does provide security for adolescents, it requires that the individual conform to the group, and this clearly prevents the development of independence.

Slum dwellers in cultures of poverty and the lower socio-economic classes tend to neglect the dependency needs of the young; in addition, they suffer from lack of adequate resources to care for the young. The consequent failure to develop skill in postponing gratification is not made up for by the development of group ties, as it is among the Africans. As a result, one finds a high frequency of impulse disorders and oral deprivation patterns.

In most societies, women have considerable difficulty in developing independent patterns. They are not expected to contain their frustrations; indeed, they are encouraged and expected to be emotionally labile and expressive. As a result, expressions of distress, unless they are exaggerated, as in hysterical symptoms, tend to be ignored or to be attributed simply to feminine behavior.

Along these lines, Yap[34] has noted that hysterical behavior is most frequently associated with small cohesive groups, where face-to-face and communal cooperative patterns prevail, so that individual expectations of help are high, while individual striving for achievement is not stressed. There is a greater expectation of dependency-need satisfaction in such groups, than in the larger and less personalized groupings of an urban industrial society.

Parker has also suggested that hysterical behavior may be more prevalent in societies where the process of early socialization is not severe, and there is minimal repression of dependency needs and sexual drives. Because of the relatively high gratification of dependency needs in these societies, the superego structure will not be severe or rigid, and the individual may instead become fixated at an oral infantile level. Hysterical behavior may also be more prevalent in societies that provide models of it in such institutionalized religious practices as spirit possession.

Hysterical disorders appear to be precipitated by the same non-specific environmental stresses that contribute to the production of various other disorders. Which specific disorder develops will depend on the patient's constitutional predisposition, as well as on the sociocultural factors that are present both in the early socialization period and in adulthood—particularly factors that are associated with dependency needs, frustration tolerance and self-reliance. Cultural factors affect both the adaptive mechanisms and the frequency distribution of those non-specific stress situations that may influence the development of disorders. The basic mechanism of the hysterical reaction operates on a biophysiological level; once the mechanism has been set in motion, by the interaction of an external stress with a vulnerable individual, it follows its own course. Physical factors can play a part in such non-psychotic states, as they do in psychotic or confusional states. The psychosomatic disadaptation syndrome among Andean Indians that was described in Chapter One clearly demonstrates the contribution of biological factors to psychophysiological symptoms.

Data on mass hysteria and collective epidemics have also been used to support the view that hysteria is frequent in developing societies. This is among the most interesting material in the literature on transcultural psychiatry. In 1964, Kagwa[35] reported on an epidemic of mass hysteria in Mbale, East Africa. Characterized by acute onset of confusion and agitation, which later progressed to physical exhaustion, it predominantly affected 300 women in the 15-to-30 age group. The first three days were characterized by agitation and assaultive behavior, in response to hallucinated orders of ancestral spirits. This was followed by several weeks of physical exhaustion, quietness, somatization and continued belief in the quasi-delusional hallucinatory system. In the third stage, the mood improved and affability returned, yet belief in the original hallucinatory ideas persisted.

Similar epidemics have been recorded in recent years. A laughing mania appeared in January 1962 in Buoba, Tanzania. Another, associated with violence, occurred among 600 individuals in Kitezi in July 1963. In each instance, these epidemics took place among members of the same tribe and culture, even though they were living on different sides of geographical boundaries.

A viral or parasitic etiology for these epidemics could not be proved; Kagwa has attributed them instead to the psychological conflict that is generated by rapid development. Whereas conflict is manifested among the educated in political, economic or educational areas, exposure of the uneducated to sudden religious and political changes tends to produce conflicts in the area of religion.

Yap has suggested that the jumpers and barkers at revival meetings in the late eighteenth-century United States were manifesting group hysteria. The fact that such behavior could be ritualized supports the thesis that it is possible to induce irrational phenomena. Irrational, albeit stereotyped, group behavior may be precipitated by a range of stimuli in various situational contexts: one single hysterical person is able to produce a "spontaneous" outbreak of hysteria in a susceptible crowd.

People require consensual validation from others about the

state of the world at any point in time. If irrational behavior can be attributed to a shared and acceptable source of anxiety, and as such regarded as understandable, it is difficult for individuals to dismiss it as deviant or to ignore it. The tendency is to accept the fears of others as valid, to suspend rational judgment and to respond to the environmental cues that have been focused on, so as to meet the expectations of others.

The pressure to conform to the group consensus, which is derived from the fundamental human need to be accepted, may also be far more powerful than the ability (usually underdeveloped in most people) to suspend the decision to act until further information is available. That ability rarely develops in preliterate societies, where it is peers, rather than individual conscience, that determine the standards of behavior. This is also true for adolescents—especially those in transitional or industrial societies—who have no specified boundaries or explicit social roles, and are therefore considerably influenced by peer group pressures.

It is difficult to pinpoint the causes of psychological epidemics. The most useful procedure at this stage of our knowledge is to turn our attention to such characteristics of epidemics as patterns of spread, symptom changes over time, and frequency distributions of particular symptoms. Hysterical contagions should, for example, be studied in terms of susceptible age, sex and membership in those tribal groups that are likely to spread aberrant behavior patterns, because of the lack of adequate inner strength or ego control. Susceptibility to hysteria has generally been explained, psychologically, in terms of intense affects and ideas that, while they are excluded from consciousness, nevertheless impinge on the somatic nervous system and influence behavior. Some groups are more prone than others to utilize this mechanism, and are therefore likely more often to manifest susceptibility to hysteria.

This does not explain the contagiousness of the phenomenon. For that, we must utilize psychosocial linking concepts, such as empathy and identification with the disturbed. Increased anxiety about succumbing may precipitate a panic state and loss of rational control. It is the other-directedness and the suggestibility of adolescents that account for the greater frequency among them of these empathic phenomena.

Most discussions of psychiatric epidemics have focused on reports of dramatic and bizarre crowd phenomena, such as lycanthropy in the Middle Ages, the hysterical outbreaks of schoolgirls

in restricted environmental situations, epidemics of St. Vitus'
dance, and other group patterns with a distinct element of contagiousness. These are not, however, the only disorders that occur
in epidemic proportions—that is, at rates greater than might be
expected from chance alone. Auto accidents, alcoholism, drug
addiction, and mental illness can all be studied in terms of their
epidemic proportions. It is likely that depressive symptoms such
as insomnia, irritability, psychosomatic disorders, disturbances
in appetite and eating patterns are increasing in frequency in the
developed and developing societies and in some places are reach-
ing epidemic proportions.

RARITY OF DEPRESSIVE DISORDERS

Reports of the rarity of depressive states in preliterate and
developing societies may have to do with social attitudes about
depressive reactions rather than with an actually lower incidence
of such conditions. They may also be concerned with the age distribution of the population in developing countries. The duration of life is shorter in the developing countries: the majority
of the population do not reach the forties and fifties, the ages of
greatest risk for developing these disorders. In addition to this,
there are a number of other cultural factors that appear to be
important with regard to the reported low incidence. Much of the
symptomatic behavior that is associated with depressive disorders is, for example, secondary to the response made by the patient and others to his basic symptoms. That response may intensify existing symptoms and lead to the development of new
ones. If a patient is too pressed by the social response to his
illness, simple suspicion may evolve into ideas of reference, and
even delusions. The fundamental propensity to such perceptually
disordered thinking is undoubtedly there from the start; but it
is detectible only by astute clinical assessment of the initial suspiciousness.

Phenomenologically, depression may be experienced as a
sense of personal decay, decline or retardation, along with cessation of the body machinery. How the individual describes this
experience of energy change is clearly influenced by his perception of the declining drive in himself and of the world about
him. To the extent that the culture offers myths and symbols that
reflect the nature of these perceived inner and outer experiences,
the individual may describe or interpret his experiences in those

cultural terms. This may lead to a reduction of anxiety about the condition; but it is also likely that it will contribute to the non-recognition of illness in the patient, and the assignment of his communications to some other category of experience—for example, deviant role, chronic sick role, and divinely inspired role. The *windigo* psychosis among the Ojibwa Indians (see Chapter 4) is a manifestation of this; another manifestation is provided by Yoruban and Ghananian women, who often claim to be witches when they are clinically depressed. Since the idea of witches is culturally valid and, in fact, rather commonplace, depressed patients may as a result go unrecognized.[36]

Beliefs and customs not only provide alternative explanations; they also furnish channels of expression for psychopathological disturbances, thereby rendering them psychodynamically understandable and ego-syntonic. To the extent that psychiatric disorder may thus go unrecognized or may be "explained away" without treatment, complications may develop when the individual's culturally acceptable behavior involves him in potentially noxious experiences. Conversely, beliefs and customs may lead many persons who have minimal situational problems—for example, in love, work and fortune—needlessly to seek help from fortune tellers, soothsayers and others who skilfully exploit the dependency needs of the troubled.

What varies from culture to culture, yet can be ascertained at this stage of our knowledge and technical development, is the attitudes that are prevalent toward nuclear and secondary symptoms of psychiatric disorders. These attitudes include: recognition of the patient's symptoms as symptoms; criteria qualifying him for entry into the appropriate role—for example, deviant, sick, criminal, sacred or profane; and what is thought to be appropriate treatment. Study of these attitudes may shed light on the experiences and the suffering of depressed patients in different cultures, and may in that way help in the prediction of prevalence patterns. One might expect, for example, that loss of energy and easy fatiguability would not be as great a problem in an urban slum, where jobs are scarce, as it would be for field workers in an agrarian society. It is likely that depressive complications will be less often reported and less often treated (even when reported), in societies in which the symptoms and the associated disability of depressive illness are of little social or economic concern.

Further, depressive symptoms may not lead to the adoption of the sick role in cultures that institutionalize certain experiences or symptom states, with the result that they are not ego-alien to the members of that culture. Where depressive symptoms are viewed as normal accompaniments of the "hard life," man's fate, or human nature, they are not likely to lead to the sick role or treatment; the same thing holds true when they are regarded as being characteristic or normal for particular age, sex, class or occupational groups.

In some cultures, institutionalized orgies or mourning customs following death may act cathartically to prevent the development of depression. Africans and other tribal groups learn to shift responsibility to supernatural powers, and to minimize ideas of free will and personal responsibility, to such an extent that they rarely express self-reproach or experience guilt when they have depressive illnesses. According to Amara, patterns of reliance on peer groups and on the community onto which the guilt is projected also tend to mitigate against guilt and suicidal feelings in depressed patients. The medical model of depression also minimizes the patient's responsibility for his symptoms, undoubtedly reducing guilt and anxiety thereby, and perhaps accounting for minimal overreaction to and speedier recovery from depression in the developing countries.

It is likely that such patterns influence the recognition and reporting of depression, as well as the complaints of the patients themselves. In Kenya, for example, both psychiatrists and natives have expressed the belief that there is little depression. Thus, there is an overall "set" not to diagnose depression. If a case does appear, it is likely to be rationalized in some other way. This general atmosphere of tolerance of depressive symptoms contributes to non-reactivity or a lack of alertness to them, and consequently to a reduced reporting of cases. Carothers noted that mild depressive disorders went unrecognized in African culture because of their similarity to the cultural background itself— that is, to the apathy and lassitude that are the sequels of malnutrition and parasitism. Cultural focus on certain symptoms leads to viewing depressive symptoms in other frames of reference. Murphy, et al.[37], state that depressive mood, insomnia, and loss of interest are reported for depression in Asia. Diurnal mood changes, anorexia and constipation are, by contrast, uncommon among Indians, while preoccupation with body and mind, religion and family, as well as loss of libido and theatrical grief, are common. Guilt feelings are rarely reported in the Philippines and in Japan; indeed, ideas of sin and suicide are infrequently reported in any of the non-Western societies. A preliterate tribal African or Peruvian Indian will rarely complain of concentration difficulty; depressive mood is also a rare complaint among those who have a pessimistic or fatalistic world view. Among Africans, depressive illnesses are frequently associated with confusional symptoms and are of shorter duration, while in Japan and other advanced societies, they are commonly associated with obsessive-compulsive disorders.

To understand the prevalence of depression in a culture, as well as its impact on it, it is important to understand the attitudes that are involved in its recognition; this has more to do with the management of disorders and the prevention of complications than with their basic etiology or with the stress systems of the society. An important facet of the underrecognition of depressive disorders is the reduction of secondary, complicating responses to them; they themselves may thus become more problematic than the original problem or illness. Few social processes are brought to bear in labeling depressed patients. Such a "wait and see" attitude exercises a salutary effect by reducing the pressure to function, which so often induces guilt and other secondary symptoms. The depressed person may not be greatly inclined to examine the reasons for depression. Such self-examination, which is a culturally patterned or learned behavior, often initiates a self-cycling series of ruminative preoccupations and unsuccessful efforts to resolve those social or interpersonal difficulties that appear to be serving as causative factors. These social epiphenomena may lead to discomfort or shame, and even to suicide. An examination of differences in the cross-cultural reactions to the depressive state provides a clearer view of which depressive phenomena are psychological complications, arising out of the interaction between the patient and his social world, and which are characteristic of the depression itself.

Running amok and confusional excitement, both of which may reflect the existence of underlying manic-depressive disorders, have more social impact than depressive symptoms. The use of limited hospital resources for control of the violent and the potentially violent contributes at the same time to neglect of quiet or retarded patients.

Murphy, et al. (see [37]) found that diurnal mood changes, insomnia, early morning wakening, and a falling-off of interest in the social environment were almost universally regarded as the core symptoms of depressive states. Fatigue, loss of sexual interest, self-accusatory ideas, anorexia and weight loss were associated with these core symptoms among Europeans, but not among persons from developing countries. The association between guilt feelings and depression was independent of the frequency of depression, as well as of the association between depression and suicidal ideation; this suggested to the McGill group that guilt feelings were related to the Judaeo-Christian emphasis on sin and guilt and to internalized standards (superego) of behavior, since they did not appear in patients from other religions.

Clinical experience certainly suggests that the individual's personality plays a large part in his ability to tolerate and to cope with a depressive illness. Some unstable and obsessional patients may be incapacitated for many years by a depression, while others are able to function adequately during periods of remission from recurrent depressions. The response to depression ranges from an exacerbation of psychotic symptoms and family pressures in infantilized schizophrenic patients, through a sense of emptiness, numbness and loss of feeling among obsessional patients, to histrionic helplessness, clinging, demanding, and increased dependency among hysterical patients. Cultural factors influence the characteristic ways of dealing with depression in much the same way as these personality factors do.

The rarity of depression has also been explained by way of the psychoanalytic hypothesis that depression is caused by ambivalence toward the loved object and by the turning inward of aggression, following loss of the loved object. Where ties to individual parents are not intense, because of the presence of numerous surrogate parents, as in Africa, the ambivalence that is felt toward them and toward subsequent objects is less. As a result, the loved object has much less emotional significance for the person involved, and it therefore takes very little for him to introject anger, and to produce thereby the concomitant of depression.

Lambo[38] has suggested that depression is to be found in those cultures that enforce social control by way of abstract and situation-centered moral teachings, which are predicated on moral obligation. It is his notion that the individualistic, competitive and aggressively striving Protestant cultures may specifically produce unusual psychological stress, and that belief in original sin probably intensifies oppressive self-reproach in a superficial, pathoplastic manner. In describing "laughing" depressions Lambo has indeed emphasized that the classical form of depression does not occur in Africa.

Most studies have relied on *ex post facto* explanations of stressful experiences to explain observed rates; few have undertaken to predict the frequency and distribution of disorders on the basis of measured stress. Such a study ought ideally to be based on a theory of stress and its relationship to disorder, as well as on an independent measure of stress and of disorder, so as to see how these are distributed in a society.

The usual measures of social stress and of demographic variables generally tell us little about the phenomenon; frequency of prayer and attitude toward the supernatural may be more important than the specific denomination. It is probably the clustering of factors, interacting in synergistic ways, rather than single factors by themselves, that accounts for human and cultural effects. It is important, therefore, to determine these clusters for predictive purposes.

Asuni[39] has suggested that, while depression is common in Africa, suicide rates are low because of the lack of inwardly directed aggressive acts based on guilt, a sense of unworthiness and self-reproach. According to Baasher,[40] one-third of the patients seeking psychiatric aid in Khartoum, North Sudan, suffered from depression of one kind or another.

The rarity of depressive illnesses, as seen by earlier writers, could be attributed to failure to recognize the cases because of the application of Western standards. According to Amara,[41] "Most patients with depression exhibit florid symptoms of hallucination and delusions, even in what may appear to be mild conditions. The hallucinations may involve any of the senses but are mostly tactile and visual. Occasionally one sees a classical depressive syndrome, but this is rare. Neurotic symptoms are very often superimposed on the depression, with frequent somatic manifestations."

In view of the close correlation between depression and suicide, it is of interest that the reported incidence of suicide in Africa and other developing countries is considerably lower than in developed societies. Laubscher (see [14]) found in South Africa only 14 cases in a population of 870,000, over a two-year period. Benedict and Jacks[42] in 1954 found a suicide rate of something like 1 per 100,000 in Africa; this is very low, as compared with 10 and 25, in the United States and in Denmark respectively.

While the material in this chapter has pointed to a variety of ways in which culture influences the development, the form and the natural history of psychiatric illness, there is no certainty about the extent to which culture influences the fundamental structure or nuclear features of such illness. The cross-cultural differences in the symptoms of schizophrenia are a case in point. Catatonic rigidity, negativism, and stereotypy are common in Indian schizophrenics; aggressiveness and expressiveness are common in patients from Southern Italy; African patients are reported to display a tendency to be quieter than patients in the Western world. The withdrawal of Indian schizophrenics has been related to the formal, hierarchical Indian culture, which has high regard for introversion and emotional controls, while the barrenness of the clinical picture in preliterate Africans has been tied to the paucity of their cultural and intellectual resources, and their difficulties in dealing with abstractions. While such cross-cultural differences suggest a tie-in between symptoms and culture, four out of 26 symptoms and signs were in no instance reported as being infrequent in the schizophrenia cases dealt with in the McGill survey: social and emotional withdrawal; auditory hallucinations; delusions, and flatness of affect. The importance of these findings is that they suggest the possibility of there being nuclear features of schizophrenia that are not culturally determined, and may be distinguished from those that are.

The same kinds of consideration are applicable to depressive illness. Thus guilt, self-reproach and suicide have been reported as being rare among the depressed in primitive societies; this suggests that these symptoms may in fact be culturally determined. At any time, in relation to a neurotic illness, conditioned or institutionalized fears may be selected to explain psychopathological phenomena. It is also just as likely that present stresses, by their interaction with generally vulnerable personalities, precipitate anxiety episodes, and that these are then explained in terms of culturally acceptable ideas. Depressed patients commonly attempt to account for their symptoms by external factors; depending on the culture, they may focus on only one symptom, such as impotence, anxiety, anorexia or anergia. Inability to work, as the result of lack of energy, is a major complaint among Western patients. Obsessional patients tend to complain of their morbid thoughts, while hysterical patients speak of the dulling of their emotions and of their need for stimulation to give them "a sense of being alive." Each patient focuses on those symptoms that are most disturbing to his normal psychic needs or to his self-image. This is frequently determined by the patterns that are emphasized within the culture; these are often culture-specific variants of universal conflicts, such as the struggle between generations, between fathers and sons, or between husbands and wives.

These cross-cultural studies are of value in helping us distinguish between the minimal fundamental elements of certain psychological disorders and those aspects of these same disorders that are influenced by cultural factors—that is, by pathoplastic features. An examination of psychiatric disorders in different cultures suggests the existence of universal symptom patterns in major psychiatric disorders. What differs from culture to culture is the cultural coloring of beliefs, delusions and behavior patterns, as well as differences in the kind, severity and location of pathogenic factors.

The fact that cultures reward and encourage different patterns of behavior, which then color the external manifestations of the psychiatric disorders, becomes strongly apparent when one examines the culture-bound or exotic disorders, as we shall do in the next chapter.

CHAPTER 4

CULTURE-BOUND
DISORDERS

THE LINK BETWEEN CULTURE AND THE
structure of psychiatric illness has often been substantiated by
reference to studies of exotic or culture-bound disorders. More
than the illnesses described in the previous chapter, these reflect
the effects of culturally conditioned compensatory responses to
the basic symptoms of mental illness.

The study of any one of these culture-bound disorders is
relevant to a number of different issues and problems in psychiatry. Such a study can throw light on both the stress points
and the susceptible groups in a particular culture; it can also be
useful in increasing our knowledge of how cultural factors contribute in general to mental health and illness. This is of particular relevance to the development of an operationally valid theory
of social psychiatry, such as differentiates between internal and
environmental factors in order to study their interrelationship.
In the planning of services, it is highly desirable to understand
the different forms that psychiatric disorders can take in non-
clinical settings—particularly since these various forms of illness
are often socially acceptable patterns of behavior, not necessarily
regarded as manifestations of illness. Insofar as the processes of
modernization may lead to a change in the incidence of these
conditions, it is important to investigate them before their highly
visible and dramatic forms disappear. Such an investigation will
be of conesiderable value for an understanding of the interplay

Notes for Chapter 4 will be found on pages 201–202.

between culture and psychological defenses or adaptive mechanisms, and it may for that reason be relevant to prognosis, as well as to diagnosis.

Culture-bound disorders are for the most part variants of the severe functional psychoses and of various neurotic syndromes. They can be connected with the context in which the syndrome develops, the content of the symptoms, or the response to and management of the syndrome. These are not new diagnostic entities; they are in fact similar to those already known in the West. For the purposes of this discussion, they are grouped here according to conventional psychiatric categories.

ANXIETY STATES

There are a variety of neurotic syndromes that focus on fear of death, castration anxiety, and beliefs about male sexuality. *Koro* in Southeast Asia, *susto* in Spanish-American culture, and *bewitchment* in Nigeria are three examples of these.

Koro

It is possible to look at *koro* from the standpoint of those universal psychodynamic factors that are manifested differently from one culture to another. In Chinese culture, victims of *koro* fear death: they have the somatic delusion that the penis will retract into the abdomen and ultimately cause the death of the victim, and they therefore take steps to prevent this from happening. Psychodynamically, the fear has been connected with unresolved Oedipal conflicts, Chinese concepts of sexuality, and the oral orientation and fear of oral deprivation that is characteristic of the Chinese. Yap[1] attributes *koro* to Southern Chinese beliefs about improper balance between *yin* and *yang* humors, emphasizing that these beliefs are not "simply pathoplastic but pathogenic in effect, much in the same way that a belief in hell-fire can help to bring about depressive states of clinical severity under certain circumstances."

Belief in *koro* intensifies ordinary guilt and anxiety over real or fancied sexual excess, especially autoerotic activity, producing panic and depersonalization of the genitals. *Koro* occurs most often in immature, anxious people who have been exposed to a sudden fright.

The following case report[2] from *The International Journal of Social Psychiatry*, illustrates the central features of *koro*:

T. H. Yang, a thirty-two year old single Chinese cook from Hankow in Central China, came to the psychiatric clinic in August 1957, complaining of panic attacks and various somatic symptoms such as palpitation, breathlessness, numbness of limbs and dizziness. During the months just prior to his first visit he had seen several herb doctors, who diagnosed his disease as *shenn-kuei,* or "deficiency in vitality," and prescribed the drinking of boy's urine and eating human placenta to supply *chih* (energy or vital essence) and *shiueh* (blood) respectively. At this time the patient began to notice also that his penis was shrinking and withdrawing into his abdomen, usually a day or two after sexual intercourse with a prostitute. He would become anxious about the condition of his penis and eat excessively to relieve sudden intolerable hunger pangs. He was treated at the O.P.D. for seven months.

The eldest of five sons, the patient was brought up in a small town on the Yang-tze river. His father worked on a junk with eighty other men and, as they went up and down the river for trade, was home only a few days every six months. When the patient was seven, the father, then about thirty years old, died of an unknown disease. This occurred shortly after the fifth son was born. The patient was a favorite with his mother, who taught him a little reading and arithmetic. She subsequently remarried a man who disliked him and favoured the youngest brother. Because the patient was disobedient and unruly, he was frequently beaten by his stepfather, who ordered him to go to work to support the family. His mother objected and took the boy to live with her brother, but he also treated him badly.

He became an apprentice barber at eleven, and was able to support himself at fourteen. He gambled a great deal. When he was sixteen he started to learn cooking, and within a few years he was a skilled cook in a restaurant. He gave some money to the support of the family but spent most of it in gambling dens and brothels, upsetting his mother greatly, and she beat him on account of his behaviour. He felt sorry for a while after losing some of his mother's money, but eventually broke with her and left home. He could not keep a job during the Sino-Japanese war; finally he started working as cook on a steamboat in Shanghai at the age of eighteen. According to the patient, he became emaciated and jaundiced on the ship because of his excessive masturbation. To control himself he took more than twenty kinds of herb medicine with no relief, until he started drinking a cup of *hwei-long-tan torn-biann* (his own first urine) every morning, which cured him in four months.

At the end of the war, at the age of twenty, he was still working on the ship. For a time he sold morphine to earn extra money. He enlisted in the army at age twenty-two, where he received little pay, and migrated to Taiwan in 1949. He then left the army to work in a bakery. Once again he started gambling and when he lost, going to brothels. For a prolonged period he had sexual intercourse every night to relieve the mounting sexual tension. The thought of saving money and marrying never occurred to him. His job kneading dough at a restaurant was dull.

In July 1957 he had his first attack of breathlessness and palpitation. He felt dizzy, and suffered from weakness in limbs and muscular twitching. He also complained of dryness of the mouth, nausea and vomiting. Physical examination was largely negative; he was given vitamin B injections. He recovered in two weeks, started going to brothels again and had another attack within a few days. Attacks came on more frequently and lasted longer.

The patient, in a state of panic, wandered from one herb doctor to another having vitamin injections. He was told by one doctor that he was suffering from *shenn-kuei* or *yin-kuei,* a sexual defect, and that he would eventually die if he continued going to prostitutes. He thought that his symptoms were caused by *yin-kuei,* a disease supposed to be due to poisons secreted in the uterus which penetrate the penis. At this point he quit his job to save his strength; in August 1957 he was referred to the psychiatric clinic by a medical doctor.

Almost irresistible sexual desire seized him whenever he felt slightly better; yet he experienced strange "empty" feelings in his abdomen when he had sexual intercourse. He reported that he often found his penis shrinking into his abdomen, at which time he would become very anxious and hold on to his penis in terror. Holding his penis, he would faint, with severe vertigo and pounding of his heart. For four months he drank a cup of *torn-biann* (boy's urine) each morning, and this helped him a great deal. He also thought that his anus was withdrawing into his abdomen every other day or so. At night he would find that his penis had shrunk to a length of only one centimetre and he would pull it out and then be able to relax and go to sleep.

In 1958 he became frightened at the sight of women, and discontinued his visits to brothels for five months. By that time he was unable to work. To cover his heavy expenses he raised a loan from friends from whom he had sponged in many other ways. Eventually they turned away from him, disgusted by his greedy habits. Subsequently, as there was no improvement in his condition, he started eating human placenta upon the recommendation of a herb doctor. He ate five placentas and felt better afterwards, but the improvement lasted for only two days. Frequently he lost sleep because of intolerable hunger pangs, and thought that he had a "hunger neurosis." He tried to prevent nocturnal emissions by holding his penis, as he was afraid of losing *chih* (vital essence) through emissions.

The patient was over-concerned with his body and would present himself at the emergency clinic frequently, in a state of panic, with various complaints and requests for laboratory examinations to prove that his illness was somatic. All the examinations made showed negative results. The patient was dependent, demanding, theatrical, exaggerating and hysterical. He would talk endlessly about his own theory of illness and ancient Chinese medical views. He said that he took thousands of dollars' worth of herb medicine to treat *shenn-kuei,* but he was very dependent on our medications. He often aggressively requested laboratory examinations and injections. His description of his symptoms was very exaggerated: "Hands tremble, anguish in the abdomen, penis withdrawing, heart pounds *kag-kag, kazu-kazu,* I am scared . . . Herb men told me that my nerve got *leng* (cold), *hern* (coolness) and *feng* (wind) . . . Have Western doctors such thing? . . . My body trembles at night, it moves, blood does not come up, my body stops moving, my lung gets hot and my head too, my mouth will dry up so that I drink a cup of tea and then I have to urinate . . . I cannot breathe at night, my heart pounds, my head aches if I talk too much, my heart sounds *kok, kok-kok,* my head sounds *zuzu-zuzu* . . ." He accompanied this description with many gestures.

During the last period of therapy (the eighteenth to twenty-second interviews) the patient became anxious about his friend's criticism of his deteriorated behaviour, and he attempted to find a light job in a restaurant and avoided prostitutes to save his strength.

Carstairs[3] has reported on a *koro*-like syndrome among Indian males; it is characterized by chronic anxiety, exhaustion, inertia, inanition and a belief in the leakage of semen, which is the reservoir of health and strength. This was the most common form of anxiety neurosis found among men in the Indian communities he studied, and he attributed it to unresolved oedipal tensions and fear of the all-powerful father. Deference to authority, emotional restraint and restriction of independence operate even after a man has married; these conflicts are resolved when the son becomes the head of the household following the death of the father.

Susto

Susto or *espanto* is an anxiety syndrome, believed to be caused by sudden fright, evil eye, bad air, black magic or witchcraft, all of which produce "soul loss." It is characterized by irritability, asthenia, anorexia, insomnia, phobias, reduced libido, retardation, nightmares, trembling, sweating, tachycardia, diarrhea, vomiting, other symptoms of anxiety and depression, and the belief that if the "fright" reaches the heart, death will occur. Rubel[4] has described two cases among Mexican-Americans:

On a Sunday outing Ricardo, the older boy, suffered an attack of *susto*. The rest of the family romped in and about the water of a local pond, but Ricardo demurred. Despite coaxing and taunts, especially from his sister, Ricardo would have nothing to do with the water but climbed into the automobile and went to sleep. He slept throughout the afternoon and did not even awake when he was taken home and put to bed. That night he slept fitfully and several times talked aloud in his sleep.

On the following morning the parents decided that Ricardo had suffered *susto*. It was caused, they reasoned, not by fear of the water but by the family's insistence that he enter the pond—a demand to which he was unable to accede. They brought him to a local curer to have his soul coaxed back to his body and thus to he healed of soul loss.

The second case involved Antonio, a young married man about 25 years of age, likewise a native-born American citizen, who could neither read, write, nor communicate in English . . . On one occasion Antonio was sent to a hospital with a diagnosis of double pneumonia. His fever was successfully controlled, and he was placed in a ward for a recuperative period. One night he noticed a change in the condition of a wardmate; he became alarmed and tried to communicate his concern to the attendants, but for some reason he was unsuccessful. Some time later, they discovered that the wardmate had died, and that the corpse had been removed from the room. Antonio was much upset by the incident. He became fitful, complained of restless nights, and exhibited little interest in his food or surroundings. Moreover, he found his body involuntarily "jumping" on the bed while he lay in a reclining position. After leaving the hospital he went home and asked that his mother, who lived in Mexico, be brought to his side. When she arrived, she immediately began to coax his soul back to his body by means of a traditional cure.

Susto is found throughout the Latin-American world. It encompasses numerous clinical conditions and beliefs pertaining to various magical substances that enter into the body and alter its natural balance. Despite these "superstitious" beliefs, the theory shares with modern theories of abnormal behavior the notion of environmental stress; of the patient's vulnerability to illness or misfortune, which may be brought about by the patient's own behavior in relation to cultural norms; and of illness as a reflection of the alteration of something vital within the individual.

Bewitchment

Among Yoruba males, sexual difficulties are frequently attributed to witches, and men often dream of an assault against their genitals.[5] Impotence, which is common among Yoruba males, occurs when a witch uses an individual's penis in order to consort with his wife or with another woman, and then returns it in an altered, now functionless form. The woman who has been seduced by the witch may as a result become barren. Witches are also thought to control the menstrual flow of women and the expulsion of the newborn child from the womb. Menstruating women and witches share the power to render powerless both magic and the native medicines. The touch of a menstrual cloth may bring bad fortune. Such attitudes about the potential power and evil of women are commonly encountered in traditional societies; they may be explained as projections of unconscious fantasies developed early in life, or as dissociated images of the "bad" mothers, although there are undoubtedly other explanations.

OBSESSIONAL-COMPULSIVE NEUROSES

The basic features of obsessive-compulsive neuroses appear to be the same in all cultures. They differ in terms of those central preoccupations and beliefs, associated with them, that are generally held to be causative.

Frigophobia

Frigophobia (*pa-ling*) is an obsessional neurosis characterized by morbid fear of the cold, preoccupation with the belief that heat deficiency is detrimental to vitality, fears of the wind, and an obsessive need to wear several layers of clothing in order to keep out the cold. In one case the patient became completely incapacitated as the result of his constant need to change his clothes, in order to protect himself against the loss of vital energy.

This condition, according to Yap,[6] shares with *koro* a core symptom: extreme fear of the loss of vital strength, as a result of disharmony between the *yin* and *yang* elements so necessary for health. Frigophobia patients are preoccupied with death as the possible result of this loss; they are inhibited and socially withdrawn; and in a counterphobic way they attempt to protect themselves with excessive clothing.

Frigophobia has all the elements of a classical obsessive-compulsive disorder, complicated by an affective illness. Persons suffering from it focus on culturally meaningful fears, such as cold and sexual impotence, after the disorder has developed. These fears are perpetuated or reinforced by other persons, who regard these fears as legitimate, in view of their links with accepted beliefs. Comparable disorders, with similar preoccupations, can be found in Western culture.

Shinkeishitsu

Shinkeishitsu, an obsessional neurosis of young Japanese, is characterized by anxiety, obsessive-compulsive symptoms, hypochondriasis, fear of meeting people and feelings of inadequacy.

According to Takeo Doi,[7] it develops when the basic need to be loved and protected has been frustrated. What is of particular interest is the fact that its occurrence in a particular age group has been singled out for special attention. One possible explanation for this is that the increased demands placed on young people in modern Japanese sociey have created conditions of performance that certain individuals, who were previously well adapted, are unable to meet; this brings to attention the existence of obsessional neuroses that were not incompatible with earlier societal conditions. It is also possible that the same set of symptoms may be interpreted differently when they appear in a different age group, thus leading to a social response that is other than the sick role. *Shinkeishitsu* is generally treated with Morita therapy, in three stages: a period of semi-isolation, a period of involvement in simple normal labor, and finally an active training in the development of attitudes of self-acceptance.

HYSTERICAL DISORDERS

Hysterical disorders occur more frequently than any of the other conditions described in this book. Most common among women, these conditions take a variety of forms, depending on which symptoms are accentuated by the patient and the culture. Hysterical disorders are frequently difficult to differentiate from borderline schizophrenic and schizophreniform illnesses. This is particularly true where hysterical or schizophrenic conditions are manifested in culture-bound disorders such as *latah*, which may in this sense be viewed as a final end-state syndrome that may result from hysterical disorders and occasionally from schizophrenia.

Latah

Latah is characterized by hypersuggestibility, automatic obedience, coprolalia, echolalia, echopraxia, echomimia, altered consciousness, disorganization, depression and anxiety. Yap[8] has also described dementia and "flights of fatuous euphoria" in cases of *latah*. These symptoms develop in progressive states in response to a wide range of stimuli; most of the cases reported have involved lower-class women who were exposed to sudden stress. Yap says that echo reactions are the simplest responses available to psychologically disorganized individuals, who cannot readily develop definite psychological sets towards dangerous objects in the environment, because of their diffuse and pervasive fear and as a result of their weak egos, which impair their consciousness.

Latah is known by a variety of names. According to Yap:[9]

Those of purely ethnic interest are: Miryachit (Hammond), Amurakh (Czaplicka), Meriatschenje (Tokarski), Olonism (Shirokogoroff), Ikota (Schrenck), Imu, Imubacco, Toconibacco, Young-dah-hte (Manson), Bahtschi (Scheube), Yuan (Bastian), and Mali-mali (Musgrave, Sison). These are all local names, used in different parts of Siberia, Hokkaido and southeast Asia. In other parts of the world where the reaction is found, e.g., on the southern fringes of the Sahara, there is no local term for it. Other names by which the reaction has been described are: Schrekaffekt (Moreira), Echomatism, Mimicismus (Stellani), and Arctic Hysteria (Hammond), all of which have psychopathological or psychodynamic connotations. In addition, this subject has in the past been linked with Convulsive Tics (de la Tourette), to which latah is quite unrelated and also with Jumping (Beard), with which latah is definitely identical . . .

Uchimura attributed the incidence of *latah* or *imu* among the Ainu in Japan to constitutional factors and to a suggestibility that has been fostered by tradition. He considered it to be phylogenetically an intermediary stage between the primitive defense reactions of lower animals and the hysteria of civilized people.[10] He also noted that certain sociocultural conditions, particularly in undeveloped countries with little technology, may produce a "passivity of mind and an unpreparedness for sudden decision and action" that predispose individuals to the fright reaction.

According to Yap,[11] disruption of the ego by fear creates a nondiscriminating, impulsive and rudimentary state of mental functioning. The introduction of cultural forces at this point can build up distinct patterns of abnormal behavior. In line with Kretschmer, Yap emphasizes the relative ease with which hysterical fear reactions can develop at this particular primitive level of mental functioning, in simple folk societies that are at the mercy of the environment and live in a psychologically hostile world.

The following cases reported by Yap illustrate the main features of *latah:*

(1) A *nonya* (woman of Chinese racial extraction who for two or three generations has largely adopted Malay speech, customs and manners), aged about 40 and living in Malacca, had long been regarded as eccen-

tric, and was called *goreng pisang* (fried banana) by way of a nick-name. She was employed as an odd-job cook during festivals, and had a daughter and a son, who was also regarded as "silly." Her husband was a stall-holder, selling sweetmeats.

She was markedly histrionic and sensitive to attention. When persuaded she would, after a show of reluctance, start to walk about with exaggerated swaying of the hips and dance the *ronggeng* (a recognized folk dance). At the same time she would sing snatches of a love song, facing me (Yap) all the time. After a little while she stopped, saying in a mischievous way that her testicles were dropping. When asked to bow, she did so repeatedly, advancing all the while, and raising hails of laughter from those around. When tickled, she would start to strut about, as though making determined and demonstrative attempts to stride away. She was not echolalic, but when she wanted to leave and was, with some physical pressure, made to remain, she showed the confusion in speech which is typical of persons in the latah state. She had been hoping to win some money, and kept on reiterating this idea: "Good-night, eh, good-night, untong-lah, kanah lottery, eh, kanah lattery, eh, good-night . . ." (which may be rendered: "Good-night, eh, good-night, shall have to owe money then, win a lottery, eh, win a lottery, eh, good-night . . .").

She had developed these peculiar mannerisms and exhibitionistic personality traits from childhood, and her latah symptoms hardly ever went beyond this. She appeared to be a gay, mischievous and fairly intelligent person, not unusually nervous or anxious. The most genuine symptom she showed was decomposition of speech when embarrassed or discomfited.

(2) The second one was also a Malay woman of about 40 from Malacca. She was the wife of a fisherman and had two children. A slow, stupid woman of rather elementary mentality, she was not easily drawn into conversation and would not reply to questions. When prodded in the ribs or teased she would make little attempt to defend herself other than to say, in a slow, deliberate drawl, "puki" or "butol" (vulgarisms for female and male sexual organs). She would not budge from her squatting position on the floor, but kept on eyeing one in a rather puzzled manner. When commanded "bukol!" ("Strike!"), she immediately said, " Bukol lu, Bukol lu" ("Strike you, strike you"). When I accidentally dropped some coins, she at once exclaimed "Duait Kechil, ah, duait kechil" ("Small money, ah, small money") in some excitement, as though she was startled by the noise of the dropping coins, and had to verbalize what suddenly attracted her attention.

These coprolalic and mild echolalic symptoms were elicited without any preceding attempt to frighten or startle the patient. Nevertheless, although the patient carried on a normal life as a housewife of humble station, there was no doubt that she was a mild or incipient case of latah. I was informed, although I had no chance to test it, that she was known to be capable of rather more definite symptoms when really confused and frightened. It was difficult to determine whether she had any nervous symptoms because of her unintelligence and lack of co-operation."

In sophisticated people, with more complex mental organizations, the same biologically primitive impulses, upon being stimulated by stress, lead to the formation of hysterical conversion symptoms. In Western cultures, such fear reactions occur in immature or mentally deficient individuals; similar fright reactions have been reported for other pre-industrial societies. Variations occur in the symptoms, the groups affected and the type of trigger events that precipitate these reactions. Among natives of Nyasla and Isala these symptoms are characterized by a brooding, histrionic running amok and by a harming of others.[12] Frustrated or frightened adolescent Congolese girls suffer from *banga,* which is similar to *misala* and includes speech disturbances and convulsions.[13]

Latah is, in my opinion, attributable to sudden, overwhelming stress; it might be characterized best as an "acute catastrophic reaction." Such a reaction does not generally occur in the Western world, except in special stress situations of war, natural disaster, or drastic social change. Indeed, many of the features of the modern industrial world may be looked upon as attempts to protect man from the overwhelming stresses of the environment, thereby maximizing his capacity to adapt to a variety of environments.

PHOBIC STATES

Phobic states, in which the incapacitating anxiety produces more distress than the feared stimulus object, commonly center around culturally significant objects. The obsessive thoughts and compulsive behavior are often ritualized and reinforced by culturally meaningful belief systems, as in the case of the evil eye and the curse.

Evil Eye

Mal ojo or the "evil eye" involves controlling another person by way of strong glances.[14] It is the culture that determines which individual is to be the victim and which the cause. Children are frequently selected as victims, while strangers and women are thought to cause it most often. Why strong stares should have universal significance as a stressor is difficult to say; it may be that strong looks generate in the vulnerable intense transference reactions.

The manifestations of evil eye also vary from culture to culture. They include otherwise unexplained illnesses, brief fevers, and emotional disturbances. "Evil eye" has many features of a classical phobic disorder, except that the particular objects and experiences feared have cultural as well as idiosyncratic significance. In all cultures, certain events are heavily invested with negative power or valence and are assiduously avoided, because they are believed to be harmful. They become especially significant as culturally accepted explanations of unpleasant or uncontrollable events, such as illness. Careful analysis of "evil eye" or *mal ojo* among Mexican-Americans suggests that anxiety about a supposedly harmful event usually develops after the onset of illness has initiated a search for culturally defined explanations of the patient's difficulties. The folk explanation, however, offers an answer to the question of *why* something has occurred rather than *how* it has occurred, the latter being the fundamental question that is asked in scientific approaches to problems of the unknown. The *fellahin* in Egypt, who suffer from malnutrition, bilharzia (which affects 75% to 95% of the population), glaucoma, trachoma and other serious conditions, are in constant fear of the evil eye. According to their belief, envy on the part of others may endanger one's wealth and health: an admiring glance may serve to introduce the evil spirit into the admired person or object.[15]

To avoid the evil eye, people refrain from boasting of their good fortunes and practice various magical or counterphobic maneuvers—e.g. stretching the right hand towards the glance of the envious and saying "*khamssa*" five times, covering objects with blue paint, and wearing charms. Compliments are negated by magical phrases. "Evil eye" has something to do with the invasion of private space, and the projection of hostility toward the imposition of forced dependency; as such, it is treated by maneuvers that enable the victim to reestablish the appropriate distance from any person who has overstepped these personal boundaries.

Treatment procedures vary considerably. Human figures may be cut from paper and punched with a pin, while the names of recent visitors are recited. The paper is then burned, with the victim looking at it, after which alum is rubbed on his forehead and he is passed over the fire seven times. Alum bubbles form, burn, and then burst, presumably releasing the victim from the evil eye. The reason why this procedure is able to allay anxiety may be that it engages the person in an activity that forces him to concentrate on another track and therefore to begin a new obsession, with a specified behavioral outlet. It thus serves to repress, neutralize, or dissipate his original fears.

It is sometimes useful simply to watch the behavior of people who are involved in these maneuvers, without at the same time listening to their explanations. One could base inferences solely on observations, although it is not possible to tell in that way when psychological space is being invaded.

In Israel, "evil eye" is one of two classes of mental illness that are identified by the Mori,[16] the other being made up of those disorders that are caused by or accompany physical conditions. Evil eye is associated with depressive symptoms; it is considered to be less serious than schizophrenic, retarded and bizarre psychiatric disorders, which are attributed to spirits.

While in complex industrial societies experiences are more idiosyncratic and thus a greater variety of factors are believed to be responsible for the development of psychiatric disorders, explanations of illness in the more circumscribed traditional villages tend to be rather homogeneous. Also, in this setting there is a greater likelihood of the need for distance, as well as a greater chance for invasion of territory and inner space.

The description of *mal ojo* by a Mexican-American informant of Rubel[17] illustrates this invasion of psychological territory.

Once I went hunting for rabbits with my compadre. It was he that wanted to hunt, although the area was swarming with rattlers. Anyway, we arrived at the grounds where we had planned to shoot and soon saw a rabbit running across our path, first in one direction, and then in another. I pointed out the running animal to my compadre and told him to shoot it. He fired once and then a second time, but each time the bullets skittered harmlessly by. I told my compadre: "Don't shoot again! There must be a snake nearby that has the rabbit in his charm (*liga*)." Sure enough! In a moment we saw a tremendously long rattler coiled by a rock, with its jaws wide open. That snake had the rabbit in his charm and was bringing it closer and closer until finally it could devour the creature. That's what *mal ojo* is like.

Last week my cousin's cute little baby had *ojo*. In the hours of the late afternoon my cousin was holding her child out in their front yard. One of the neighborhood men returning from work stopped to talk with the couple, remarking on the child's cuteness. Then he went on his way. That night when they put the child to bed, it began to cry and remained inconsolable through most of the night. Even though I slept in the other part of the house, I could hear them moving about with the child. Very early the next morning I could hear my cousin leave the house, as she went next door to speak to our neighbor, to do her the favor of requesting the man to stop at our house on his way to work. The neighbor went and roused the man with strong eyes. On his way to work, that man stopped at our place and went into the other room, where he ran a hand over the child's face and forehead, cooing to her and talking to her. He didn't remain any longer than about five minutes. When he left, the baby had stopped crying.

Folk syndromes are defined by the social circumstances under which they occur. In Mexican-Americans, a person becomes vulnerable when he permits another person to override his personal autonomy. Eating food out of politeness to one's host; a lover's spat; an unrequited love affair; or evidence of invidiousness between members of a nuclear family—all these may provide the setting for witchcraft or for the development of folk illnesses. One always has to try to determine whether the individual's life space or territory has been physically or psychologically intruded upon, thereby setting in motion the particular folk illness. To the extent that this happens in every human culture, there is rarely any difficulty in finding an explanation retrospectively for any illness that develops.

A "self-fulfilling pattern" may also operate in the development of "evil eye." The mere belief that one has been exposed to specific stresses may lead to symptoms that are likely to be interpreted as having been induced by the evil eye. The development of anxiety by way of "curse" is one manifestation of this phenomenon. The Yoruba believe that uttering the name of something may cause it to come into existence—not only in the mind and body of the individual who has uttered the name, as well as of the individual who has heard it, but also in the physical world. This is particularly true of potent ancestor words, such as *oronyinle;* simply mentioning such words will cause what they denote to come into existence. *Sopono,* the word for the smallpox god, is avoided by the Yoruba; it is mentioned only through the substitute abbreviation of SP, by way of some such euphemism, because naming the god might offend him and thus call up the disease. It is also offensive to tell someone he is sick, for this may make him sicker. Mentioning the name of an older person or of the senior person in a family is also a taboo. A man is not to be called by his name by his children or wives; if that does happen, another word must be spoken, in order to undo its potential harmfulness. Prince[18] has emphasized that these phenomena are due to the suggestibility of the Yoruba; but my own impression is that these are universal phenomena, deriving from the reinforcement of early socialization experiences by means of various beliefs. Not all taboo violators became anxious and fearful; those who do so are predisposed to it by virtue of their constitution, their early experiences, and their exposure to stress.

In all societies, there are superstitious beliefs that harm will come to those who have violated apparently harmless taboos. It is rare, however, for everyone to adhere to these taboos; it is only in retrospect, after an illness has developed, that the patient and significant others look back upon past mistakes—including taboo violations—as possible causes of that illness.

Voodoo Death and Curse

The most dramatic result of taboo violation is voodoo death. Voodoo death, according to Cannon,[19] results from excessive sympathetic activity, which produces vaso-constriction and damage to the capillary endothelium of the visceral blood vessels, loss of blood plasma volume and pressure, and ultimately death. Cannon compared this to death from surgical shock and from sympathetic overexcitation in the decorticated cat. Sudden death in laboratory rats has recently been explained in terms of excessive parasympathetic stimulation.[20]

No one has convincingly proven the validity of Voodoo death. Most observers have uncritically accepted "natural" explanations of unexplained deaths, without having sought more universal and objectifiable variables, such as starvation, chronic fear and exhaustion in the patient, or group processes and methods of sanction in the cultural environment. It is only by way of delineation of these variables that such studies will add to the general body of psychiatric knowledge. Studies of indigenous therapy, which is able to stem the course of the progressive deterioration that frequently follows bewitchment, should also prove useful in explaining the negative initial aspect of this phenomenon.

Although variations of the Voodoo death phenomenon are widespread, observers have focused on such aspects as the curse or the context, rather than on the victim; as a result, these variations have not been widely reported. The pattern of curse varies from culture to culture. There are several species of curse, for example, among the Yoruba[21]. *Epe* is used when the victim is in view: black medicine and a red feather or a cobra fang are put in an animal horn, after which the sorcerer licks the medicine in the horn and speaks the curse. In an *omoge* curse, certain tree roots in the mouth of the operator will ensure that what he says will come to pass. In an *ofoshe* curse, medicines are rubbed into a cut made below the lower lip, and to curse someone, the lower lip is licked. The Yoruba believe that these curses can produce psychosis, illness or death, even when the victim is unaware of the curse. It is likely, however, that the psychological effect of knowledge of the curse leads people to withdraw from the victim, or to alter their behavior toward him, and this no doubt has an effect on the victim when he responds to these subliminal cues.

Prince has reported cases in which a curse was said to have precipitated neurosis and psychosis; in each instance, the victim had heard the curse uttered or had been made aware of it by others. Upon finding his own protective medicine ineffective, he usually developed panic, loss of appetite, insomnia, nightmares (of *egunguns* or masqueraders [spirits] chasing him, or of being drowned in a river), hallucinations and psychosis. Prince was unable to document the popular belief that a curse can cause death, and further noted that not everyone seemed to be susceptible to it. This last observation is important, suggesting as it does that a curse may merely serve to intensify difficulties that have already been developed. Thus the depressed individual may be less able than others to cope with the stress of curse, and therefore more likely to feel worse if it is added to his burdens. Disturbed individuals are also likely to be more dependent and suggestible, as well as more responsive to negative self-fulfilling expectations; they will therefore be less able to reject notions of curse.

Patterns of curse intensify anxiety and contribute to the development of compensatory or pathoplastic symptoms; they do not, however, cause defects in perception, cognition or emotionality. When such defects become apparent or such symptoms are manifested, efforts are made to explain them in terms of such cultural concepts as curse. Even if no history of curse exists, the symptoms can be taken, it is believed, as proof that it has occurred. The group's acceptance of these beliefs or rationalizations reinforces the patient's anxiety, thus producing secondary anxiety and additional identifiable symptoms. While this is distressing, it also assures the patient that he will receive help, since he can now be identified as a victim of those forces that are threatening everybody in the community. In that sense, the community has a major stake in the patient's recovery from his illness.

Collomb[22] has reported that, while voodoo death is in fact uncommon in Africa, everybody has seemed on some occasion to have witnessed it. At times, it may be the only solution to a conflict situation, the unavoidable consequence of a broken taboo, or the compulsory realization of an all-powerful threat. According to Collomb, vital forces may be withdrawn from the patient by man-eating magicians or by tribal ancestors—this being carried to the point of death.

The experience that is associated with curse has been described by one victim of group vengeance in the following way:[23] "The body lives but is uninhabited. There is no longer anything inside. It is not a matter of the organs failing to work; everything is functioning—the heart, the stomach and so on and in their places; it is life itself that is gone. Intelligence remains; the mind is capable of understanding, reflecting and reasoning, but life is something else again."

The withdrawal of group support from those who are markedly dependent on a group—e.g. the tribal African—can be truly terrifying to them. Here the culture-specific stress of group withdrawal is clearly related to the cultural support systems and to the maintenance of control by the group. It is also a possible consequence of failure to live up to their expectations, even though the person's failure was not intentional.

These patterns are relevant to other physical and psychiatric disorders. They vividly demonstrate the power and force of the psychological leverage of the group over the individual, and the significance of the label or role that the group assigns to the individual. Assignment of the patient to a particular role evokes a specific response from the group, which may in turn have significance for the development of the patient's mental state. The group supports the sick role and condemns the deviant role. Behaving in accordance with role requirements thus engages the individual in a special interaction with the group, which not only insures support but guarantees that the patient will go through a series of traditional or ritualized steps that will lead to recovery. Thus there is built into the patterning of exotic illnesses elements that relate to the treatment process. It is this that explains, in part, the existence of manifestations of disorder that are universally found to be recognizable by members of the particular culture but not by other observers

DEPRESSIVE REACTIONS

Depressive reactions are not uncommon in pre-industrial society, and mild to moderate depressive reactions probably provide the background for many of the disorders already described. As was noted in Chapter 3, however, other symptoms are more prevalent here than depressive symptoms, so that the condition is likely to be labeled in other terms than depression—that is, in terms of the symptom, of the individual affected, or of the natural or supernatural etiological agent.

Disorders do, however, make their appearance in which depressive symptoms predominate and here the folk explanation focuses on the depression itself—as, for example, in the Mohave "heartbreak" syndrome.

Hiwa: Itck

Hiwa: Itck or "heartbreak" syndrome (Hiwa = heart) is a depressive syndrome found among elderly Mohave men who have been deserted by young wives. Devereux[24] has described it extensively:

Case 1. Kaly Yahway ("Tomahawk") of the Mo: se gens was born about 125 years ago and died an old man. The episode about to be described occurred when he was about 45 years old. He was married to a woman his own age. This woman left him. He then married a young girl, who also left him. He thereupon began to say that he was all the time thinking of killing. He talked about this until he went insane (*yamom*) from Hiwa: Itck. When he had his psychotic episodes, he painted his face black, the way warriors do who prepare to go on the war-path. On these occasions he believed himself to be going on the war-path. People began to notice that he was acting "queer," and suspected that he had become a shaman. In this they were apparently mistaken, since he never cured anyone. (The first manifestation of shamanism is a fugue resembling a psychotic episode.) It is not reported whether he recovered.

Case 2. Amo: Nomak ("mountain-goat lost") was a member of the Noltc gens. He died many years ago, a very old man. He was old when the episode about to be described took place. He had been married to a girl much younger than himself, named Mo: se of that same gens. She just "got up and left him, because she got tired of him." (At this moment informant and interpreter began to speculate on whether she left him because she wanted a man with a larger penis, or whether she merely wanted a "stronger" (i.e. more potent) husband. No decision was reached.) He showed no untoward reaction, until news reached him that the girl had settled down with another man. He thereupon became insane (*yamom*) from Hiwa: Itck. He cut off his long braids of hair, as mourners do. Then he painted his face black. (Here interpreter remarks: "Cutting his hair off makes me laugh.") He went into the winter-house (*ava hatcor*) and sat down. He then laid out his bow and arrows, and declared that he would kill anyone who tried to enter his house. No one dared to enter the house, and that is why no attempt was made to "doctor" him. People were afraid of him. (Here interpreter and informant laughed out loud.) He stayed in his house for two days. Then he made a spontaneous recovery. He even picked up the braids he had previously cut off, and tied them back to his remaining locks. (Interpreter and informant laugh. Interpreter states: "It seems funny now." Informant replies: "At that time it was not funny at all.")

Case 3. Katcioomp belonged to the O: otc gens. He died at Needles, California, at the approximate age of fifty, about half a century ago. He was about thirty years old when the following events took place at Parker, Arizona. He was married to Hualy, of the Hualy gens. They seem to have had two children, but both children had died. They had lived together for a long time. Eventually she got tired of him, and deserted him. Three days later she married another man, named Hamouly Kuoap (a kind of lizard which lives on the mesa, split open). When he heard that she had married again, he became afflicted with Hiwa: Itck. He lost his appetite and neither ate nor slept for three days. During these three days he ran around constantly.

Starting from his house, he ran to a lake known in English as Twelve Mile Slough, and in Mohave as *Anakkroo* (iron railed, or fenced). Thence he would proceed to the Colorado River, and eventually return to his own house. He ran this circuit for three days, stopping once in a while at the houses of relatives who tried to press food on him. He would not eat. He was never "doctored" for his mental disorder, but made a spontaneous recovery. (Here author commented: "You women are the devil!" Informant replied: "Your own girl must be *hukoar*." [This word means properly coyote, and by extension, "crazy" but not insane.])

The Mohave psychodynamic formulation of Hiwa: Itck, as described by Tcatc, one of Devereux's informants, is remarkably similar to Western psychodynamic formulations.

Some people alternate between excitement and depression. This is caused by too much worrying. It goes to such an excess, that they are almost out of their minds. When people are very deeply in love, even though they be far apart they see each other, because of their great love. Among the Mohave there are cases of men loving their women so much that it causes their death . . . their hearts break. Such cases do not occur among the unmarried, but among the married only. People marry those whom they love very much. If the woman then starts going with some-one else, it breaks their heart. They keep on living with her until she deserts them, because they cannot help loving her, even though it hurts. Recently a few men even went so far as to commit suicide. Hiwa: Itck is generally limited to cases in which an older man married a younger girl. The bride's father or mother may have advised her to marry an old man, because the older people are more likely to be faithful to their wives. They also know more about planting (by which, be it understood, the bride's parents would profit), and they had maturer notions about marriage. They were less likely to desert their wives. Such marriages were not always successful, however. If they broke up, the old men got Hiwa: Itck. His relatives would advise him to forget about the faithless wife, and to think of some other girl. They would tell him that thinking of the deserting wife would make him feel just that much worse. They did not doctor such cases.

The Windigo Psychosis

The *windigo* psychosis has been reported[25] among the Algonkian-speaking Indians of central and northeastern Canada, the Ojibwa, the Saulteux, the Cree, the Beaver and others. The disorder is supposed to produce a compulsive desire to eat human flesh. A sorcerer, or a *windigo* spirit-helper, appears in a dream and transforms a man into a *windigo*. Only specific treatment can produce recovery.

This is a classical depressive disorder, showing a specifically prominent secondary symptom of self-depreciation and need for punishment, with a culturally available explanation. These Indian groups suffer from limited food supplies, and they have developed elaborate myths about hunger and cannibalistic monsters that influence their response to depressive illness. To the extent that others accept the patient's account and desire to be killed, as a result of their own fear of engaging in cannibalism, a vicious cycle is set in motion. Fear shown toward the patient may, for example, intensify the patient's fear of himself, and thus incline him to act even more explicitly in terms of culturally prescribed patterns of illness. This produces a growing conviction on the part of others that the patient is indeed a *windigo* monster.

Starvation may indeed lead some to the practice of cannibalism; this is then followed by depression and by the delusion of being a *windigo*. The same belief may develop within the setting of a depression, which may stimulate morbid thoughts of being a *windigo*. Schizophrenic and manic illness can quite clearly also be associated with *windigo* delusions. There is no evidence available that the form of the illness is caused by cultural factors, nor any evidence that the *windigo* belief itself has an etiological role.

The dependency needs of the Ojibwas are early and severely frustrated, leading them to react in a depressed or hostile way to misfortune: they interpret it as being the result of hostile rejection by those around them. Social institutions further curtail, and set up negative sanctions against any direct attempts to express dependency needs and repressed hostility. This creates pressure for Ojibwa men, who try to seek the support of others while at the same time giving expression to their own masculine aggressiveness. According to Parker, the Ojibwa male fears failure to live up to the rather narrow and rigidly defined masculine role, but he also fears the social rejection and envy that come with outstanding achievement and success. A failure in hunting will produce depression and anxiety in the Ojibwa male. Faced with this failure the individual feels abandoned, worthless. "For the windigo victim the usual masochistic devices to insure dependency satisfaction and the normative cultural channels for an oblique expression of hostility no longer suffice to relieve anxiety and depression. Under these conditions, the dam (constituted by ego defenses) is shattered and the repressed cravings for the expression of dependency and aggressive needs burst forth. The depressive conflict between the rebellious rage and the submissive fear is resolved . . ." The morbid depression and paranoid ideas that follow, of bewitchment and possession by the cannibalistic and homicidal witiko monster, are thus ultimately, according to Parker, a form of pathological adjustment of the modal Ojibwa personality and serve environmental and other pressures.

While many of these formulations make sense, they should, I believe, be viewed only as tentative and useful formulations rather than demonstrated truths. It is likely that there are many societies, with the same environmental conditions and early socialization experiences, in which this kind of thing does not develop.

Malignant Anxiety

Malignant anxiety[26] is characterized by chronic anxiety, tension, hostility, moodiness, restlessness, a preoccupation with witchcraft and confusion, excitement, social disability, homicide and suicide. It is also marked by impaired perception, fear of bewitchment, confusion, disorganization and, occasionaly, ritual homicide or suicide. Malignant anxiety is seen most commonly in marginal Africans, in Western contact areas such as labor camps, new industrial settlements, and artificial villages. The recent epidemics of it in Kenya, Eastern Nigeria and the Congo have generally been initiated by abnormal individuals with social position and authority or aggressive power, who have intimidated some weak individuals into joining antisocial secret societies. Unlike manic-depressive disorders, malignant anxiety is not phasic; it may occur without excitement. There is no flight of ideas. By contrast with the situation among catatonic schizophrenia patients, genuine schizophrenic symptoms do not emerge after the excitement. It is difficult to differentiate malignant anxiety from acute schizophreniform psychoses, running amok, or acute catastrophic reactions.

Yap considers it to be a clinically undifferentiated form of the hypereridic state, in which hostility accumulates without being converted into depression or psychoneurotic symptoms, ultimately leading, as a consequence, to destructiveness. *Negi-negi*, which follows the death of a relative or severe frustration, is similarly characterized by transient aggressive behavior, homicide and fears of the departed; it is said to be caused by spirit possessions.[27] The altered consciousness, amnesia, violence, and hyperactivity of amok is similar.

DISSOCIATIVE STATES

Dissociative states occur most often in connection with hysterical disorders and drug abuse. They may, however, be a major feature of manic or hypomanic excitement states, such as amok, and are at times difficult to differentiate from transient schizophrenic disorders.

Amok

Amok, an acute homicidal form of mania that terminates in exhaustion and amnesia, has been attributed to epilepsy,[28] malaria,[29] cerebral syphilis, the intake of hashish, poisoning, sunstroke and mania. Carothers[30] suggested that amok is a primitive reaction that corresponds to the outbursts of psychopathic persons in developed cultures. Van Loon[31] has considered it to be specific to the Malays; Van Wuefften-Palthe[32] regards it as a standardized form of emotional release. In Polynesia it is called *cathard;* in the Sahara, *pseudonite.*

According to Pfeiffer,[33] amok is the consequence of environmental stress, chronic illness, infections, sleep deprivation, heat, alcohol, sexual excitement, fear and anger. Its initial phase is characterized by neurasthenic features, while the second phase is marked by depersonalization, derealization, persecutory ideas, anxiety, rage, and vegetative and motor symptoms. The third or amok phase is characterized by automatism, amnesia, sudden outbursts of motor action and screaming, along with violent attacks on people, animals and inanimate objects; it is followed by exhaustion, calm, depression and the return of consciousness.

Amok-like behavior may occur in delirium, agitated depression, acute anxiety reactions, acute catastrophic reactions and disinhibited aggressive states. Like other exotic disorders, amok does not require a unitary disorder to explain it. Its sudden pathognomonic onset is usually due to the fact that previous symptoms of distress have gone unnoticed, rather than to their sudden appearance.

Alterations of consciousness, manifested by dissociation, automatism, glossolalia and semi-purposive behavior, are also characteristic of possession states throughout the world. These states usually occur in depressed and anxious individuals.

Hsieh-ping

Hsieh-ping or double-sickness, among the Chinese, is a trance state in which the individual identifies with the dead. The seizure lasts anywhere from a half hour to many hours and is manifested by tremor, disorientation, clouding of consciousness, delirium, glossolalia and visual and auditory hallucinations. The patient is believed to be possessed by dead relatives or by friends in the afterworld, to whom he has shown disrespect through inadequate offerings. According to Lin,[34] belief in the power of dead ancestors to bring sickness or disaster as punishment may in and of itself lead to abnormal reactions. Most cases occur in uneducated hysterical females from religious homes, who are exposed to conflict. Treatment is performed by the Wu priest, who enters a self-induced hypnotic state and drives out the ancestral spirits by mediating between the god and earthly people.

Hsieh-ping is a hysterical syndrome, precipitated by social pressures on non-conformists. The dissociative state constitutes a confirmation of punishment; it is followed by a reduction of social pressure and by reintegration of the patient into the group. The valid supernatural explanation for such dissociative behavior frees the individual from responsibility for social conformity, even though such secondary gain is not likely to be the original motive for the symptoms.

Piblokto

Piblokto among Eskimo women is characterized by depression with brooding, tremors and anxiety, screaming and crying, wild running in the snow, and jumping into the water. Symptoms may also include self-destructive or violent homicidal behavior. According to Gussow,[35] *piblokto* is also characterized by seizure-like alternations of consciousness, fatigue, depression, confusion and amnesia—the consequences of an attempt to restore balance to an ego that has been threatened by a severe cultural-typical stress. It provides a defense against panic, sudden fright, feelings of being lost, brooding over dead relatives, fear of the future, threat of starvation and accidents.

These symptoms have been attributed to the stillness and the sense of impending doom that are characteristic of the arctic climate, as well as to sudden fright, frustration, shame or rebuff—elementary instinctive responses to acute stress.

Spirit Possession

Boufée delirante aigüe is an acute confusional psychosis, found among Haitian peasants, that in many instances then goes on to become a chronic schizophrenia. Native priests or *hungans* interpret such illnesses, which occur most often in individuals who are several generations removed from the soil, as forms of possession (spirit), resulting from the patient's unwillingness to accept the call of the voodoo deities to join the voodoo church. They believe that reintegration into the voodoo church will bring about the individual's recovery. Sanseigne,[36] who has had the opportunity to treat such illnesses in a modern clinical setting, has suggested a different view:

Clinically, the picture met most frequently is an acute psychosis, such as the "boufée delirante aigüe," sudden attack, marked confusion, psychomotor excitation, with denudative and aggressive behavior, and sometimes religious delirium, visual and auditory hallucinations; the whole thing for a short period of time, without deterioration. We often wonder if this is not an hysterical episode, but by searching out similar attacks in the histories of our chronic schizophrenics, we find almost constantly that such episodes have occurred many years prior to the appearance of definite schizophrenic signs.

Boufée delirante aigüe demonstrates the tie-in of acute psychotic behavior with learned institutionalized patterns of behavior. To understand this condition properly, it is necessary to understand the role-playing aspect of the possession phenomenon in Haitian culture and its characteristic manifestations in non-psychotic individuals. As noted above, the native doctors interpret this illness in terms of spirit possession, and it is of interest that this explanation and the patient's behavior do correspond to the sought-after possession experience of voodoo priests and congregants. There are some differences, however. Ritual possession is usually characterized by a reduction of higher integrative functions, such as articulate speech, social inhibitions and muscular coordination, with a concomitant increase of reflex behavior, such as trembling, convulsive movements, muscle-twitching, teeth-grinding and sucking movements.[37] In many instances of possession, a sensory anesthesia exists, which permits the individual to expose himself to noxious stimuli that would normally be harmful. The *hungan* or healer enters into a well-controlled, learned, complex and redefined, self-induced trance, by means of autosuggestion. Possession in the *hunsi* or congregant has the quality of a dissociative state, precipitated and reinforced by a highly charged emotional atmosphere, which is accompanied by an excessive barrage of sound, light and drug stimuli. By contrast, *boufée delirante aiguë* would seem to represent a disorganizing psychotic illness in a culturally alienated individual.

The concept of a culturally recognized and accepted way of "going crazy," which was examined in Chapter 2, best explains the link among these various behavioral patterns. The role of the possessed is applauded in ceremonies and tolerated in public marketplaces, but it is frowned upon in other contexts and when it differs in degree. It offers an opportunity for the expression of ego-dystonic feelings and thoughts that have been repressed and suppressed.

Indeed, from an early age the peasant child is exposed to ceremonial possession. He is made aware of the prestige of the *hungan* and the possessed; he sees how applauded are the possessed and he learns of their good fortune. Observing the possession of his elders, a Haitian peasant child grows up with the hope that some day he too will be possessed. As one well-educated Haitian told me: "Everyone in Haiti is trying to catch a *loa*." It is obvious that, for the non-literate uneducated peasant, "catching a *loa*" by possession is far easier than it is for those who are more educated, intellectual and sophisticated.

In essence, possession is a useful and culturally sanctioned form of role-playing, which serves public as well as private needs, and is legitimized only insofar as it occurs within the context of voodoo and in the correct proportions. For those who are out of touch with voodoo, or for those whose possession lasts longer than the ceremonials warrant, it is not legitimized but regarded as a form of *folie*. The similarities between explanations of possession phenomena and psychiatric illness, and those put forward for *loa* possession and supernatural *folie* suggest a strong relationship between the two; they add weight to the conception of ritual possession as an acceptable form of "going crazy."

DISCUSSION

In an attempt to unify the mass of anthropological data that deal with psychological and social aspects of personality, child training, socialization experiences and psychopathology, Devereux[38] has formulated what is perhaps the clearest theoretical statement on the subject of ethnic neuroses and psychoses, the essential element of which is the idea of an ethnic unconscious. "This is that portion of the total unconscious segment of the individual psyche which is shared with most members of a given culture in that . . . society or culture permits certain impulses, fantasies and the like to become and to remain conscious, while requiring others to be repressed. The members of a given culture are likely to have repressed the same things and thereby to have certain unconscious conflicts in common."

It is Devereux's view that there are emotionally disturbed persons in whom the unconscious segment of their ethnic personality has not become so disorganized as to incite them to wholesale rebellion against all social norms. While they are genuinely ill, such persons tend to borrow from their culture the means for implementing their subjective derangement in a conventional way. According to Devereux, the classical examples of such ethnic illnesses are *amok, latah, imu, windigo, koro,* etc.—syndromes in which disturbed people in certain cultures conform to the behavior patterns that are actually expected in that society from disturbed people. He says:

We might add that the symptomatology of the ethnic psychoses conforms to cultural expectations, chiefly because conventional ideas on "how to act insane" are determined by the specific nature of the conflicts prevailing in certain cultures, and also by the nature of the defense which culture provides against such culturally penalized conflicts and impulses.

In other words, whereas, in view of the nature of Crow culture, the psychically traumatized Crow Indian can, because of his distinctive ethnic makeup, and because of the nature of his culture and culturally determined tensions, find relief by running amok, it is the cultural conformism manifested by such psychotics which often causes us to minimize the seriousness of their basic derangements.

Devereux's notion that the patient needs to select a particular form of culture-bound disorder that will enable him to "act crazy" in a culturally acceptable way ignores the fact that the cultural patterning of abnormal behavior has to take place, to begin with, on the basis of individual psychological or psychiatric dysfunction. Devereux overestimates the degree of self-control open to the patient and also exaggerates his freedom of choice in the expression of his disability. In addition, the formulation exaggerates the psychogenic origins of psychiatric disorder and ignores its structural aspects.

Thus, there is a good deal of controversy as to how to regard these exotic disorders. In my opinion there has been too great an inclination to accept native notions of etiology and nosology. Thus, in so far as the content of an illness such as *windigo* was linked with beliefs about taboo violation, it has been thought likely that it was belief in the taboo and the consequences of its violation that led to anxiety, and this in turn led to the illness. Such studies, however, have generally failed to recognize that taboo violation is such a common event in the lives of most people that difficulties will in most instances be explained by just such an acceptable, culturally shared phenomenon. While this may lead to prompt diagnosis and treatment, it is in itself insufficient evidence of causation.

What is crucial here is the fact that the absence of such explanations for psychiatric symptoms often leads not to treatment but to the neglect of the troubled individual, since the culture defines within specified limits what patterns of disturbed mood, thought, and behavior are to be regarded as illness. Anxiety that is caused by seeing a ghost is diagnosed as *susto* and leads to treatment among Mexican-Americans. Fear that is not linked to a specific kind of culturally meaningful situation, however, tends to be ignored or criticized, and does not generally lead to treatment.

While different factors may produce the same clinical picture, the same etiological factors and psychological mechanisms may also produce a variety of clinical pictures. This is certainly true of the degenerative organic psychoses and the symptomatic psychoses, both of which present themselves in an extraordinary variety of ways; it is also true of hysterical disorders and, to a lesser degree, of other psychiatric illnesses. Of interest in this regard are conditions that have the same underlying psycho-dynamic mechanisms, but whose differing clinical manifestations and symbolic content reflect differences in the culture. Thus, castration fear, dependency needs, and inferiority feelings, which may be expressed either in the Don Juanism of Western culture or in the *machismo* complex of Mexican-American culture, may also take the form of fear that the patient's penis will disappear into his abdomen, and that he will die, as in *koro* in Southeast Asia.

In this connection, it is Devereux's formulation regarding the universality of basic psychodynamics that best accounts for clinically observed differences in individuals with similar under-lying psychodynamic conflicts:

The same defense mechanisms are present in the normal and in the abnormal personality, as well as in members of various cultures. The normal differs from the abnormal and the Eskimo differs from the Bedouin, not in terms of the presence or absence of the patterning of all defenses, but in terms of the relative degree of importance which culture "assigns" to the various defense mechanisms. This "assigning" of importance is not a deliberate act, but simply a more or less inevitable byproduct of the prevailing cultural atmosphere.

It is this that accounts for the fact that the psychodynamic mechanisms, or the patterning of behavior and defenses, vary from culture to culture, and are in turn reflected in patterns of psychiatric illnesses. While much work remains to be done to validate this theory, it nevertheless provides a unified view of a diverse array of data on normal and abnormal patterns, at the same time as it takes into account both psychiatric and anthro-pological data.

The effect of culture on psychological and psychopatholog-ical phenomena is further illustrated by those culture-specific theories and therapeutic practices that are examined in the next chapter.

CHAPTER 5   PRE-SCIENTIFIC
              MEDICINE AND
              PSYCHIATRY

ALTHOUGH VIEWS ABOUT ETIOLOGY AND
therapeutic efforts are necessarily influenced by the culture, it
seems likely that most pre-scientific healers would be in agreement about which individuals are in need of help. Symptoms of
uncontrollable anxiety, depression, and agitation would be recognized almost everywhere as evidence of disorder, as would such
gross breaks in contact with reality as delirium or acute schizophrenia. In addition, it seems that most healers in most societies
are concerned first with the control of violence both toward the
community and toward the self; next with the reduction of fear
and anxiety; and lastly with the reintegration of the withdrawn
(schizophrenics and depressives) into the community. The various therapeutic institutions that have developed to deal with
the problems that are universally associated with psychiatric disorder and deviant behavior thus share many features, and examination of them may help to throw light on certain universal
therapeutic principles, as well as on the culture-specific contributions that are made to these universal healing systems.

Ever since the first travelers and missionaries reported on the
"strange" ways of primitive peoples, Western man has been
fascinated by their medical beliefs and customs. "Primitive"
societies (*naturels* or *Naturvolken*) are those that are isolated
from the mainstream of Occidental or Oriental civilization; they
are generally non-literate, and organized on the basis of either
small local or kinship groups, with simple nonspecialized econ-

Notes for Chapter 5 will be found on pages 203–206.

omies and technologies. We know from numerous studies that primitive theories of illness have a universal pattern; Tylor[1] suggested that concepts of the causation of disease through object intrusion were spread by diffusion. Clements[2] supported this view, suggesting that these concepts spread, during the Pleistocene era, from Africa to Asia and then to America via the Bering Strait. He found only four basic concepts of disease causation: loss of a vital substance from the body (soul loss); introduction of a foreign and harmful substance into the body (intrusion or possession by spirit); violation of taboos; and witchcraft.

In most societies, these concepts provide the logical foundation for the medical techniques that are used there. For example, where sorcery is suspected, countersorcery measures are employed, or elaborate witchcraft hunts are performed until the culprit is found. Where harmful substances are believed to have entered the body, on the other hand, extraction of the supposed substance is attempted by "sleight of hand," or ritualistic exorcism. From the crude magic of the aborigine to the sophisticated empiricism of the Plains Indians, medical systems of this sort have developed in all societies. To propitiate, exorcise, or coerce unwanted spirits that have taken possession of the sick, man has used prayer, sacrifice, fumigation, starvation, heat, fright, bloodletting, catharsis, and scapegoats. The recovery of lost souls (of a lost vital substance) has been undertaken with techniques of confession, expiation, and purification of the sinner, as well as by countersorcery and threats against the sorcerer. Forms of magic are also vehicles for use against the various causes of illness. J. G. Frazer[3] recognized two forms of sympathetic magic: imitative and contagious. In the former, harm is done to the individual, who then suffers in sympathy. While imitative magic acts on a man's effigy, contagious magic acts on one part of his body—nail parings, a tooth, strands of hair—being based on the notion that infecting a part will affect the whole. As noted in Chapter 4, *mal ojo* or "evil eye," the form of magic that is so common in the Mediterranean, is based on the belief that whoever falls under its spell will suffer misfortune.

PREVENTIVE MEASURES

Magical

Concepts of producing contagion by way of magical formulae have formed the basis for many prophylactic measures in preliterate societies. According to Burstein:[4]

In various parts of Africa (Nigeria, Sierra Leone, Southeast Sudan, Tanganyika), smallpox patients and contacts are isolated in separate villages built for this purpose. The patients are looked after by people who have already had the disease, as it has been observed that no one gets it twice. The clothes are buried with those that die; if patients recover, they bathe and wash their clothes in seawater before using them again. Among the Batetala of the Congo, syphilis victims are driven from the village and compelled to live alone in the bush. The Fanti of West Africa give syphilitic ulcerations a name which means "isolated," and send their patients into the bush for treatment. Where such beliefs do not exist, appropriate precautions may not be taken, so that healthy persons may be regularly exposed to sufferers from infectious diseases.

As Sigerist[5] has noted:

Sickness that strikes the individual is bad enough, but worse are epidemics that visit and decimate entire tribes. The severity of the menace drives people, civilized or primitive, to act, and for thousands of years, until the scientific era, the main reactions to epidemics have been much the same. The first impulse is to flee from the infested locality. The Kubu, who live in the forests of Sumatra, one of the most primitive tribes in existence, know of no other reaction than flight. When smallpox or some other epidemic reaches them, they move on deeper into the forest, and simply abandon their sick, who thus are dead socially before physical death has overcome them. Nomad or semi-nomad tribes obviously find it easier than sedentary tribes to flee before an epidemic. The Navahos do not hesitate to abandon their hogans, while the Hopis remain in their pueblos and die in large numbers. It was probably easier for primitive and early civilizations to develop a clear concept of the contagiousness of disease than it was for later civilizations, for the good reason that among primitives and in early antiquity we usually find an outspoken magico-religious concept of contagion.

Beliefs about the contagiousness of illness have preventive value. In Ecuador, according to Erasmus:[6]

The folk concept of contagion is different from the modern one. The major folk explanation is concerned with the fear of bad body humor. This is most commonly described as due to lack of personal cleanliness. It is a substance which exudes with perspiration and if one does not bathe frequently it may re-enter the pores and infect the blood. Not only is it a source of auto-infection, but it may also be passed between persons. Thus it may cause such ailments as skin disease, infected wound, and syphilis. Close contact, sexual relations, or seats still warm from a previous occupant are means by which it may pass from one individual to another

The notion that a disease may be passed from one human to another is the essence of the concept of contagion, even when the etiological agent is a hypothetical or magical humor. While elaborations of this notion in primitive cultures may have seemed to observers in the past to be extreme examples of superstition, similar formulations are becoming increasingly prominent in contemporary psychiatric theories, which emphasize the impact of social and interpersonal forces. The contradictory and conflict-producing effect of the implied messages of the "schizophren-ogenic" mother is a good example of a modern etiological theory of psychiatric disorder that has incorporated the notion of the transmission of disorder from one person to another in some subjective way.

Concepts of illness in pre-literate societies can also be very advanced. According to R. G. Abraham,[7] some African groups consider leprosy and elephantiasis to be inherited, and care is taken to see that the family into which a man marries has no such disease in it. The Digo have a method for preventing kwashiorkor —a protein deficiency disease of children.[8] They believe that kwashiorkor develops when a woman becomes pregnant too soon after her previous delivery to be able to continue feeding the older child. They therefore correlate the illness with her inability to devote all her attention and her milk to the first infant, thereby robbing it of its strength; the second infant, in short, becomes a danger to the first. Although the correlation of repeated pregnancy with protein deficiency is based on empirical observations, the relevance of food deprivation is not understood. The whole phenomenon is explained supernaturally, in terms of *chirwa* or the violation of sexual taboo. This belief is an obstacle to modern treatment by dietary supplements, since the tribes believe that what is indicated is supernatural treatment.

Traditional rituals can be useful prophylactically, irrespective of their supernatural explanations on which they rest. The Navaho Indians, for example, do not permit fecal material to accumulate around their living quarters, because it is feared that it might be used by an evildoer to produce harm to the individual.[9]

Objective

Primitive medicine also has many objective measures for the prevention of disease; these include the trephining techniques of the Incas, Masai surgery, and the anatomical methods of the Aleuts and Eskimos. Primitive groups have developed surgical techniques, massage, bloodletting, bathing, inoculation and cauterization. Some 25 to 50 per cent of the primitive pharmacopeia is objectively effective.[10] Chaulmoogras podophyllin, digitalis, caffeine, ephedrial, pretbram, squill, sagrada, reserpine, LSD, opium, hashish, hemp, coca, cinchona, ipecac, curare, eucalyptus, sarsaparilla, acacia, kousso, copaiba, guaiac, cascoma, bakam, jalap, podophyllin and quassia—all these are forms of naturally occurring drugs that are used by pre-literate peoples throughout the world.

Of course, a wide range of preventive measures of questionable value have also been reported. Such practices include scarification and inoculation with snake ashes; tattooing; finger amputations; flagellations; skull deformation; fumigation; circumcision; the use of penis envelopes; nose rings, and lip plugs.

Empirically effective inoculation techniques against snakebite and smallpox have been described on various continents.[11] In Africa, the serum from a pustule is applied to an incision. In Central Asia, scabs ground with water are inoculated with pins, and in China pulverized scabs are blown into the nose. The Nyamwezi and Sukuma tribes of Africa put a small amount of pus from a smallpox sore onto the bridge of an individual's nose.

Harley[12] has observed certain empirical preventive methods of the Manos in Liberia:

One would scarcely expect very advanced ideas about prevention of disease among these people, but there are a few rational preventives used. The leaf of *fla la* (*Alchormea cordifolia*) is mixed with the red palm oil and smeared on feet and ankles to prevent ground itch (Hookworm). *Ka nai la* (possibly Synclisia sp.) is used to prevent diarrhea after eating new rice. A leaf is rubbed up and the juice licked off the fingers. Juice of *bela* (*Scoparia dulcis*) is rubbed on the skin as a protection against snakebite. Leaves of *bo yidi* (*Glyphaea lateriflora*) are given to a baby when it first begins to eat rice. *Bo yidi pulu* (*Erythrococca africana*) is also used with the first solid food the child takes.

The Manos natives are essentially clean and careful, though ignorance leads them to be grossly inconsistent at times. The Mano has a hot bath every night at sunset. The woman washes her skin and the clothes of the family at the edge of the stream. Native towns undisturbed by external influences are well kept, houses are remarkably free from the type of vermin associated with bodily filth, rubbish heaps are periodically turned into gardens, and night soil is deposited in the bush, always in a different place if possible, and covered with newly pulled leaves placed upside down to warn a passerby. A clean water supply is always appreciated, and the location of the town is always determined by the accessibility of the water supply. Some diseases, at least, are recognized as contagious, and sick people in general are avoided. Food is clean and well cooked, as is indicated by the rarity of such diseases as tapeworm (five cases in the Ganta series of 6,000 patients).

Numerous preventive measures have to do with the use of food and water. Gillin[13] noted that water in a Peruvian coastal village

is considered to be essential for the irrigation of land, as useful in cooking vegetables and meats (although some cooks use only chicha), and as pleasant for an occasional bath, if convenient. But it is regarded as little short of poisonous if used as a drink by man. No doubt this is an eminently hygienic attitude, considering the fact that many available supplies of the liquid are possibly contaminated. Tea made of yerba luiza and also coffee are consumed by both children and adults, usually for breakfast only (also milk, cocoa, and soda water in comparatively small quantities by children). Nevertheless, the principal drink for all persons above the age of puberty is chicha, a maize beer.

According to Polgar,[14] food taboos were probably introduced when primitive groups learned of the allergic potential in food and its relationship to trichinosis, brucellosis and tapeworm. Food taboos are also directed at those periods of life during which visible physiological changes occur and susceptibility to illness and death are believed to increase. Numerous taboos are connected with pregnancy, lactation, infancy and puberty.

The psychological value of such preventive practices is often as important as their practical value. Most of these practices are incorporated into ceremonial and ritual contexts, to become an integral part of the social and psychological economy of members of these societies. This is illustrated by bathing practices among the Navaho:

Bathing by means of the sweat-bath or the yucca-root-and-water bath is part of both ceremonial and everyday treatment. Sweat-baths are taken to tone up the system, as well as for purposes of cleanliness, and after a doctor has seen or participated in one, so that he understands what it involves, he might find it very helpful to advise it in certain cases where he feels a general tonic is needed. Nurses and day school teachers report that if you provide a Navaho with soap and water there is no trouble in keeping him clean. When given the facilities, Navahos love to bathe, and at home it seems that only the lack of water and privacy keeps them from doing it.[15]

PRE-SCIENTIFIC HEALERS

In every society there are individuals who function as healers; who becomes the healer, and how he functions, varies from culture to culture. Healers can be differentiated, for example, by the different ways in which they enter the healing role; special dream experiences, the resolution of a psychotic illness, apprenticeship to a trained healer or inheritance, are among these ways. Healers may also be differentiated by the problems they treat: some specialize in bone ailments, poisoning or mental illness, while others specialize in the use of certain medicines or techniques. As societies become more complex, specialization of function develops and the prerequisites for taking on the healing role becomes more demanding. Skill in performance becomes a more significant criterion than heredity or special experiences, and the individual is likely to deal only with a limited group of illnesses.

There may be a variety of healers within the same culture. Healers such as the *hakims* and *vaids* in Indian villages must study complex traditional lore, like the Unani and Ayurvedic Indian traditions, a requirement not unlike those found in China and the Arabic world; snakebite healers and exorcists, on the other hand, may rely more upon unwritten traditions. Other individuals have worked in Western hospitals or dispensaries; often they establish their own practice among acculturating or modernizing groups, or function in officially designated intermediary roles, as skilled bilingual medical aides.

Healers by no means occupy the most desirable role in the society, even when they are obviously in control of powerful social forces. Although the snake healers in Indian villages have great prestige in the eyes of the villagers, they receive no payment for their efforts.[16] They may be viewed as deviant and odd—an attitude that is not infrequently encountered in other cultures as well, and that may be attributed to the fact that the healer has to deal with many different types of undesirable matter and people in his work. This same attitude is reflected in the not uncommon notion that primitive shamans are recruited from the ranks of neurotics and psychotics—which does indeed occur in some cultures, where mental aberration is a necessary prerequisite for becoming a leader. The similarity between the Haitian voodoo theory of mental illness and the Haitian voodoo pattern of becoming a healer sheds some light on the relationship between mental aberrations and the role of the healer.[17]

An individual becomes a *hungan* or voodoo priest by following and learning the practices, customs, and secrets of the voodoo cult. By observing and assisting an older *hungan*, and by traversing the hierarchy of ranks—from apprentice or *canzo*, to acolyte or *hunsi*—he may acquire the necessary skills. The selection of this career is determined in two ways. If a person is bright, has a knowledge of leaf medicine, and seeks the power, prestige and remunerative beliefs of the priestly office, he can buy that power from another *hungan*—which means that he pays for information about techniques and often for practical instruction as well. "Receiving a call from the gods," is a more common approach to the priesthood. Such a "call" may take the form of dreams, where the *loa* speaks in his head. In most instances, the first manifestations of *loa* possession are indistinguishable from *folie*. If an individual does not accept the call of the *loa*, he may be punished with sickness or insanity.

Accepting the "call," an individual usually experiences another dream ("the supernatural power of the mystery speaks in your mind") and then visits a *hungan*. A period of ill-defined apprenticeship follows. Clever devotees often acquire the necessary knowledge in one month; others take longer. The famous "mambo," Madame Laurent Mellon, said that she acquired the knowledge in two weeks through intuition. Not all who visit a *hungan*, whether they are called or themselves select the role, are given the *asson* (a gourd lined with religious beads, which is symbolic of the office of *hungan*). Failure by the individual during the ceremony of the *asson* (graduation) to receive manifestations of the *loa* in the form of recognizable possession is taken to indicate the *loa*'s refusal to accept him as a *hungan*.

It is easier for a *hungan* to develop *folie* than anyone else, because of his enormous responsibilities to the *loa*: "If one day he forgets to honor his god, the god will punish him... If during a ceremony he forgets he can become crazy." When *folie* occurs, he loses his power, usually because he has lost favor with his *loa*, but occasionally because a more powerful *hungan* sends a bad spirit. An attempt to ascertain the cause of *folie* is made in various ceremonials: if a "miracle" happens, the *hungan* is cured, if he dies, death is attributed to loss of favor with the bad spirit. Most *hungans* die of "old age or insanity." For those who have bought the power, *folie* occurs when they are unable to manage or control it.

The range of personality characteristics associated with shamanistic roles is very great. Sasaki[18] found that in primitive shamanistic communities in Japan, specific psychopathological needs are not essential for becoming a shaman. In more modern communities, however, shamanism clearly serves psychopathological needs. Thus the question of who adopts the role will depend not only on psychological predisposition, but also on the level of organization of the society; the roles that are available in it for certain types of personalities; and the attitudes toward the shamanistic role itself. In more complex societies, the shamanistic role is a peripheral one, available to the alienated of the society, who are given more freedom in dealing with both the sacred and the profane. To the extent that the shaman concerns himself with matters that other people do not, he encourages extreme attitudes of awe and hate, fear and ridicule; these further alienate him from the society and at the same time strengthen the authority of his role.

While traditional healers share many features with Western physicians, one must be aware of the differences when one attempts to substitute modern for traditional medicine. Native healers serve far more numerous purposes and functions in the maintenance of the social system than initially meets the eye. Marriott[19] has demonstrated three major differences between the Ayurvedic *hakim* or *vaid* in India and Western physicians:

The first device that the hakim or vaid uses to bridge the gulf of status between him and his patient is to cultivate a reputation for having a superior and penetrating—almost magical—knowledge of the body. This inspires the patient's confidence. The first thing that such a physician does by way of diagnosis is to grasp the patient's wrist. From the pulse— and from other astute observations which often go unnoticed—he tells everything. He asks no questions, or only indirect ones, for he is expected to know. One hakim in a village near Kishan Garhi had the reputation of being able to tell the contents of the stomach by feeling the pulse. He would take the patient's hand and inform him whether he had eaten wheat, barley, or millet bread together with sweet milk or with curds. Another vaid was credited with being able to predict anyone's life-span to the day and hour. On one occasion, he felt a very old woman's pulse and said she would die at noon that same day, all treatment being futile. Villagers swear that the woman died on the hour, as if by command. Of course, a western doctor's diagnostic skills and devices would occasionally permit him to play out much the same sort of drama if he chose to do so and similarly to create a reputation of power. Villagers' fascination with the diagnostic and predictive powers of thermometers and stethoscopes has already forced many indigenous physicians to add these to their kits, even though they may understand little about the actual use of such instruments.

A second special device which helps the hakim or vaid create confidence—to make himself a dependable man—is the theory, similar to the theory which surrounds the snake-bite curer, that he is practicing medicine for piety, for the sake of enhancing his own religious merit. The indigenous physician often seems to charge nothing for his skilled services. Indeed, he is felt to be giving his services as charity. Ragged villagers must therefore approach the lordly, white-clothed physician in a manner of worship. It is usual for the hakim or vaid to hold a free clinic each morning at which he advises supplicants as to the diet and regime that may be proper for their ailments and the season. The poor most often seek attention at these early clinics, weaker persons being carried to the physician's house on the back of stronger family members. For the physical labor of walking to a wealthier patient's home, the hakim or vaid charges a substantial fee amounting to a sum two or three times the daily wage of a laborer. One well-known hakim came from two miles away to call on a lone and injured landless laborer of Kishan Garhi; his refusal to accept payment from the lame laborer added a great deal to that hakim's reputation for selfless piety. It is believed safe for a poor patient to deal with a rich physician who is also pious, for then the physician will not exploit the poor man.

The pharmaceutical arrangements of the hakim or vaid are a third device which, perhaps even more than piety and skill, contributes to the financial and social strength of his practice. Since such a physician does not charge directly for his treatment, he must obtain most of his income through the sale of medicines. Himself he travels to distant markets to purchase what are believed to be rare materials. Himself he grinds and mixes the materials. Then when he wraps his powders in small packets and retails them at high prices, he creates an illusion of value and a feeling of confidence in the treatment, here exploiting a logic much like that used by the religious exorcist.

But the hakim goes still farther and guarantees his medicines. If a medicine is very expensive, the hakim may ask for its cost in advance, or may take a small initial payment so as to seal a contract for full later payment by the patient. Such guarantees constitute acceptance of the patient's dependency, and at the same time give the patient a sense of control over the high physician. Any suspicion that the physician is making some economic gain by exploiting the patient's illness is removed from the therapeutic situation by such a contract or guarantee. The physician assumes full responsibility; the patient is reassured; and the two parties are united in a set of mutual obligations, recognizing their respective positions of dominance and subordination.

PRE-SCIENTIFIC THEORIES OF MENTAL ILLNESS

There are a number of important lessons to be learned from an examination of the diverse beliefs and practices that are related to psychiatric illness in various cultures throughout the world. In many non-Western cultures, native practitioners to whom modern psychiatry is completely unknown are treating emotionally disturbed persons. Examination of the emotional, attitudinal, and interpersonal elements in these various forms of psychological treatment should offer psychiatrists a broader perspective from which to understand the basic components of our own systems of psychiatry and psychotherapy.

As noted above, Clements[20] found that the emergence of disorders of mood, thought, and behavior in most pre-technical, pre-literate, and underdeveloped cultures has invariably been explained by supernatural concepts of taboo violation, witchcraft, the instrusion of harmful objects into the body, or loss of a vital substance from the body and possession by angry or evil spirits. Incest and murder are taboo violations, almost universally believed to have deleterious effects on the mind of the perpetrator, with punishment in the form of insanity coming from ancestral deities or God, or from the individual's conscience. Witchcraft, by contrast, is usually associated with the nefarious activities of others, such as witches, sorcerers, and black magicians, whose special powers or use of sympathetic magic enable them to inflict insanity on the victim. Witchcraft is often thought to be responsible for the introduction into the victim of magical or foreign substances that produce illness by upsetting the natural equilibrium of the body. To restore health, these substances have to be extracted from the victim through blowing, sucking, bleeding, etc. Strange behavior is also explained by the presence of an alien spirit, sometimes sent by malevolent sorcerers, or by ancestral deities, as punishment for failure to honor the dead. Haitian peasants, for example, believe that a sorcerer can force the *gros bon ange* (soul) from the victim's head by magical means, and replace it with the soul of an insane dead man or animal, whose manifestations are then responsible for the victim's insane behavior.[21]

These etiological notions are not found at random throughout the world; rather, they occur in relation to the nature of symptoms, as well as to the prevailing beliefs and customs, and other factors present in the particular society. Thus, Field[22] found that the self-accusation of witchcraft was common among depressed Akan women in Ghana. Because this belief was not considered irrational in their culture, they were not thought to be mentally ill and were rarely sent to hospitals. Others have noted that witchcraft is more often considered a cause of mental illness in those groups that have little expectation of individual responsibility, as well as a highly developed tendency to utilize projective-adaptive measures.[23,24]

Several studies have suggested an association between personality patterns and primitive therapeutic techniques. One study of 75 primitive societies found that magical medical therapies were related to patterns of anxiety reduction that had been learned earlier, during socialization training.[25] Self-punitive practices, such as sacrifice to the spirits causing the illness, or bloodletting to remove harmful agents, were significantly associated with severe prohibitions on the expression of aggression during childhood; whereas such extrapunitive measures as witch-hunting were related to the fact that there were few prohibitions on aggressive behavior during childhood. Taboo violation, which functions as a social sanction in highly atomistic or disintegrating social groups, seems to be universally present as an explanation of mental illness; object intrusion, on the other hand, is often the explanation for acute and chronic physical pains of psychosomatic or hysterical nature. "Possession" seem to predominate in those cultures that accept and encourage such behavior in ritualistic and institutionalized situations (in Haiti, for example, "possession" is a necessary element of the priestly role).

Every society must deal, conceptually and emotionally, with the experience of death. A great number of practices have developed to prolong life, to ensure easy passage to the kingdom of the dead, or to guarantee a comfortable life in death. Since the dead are buried close to the living, their spirits have frequently been blamed as causes of illness. Because of the contagiousness of some illnesses, the dead are viewed with awe; they are placated to keep harm from coming to the living. Another response is not pronouncing the name of the dead, so as to avoid the arousal of their anger and revenge against the person who "misused the name." The proximity of burial plots to living areas also makes it difficult for attitudes to change after people have died, and this may account for the power attributed to ghosts. In any case, they serve as useful rationalizations for behavior that is actually based on preconscious motivations. According to Kligfeld and Krupp,[26]

The preservation of the belief in immortality provides certain advantage to the individual, family, and community. Essentially it permits the denial of the loved object being permanently lost and thus allows for the phantasy of eventual reunion. The anthropomorphic characteristics of both the gods and departed spirits are readily noticed: both the gods and spirits of the dead maintain their interest in the moral structure of the group in that they both direct the moral actions of the living. Although the forces may be bad at times, for the most part their role is to aid the individual and society to obtain food and to insure fertility. The dead become over-idealized and are the personnel of the sacred myths, legends and beliefs. By recognizing the role of the dead and their place in religion we are able to see once more the projection of the parent-child relationship. Therefore religious funeral rituals permit the individual to keep his parent or substitute from permanently leaving him.

Witchcraft practices are also linked with the world of spirits. In addition to maintaining the stability of social organization, witchcraft provides a conceptual and behavioral framework for the expression of a range of feelings. According to Nadel,[27] witchcraft provides for: "projection or displacement of hatreds and aggressive desires from the sphere of rational social life into one mystically sanctioned . . . through such projection and displacement, the doctrine of witchcraft both permits anxieties to become articulate (if in fantasy language) and shows them an outlet, or scapegoat."

Beliefs in witchcraft are often the focus of a patient's thoughts; they may also contribute to non-recognition of the illness. In Ghana, according to Field,[28] "Witchcraft meets, above all else, the depressive's need to steep herself in irrational self-reproach and to denounce herself as unspeakably wicked." Similarly, Spiro's[29] cogent analysis of witchcraft in Burmese culture illustrates how witchcraft beliefs function as acceptable rationalizations of aberrant behavior and anxiety, and how they evoke reparative or therapeutic responses from others.

PRE-SCIENTIFIC TREATMENT OF THE MENTALLY ILL

Attitudes toward the mentally ill vary with a culture's beliefs, its economics and resources, and other factors. In some places, the sick blend into the setting as wandering beggars; in others, they are thought to be divinely appointed and are chosen as medicine men.[30] As we have noted in Chapter 2, by viewing psychiatric symptoms as evidence of spiritual tests and special psychic powers, Puerto Rican spiritualists render acceptable such symptoms as hallucinations and delusions.[31] Schizophrenics can often become reintegrated into the community by becoming mediums; their hallucinations now serve as a source of prestige. On the other hand, where insanity is viewed as an indication of bewitchment, the sufferer may be cruelly punished in order to protect the community from the evil within him. For this reason, the mentally ill in Fiji and New Hebrides (who are believed to be possessed by frightening evil spirits) are often buried alive, while victims of witchcraft among the Bengala of the Belgian Congo are put to death.[32]

It is important to note that *diagnosis* in pre-scientific psychiatry is most often made in terms of the patient's *conforming with* a recognized marginal model of behavior, not in terms of *deviation from* the norm. When behavior does not fit any psychiatric "thought model," it is often looked upon as criminal, not insane.[33,34]

In some developing countries, the mentally ill are often put in prisons and jails, without any distinction from genuine deviants. Margetts[35] has pointed to the system of restraints that is used by healers in Nigeria. One healer, who specialized in the treatment of madness, epilepsy and leprosy, ran a private "asylum" in Akure, in which Margetts observed an excited schizophrenic man and a manic woman in remission. In this "filthy and unhygienic" asylum, the healer used isolation, physical restraints, threats, iron ankle shackles, and soporific drugs, as well as magical images, offering bowls, and other paraphernalia. Elsewhere in Africa, physical restraints have included ropes, chains, iron wristlets and anklets, log stocks, stretchers, iron stone and cement weights, and locked doors.

That in time such models of behavior can change in a society is well illustrated in Sigerist's[36] study of Tarantism, or the "Dancing Mania," which appeared in Italy during the thirteenth century. This illness, made its appearance in epidemic proportions during the summertime, was attributed to the bite of the tarantula; it was manifested in great excitement and loss of inhibitions, with the victims drinking and dancing in the streets, often to the point of exhaustion. (Music and dancing were the preferred methods of treatment.) Sigerist found that this phenomenon had originated in Apulia, where the Greeks had once openly practiced their Dionysian rites. Christianity, however, was unable to assimilate these orgiastic rites and suppressed their practice, thereby forcing them underground; the people then practiced them in secret. In so doing, according to Sigerist, "they sinned, until one day—we do not know when, but it must have been during the Middle Ages—the meaning of the dances changed. The old rites appeared as symptoms of disease. The music, the dances, all that wild orgiastic behavior were legitimized. The people who indulged in these exercises were no longer sinners, but the poor victims of the tarantula."

Kaplan and Johnson[37] have observed a strikingly similar phenomenon in the American Southwest among Navaho Indians, whose culture derives from two conflicting traditions: one is based on hunting, raiding, and personal "power" (Apache), the other on religion, agriculture, and the maintenance of social control (Pueblo).

With the cessation of hunting and raiding, Apache values came to be excluded from what the Navaho regarded as normal and virtuous, and there were no longer any vital institutions for the expression of Apache tradition. These obsolete traditions and values were then translated into patterns of deviance and psychopathology, such as "crazy violence," a form of willful and reckless assaults on others that is associated with intoxication from alcohol. According to Kaplan, this behavior simply expresses the Apache values of willfulness, honesty, courage, and the willingness to "take the consequences"—values that are no longer sanctioned in the areas of hunting and raiding.

Exorcism

Techniques of exorcism are common because of the widespread notion of spirit-induced mental illness. In Nepal, evil spirits or *boxi* are exorcised by squeezing the patient's fingers, forcing him to lick the sole of a shoe, exposing him to irritating fumes in a closed room, or applying a heated spatula to his body. It is only the spirit that is believed to suffer from these tortures.

Not all forms of exorcism are violent. T. Yonebayashi[38] has described the treatment of *Kitsunetsuki* (or bewitchment), which does not respond to ordinary medical treatment. Patients must visit the famous Shinto shrine, Susa Jingu, where the priest (*Kannushi* or *Guji*) prays for separation of the patient from the animals that possess him, and brushes off the evil spirits with his sacred sweeper (*Gohei*). A rather benign form used by Mexicans and Mexican-Americans for the treatment of *susto* has been described by one of Rubel's[39] informants:

Until I was fourteen I lived with my family on a rancho just outside of the northern town of Cadereyta Jimenez in Mexico. In those days either the family cared for its sick or else they died. There were no doctors for us to run to whenever we felt sick! Every house was furnished with a copper pot in those days, and when susto occurred to a member of the family, that pot would be put in the kitchen fire to heat until its surface became red hot. The patient would lie on the dirt floor of the house and his mother would dig holes under his head, his feet, and each of the outstretched hands. Some water would be poured into the holes, and then the muddied water would be scraped up and put into a vase. Mother would then place a bit of red ribbon, some alvaca (an herb) and a gold ring into the vase, as well as four crosses of palm leaf. After the patient had been swept with the pirul branch, he was led to the fire where he began pouring the cold liquid from the base into the red hot copper pot. The terrible hiss given off by the copper as it received the cold mixture frightened the patient terribly. He leaped back away from the fire and shrieked, and a tremor ran through his body. At that moment the susto he had suffered ran from his body into the copper pot. Then for two nights following, the patient was swept and prayed over, sweated at night, and had to drink from the copper receptacle before eating in the morning (*en ayunas*), and before retiring for the night.

The exorcism of evil spirits is generally performed in dramatic, excited settings, where excessive stimulation appears to arouse a variety of positive emotions in patients and onlookers. No more dramatic ceremony can be found anywhere than the devil dancing of Ceylon. According to Senanayake,[40] psychoneuroses are believed to be caused by the influence of nine evil spirits or invisible powers, and treatment is possible only through invocations, offerings and rituals to these devils or planetary forces:

The patient is placed in the front verandah of his house, either in a chair or on a mat. The ceremonial dance takes place in the courtyard in front of the patient. This is a square, seven arms-length broad and seven wide, built and decorated with plaited coconut leaves. At the four corners are four banana stems, which act as decorative pillars. By the side of this main square are built two platforms, four feet high and three feet square, which are also decorated with young palm leaves. On these are kept various offerings, such as coconut flowers, cracked king coconuts, rice, a freshly-killed cock, etc.

The dance begins at 6 P.M. and carries on until 6 A.M. the next day, with intervals every three hours. Frilled skirts in tiers, and a short jacket decorated with imitation pearls and tinsels, are worn by the performers. They also wear a tight waist band, and a crown of tender coconut leaves on the head, and carry tufts of leaves in their hands, which, as the dance progresses, are replaced by burning torches. The dance and song which is dialogue between the head dancer, or Kapurala, and the drummer, gets more and more furious when the flaming torches are thrown up and caught dexterously. As it becomes wildest, they leap up and turn and twist their hands, arms and body, rapidly. Now it becomes a frenzied acrobatic feat, during the course of which the chief actor, who is now supposed to be possessed, demands certain presents in compensation for leaving the patient. A raw egg placed on a coconut shell ring is cooked over a flaming torch, and placed on the plate of rice. He then calls out to the king of Yakkas and says: "Look! Here is the offering for you; now you depart and leave this place!" The offering consists of cooked rice, egg, a bleeding killed fowl, sweetmeats, etc.

The chief performer now stretches himself on a mat, reciting charms or Mantras. He pretends to be dead, and the feigned corpse is carried out and deposited among the bushes nearby, thus cheating the yakka.

After refreshments, he begins another session, probably with a mask, white, black or brown, according to the spirit he is enticing. During the dance he works himself into such a frenzy that his eyes look glazed, and he gets into a trance and swoons, completely exhausted. Burdened with different gifts, he dances the last dance towards morning. Powdered resin is thrown at the lighted torches, which burst into flame and are carried in his mouth. Then he stops suddenly, and carries the offerings, and places them in the bushes for the crows and the dogs. The ceremony ends and the patient is supposed to be cured of his neurosis.

Drugs

The use of potent pharmacological substances has played a prominent role both in daily life and in pre-scientific medicine in almost all cultures. A variety of chemically active natural substances have been used to alter consciousness and mood, as well as to assist adaptation to life stress. There are estimated to be 4,000 species of angiosperms with alkaloidal narcotic properties; these include stimulants to increase awareness, sedatives to reduce awareness, and hallucinogens to alter awareness. Some 60 of them are used for their intoxicating effects, while five have major commercial significance: cocoa, opium, hemp, tobacco, and coffee. In some settings, these substances have been used ritualistically, and have had great social and economic significance; elsewhere, they have influenced large-scale social movements and changes. They have also contributed to a wide range of medical problems, associated with habituation, addiction, secondary psychotic disorders and antisocial behavior patterns. Most cultures have made use of stimulants such as tea, coffee, khat, pitura, cocaine and Benzedrine to increase alertness and to heighten contact with the environment. Stimulants such as the cacao leaf (cocaine) are chewed by the Andean Indians of Peru, Bolivia, Colombia and Ecuador to increase their tolerance for high altitudes, hunger and hard work.[41]

Hallucinogenic drugs, like mescaline and *ayahuasca*, have been used to reduce inhibitions in therapeutic group rituals. The effects of the drugs combine with the psychologically disruptive effects of the ritual, which are produced by persuasion, reward, punishment, sleep deprivation and social isolation, so as to engender strong emotional states in already troubled patients. The combination of stresses and drugs increases the patient's amenability to the introduction of new ideas. The drugs decrease defensiveness, heighten suggestibility and faith in the ritual, and lead to increased confidence and psychological integration. Follow-through on the part of both the leader and the group reinforces the acceptance of new behavior patterns and ideas.[42]

Hallucinogenic drugs have been used to produce a variety of states. *Ololiuqui* was a popular oracle- or truth-drug among the Zapotecs in ancient Mexico. In Central and South America, tobacco has been used in liquid form, or chewed to produce visions. California tribes have used jimson weed (*datura*) in puberty ceremonies to produce visions; these are then taken as evidence that the individual has acquired tutelary spirits. Substances such as rauwolfia serpentina have been used for centuries for their tranquilizing properties. In India rauwolfia was a common antidote for snake bites, lunacy, anxiety, stomach pain, fever, vomiting and headache. Other potent drugs include ergot, which was blamed for epidemics of madness during the Middle Ages; Iboba, an ordeal poison of the Congo, and Cohoba, a narcotic Caribbean snuff; Clorines, which paralyzes the muscles, destroys the willpower and produces psychic excitement, along with a great risk of cerebral hemorrhage; Camtillo, which produces paralysis and death from suffocation; and Toloachi, which leads to temporary insanity.

Any single substance may have a wide range of uses and misuses, depending on the amount taken and the form in which it is taken, as well as on the attitudes and expectations of the group and their prior experience with it. A substance that produces a stimulant effect when it is taken in low, measured doses may in higher doses produce toxic psychosis, addiction, withdrawal effects or even chronic personality deterioration. This is true, for example, of betel nuts. Chewing betel nuts is an integral part of the social customs of the South Pacific, a customary way of establishing friendship. The nuts are chewed in pre-marital and marital ceremonies, and they are used as sacrificial religious offerings to the dead, in order to prevent illness. Chewed by some 200,000,000 people throughout the South Pacific—including Australia, Tasmania, Madagascar, India, Pakistan, Ceylon, Tibet, China, Thailand, Vietnam, Malaysia, Indonesia, the Philippines, New Guinea, Formosa, and Micronesia—betel nuts are stimulants, which can also produce addiction. Abrupt termination of the practice, followed by resumption, may even precipitate an acute reversible toxic psychosis, with auditory hallucinations and grandiose and persecutory delusions.[43]

A substance may also be used for different purposes from place to place. Nutmeg (*myristica fragrans*) is used to improve virility among Yemenites; for fever, consumption, asthma and heart disease in India; for the treatment of madness in Malaya; and as an intoxicant or marijuana-substitute elsewhere. The significance that is attached to the dissociative experiences produced by psychotomimetic substances depends greatly on the belief system of the particular group. The range of consequences that may ensue from use of the same substance in different contexts points up the significance of sociocultural influences and expectations in the patterning of behavior. This is well illustrated by the use of *peyote,* whose hallucinatory properties have been harnessed to a wide range of religious beliefs and practices through the ages. In ancient Mexico,

The *chichimekas* knew of the properties of Peyote. . . Those who get peyote take it instead of wine as well as poisonous mushroom nancatal. They assemble somewhere in the prairie, dance and sing all day and all night, the next day meet again and weep to excess. With their tears they wash their eyes and clear their brains (i.e. return to reason, to see clearly again). The prime peyote, a kind of earth nopal, is white, grown in the northern parts and produces in those who eat or drink it terrible or ludicrous visions. This inebriety lasts 2–3 days and then disappears. The *chichimekas* eat a considerable amount of the plant; it gives them strength, incites them to battle, alleviates fear and they feel neither hunger nor thirst. It is even said that they are protected from every kind of danger.[44]

Peyote has been used in various kinds of sacred rites in Mexico, and among the Texas Indians, the Mescalero Apaches, the Omaha, the Comanche and the Kiowa. The Mexicans believed it to be a divine substance; the missionaries viewed it as the work of evil.

Lewin[45] has described the use of peyote by an Omaha Indian.

Torn for some hours from his world of primitive perceptions, from his life filled only with the satisfaction of purely material wants and necessities, such an Indian feels himself transported to a world of completely new sensations. He hears, sees and feels things which, agreeable as they are, must of necessity astonish him, because they do not in the least correspond with his ordinary existence, and their strangeness must create the impression of supernatural intervention. In this way anhalonium becomes God, like the patient I have already mentioned who stated that God was incarnated in cocaine.

Peyote is central to the religion of Indians in the American Southwest. This religion made its appearance in the Great Plains area in 1870 and has since flourished among the disenfranchised Indians; it has revitalized old customs that were threatened with extinction and has thus served religious, economic, and social purposes. Peyote functions as the repository of the supernatural power given to the Indians by the Great Spirit, so as to enable them to communicate with the supernatural world through visions. The substance is usually eaten in group ceremonies, which also feature much singing, drinking and praying. The hallucinatory experiences are generally followed by baptism, and by discussion of the experience on the following day. In that way, the drug is used therapeutically: the vision experience acts to "soften up" the patient, to make him amenable to the group's suggestions. The patient thereafter has the opportunity to confess his sins, to be baptized or reborn, and to become reintegrated into the group through group discussion.

The peyote religion has successfully combated alcoholism among Southwestern American Indians, thus demonstrating that the effectiveness of such mind-expanding substances depends in part on the expectations and attitudes arising out of the social context in which they are used. Addictive patterns and pathological outbursts do not therefore develop solely from the pharmacological effects of various substances, but also from attitudes and expectations regarding its misuse.

The effect of kava-kava (piper mysticum) also depends on group expectations; these in turn depend on the form and occasion of its use—that is, whether it is used clandestinely, in a religious festival, or for medical purposes. In small amounts, kava-kava produces a state of euphoria; in larger doses, it produces sleep; it may be addicting. It is usually chewed into shreds and the juice spit into a container. Colonial authorities and missionaries have often tried to suppress the use of pharmacologically active substances, even when their use was defined by ritualistic controls. The use of *kava-kava* in the South Sea Islands as a euphoric, sedative and anodyne was actively fought by missionaries. To the natives, *kava-kava* was a divine gift, and *kava-kava* plantations were divided into sections for evil gods, gods of sleep, and the family. It was drunk during festival times. In the New Hebrides, public houses were designated for *kava* orgies; in Samoa, people prayed to the gods at public *kava* feasts for health, long life, good harvest, and success.

The increasing use of these substances among certain disenfranchised groups in the modern world has led to abusive practices and to the loss of the social control that was traditionally associated with them. The use of peyote has spread beyond the Indian reservations to urban centers and college campuses in the United States. When it is used in personal efforts at psychic integration, it has often contributed to psychotic reactions, especially if group supports were not present. Ceremonial drinking has also given way to alcoholism.

Alcohol, if used to excess, produces an excitatory state, along with a reduction in inhibitions; ultimately, it leads to a state of depression and cloudiness. Its harmful effects, when used outside a ceremonial context, are well illustrated among various American Indian groups. The Mescalero Apache in the American Southwest have lost their traditional channels of emotional discharge, and dependency patterns have been encouraged by their "protected" reservation life. According to Boyer,[46] drunkenness has become an outlet for poorly integrated sexual and aggressive energies. Among the Navaho Indians, the stress of discrimination in reservation life, along with the loss of such traditional supports as the guardian spirit, have led to increasing drunkenness.[47] However, alcohol occasionally produces some psychologically beneficial effects. The men assert themselves by acting out the role of warriors, and their women consequently experience them as men, rather than as passive, dependent "reservation Indians." Culturally valued behavior patterns, such as courage, are more readily expressed, and there is a temporary increase in interpersonal contact and group harmony.

The differential effects of active substances seem to be related to the pattern or context of their use. It may be that those individuals who use the substances without group support are already psychologically disturbed; another possibility is that the group exerts sufficient control over dissociative experiences to enable individuals to tolerate them without overreacting. Certainly, changing attitudes and patterns are in and of themselves psychologically disruptive, and may for that reason contribute to the development of psychiatric illness. It may also be that group support and its explanation of the effects of a drug is more significant than group participation as such. If so, the individual may seek contact with the drug rather than with the group, thereby increasing the likelihood that the addictive properties of the drug will hold sway.

Cults

Special mention should also be made here of the therapeutic cult groups that serve rehabilitative and prophylactic purposes in many of the developing societies. Cults contribute to group integration and to the reaffirmation of various psychodynamically significant ends. In Brazil, the Umbanda cult emphasizes good deeds (*Ligne blanche*), and the Quimbanda cult, evil or witchcraft (*Alsstein*).[48] In the *Gelede* cult of the Ebado group among the Yoruba, male dancers are provided with wooden masks and protuberant wooden breasts and buttocks, in ritualized transvestitism; this serves as a defense against a devouring and castrating mother.[49] Their preoccupation with the devouring women is suggested by the following Gelede ritual song:

All-powerful mother, mother of the nightbird
Mother who kills animals without striking
We are three whom the mother has born and placed into the world:
The first one inherited the cloth (*Egungun*)
The second one inherited the bloody buba (*Aje*)
The third one looks in the house, and looks on the road, but finds nothing to inherit;
That is why he has inherited the dance. (*Gelede*)
My mother kills quickly without a cry
To prick our memory suddenly
Quickly as the woodpecker picks the tree on the farm from his mouth,
Great mother with whom we dare not cohabit
Great mother whose body we dare not see
Mother of secret beauties
Mother who empties the cup
Who speaks out with the voice of a man,
Large, very large mother on the top of the Iroko tree,
Mother who climbs high and looks down on the earth
Mother who kills her husband yet pities him.

Beier[50] has commented on this:

The purpose of the Gelede dance is to "placate the witches". This is what every Gelede dancer says. . . The men say: Gelede is "the secret of women." We the men are merely their slaves. We dance to appease "our mothers." The witches, they say, can kill in the dark, and there is no protection from their power, "because God has already given them permission to kill. God does not mind killing, because for every man who dies he can make a new one."

One Gelede dancer said: "As I have already got three children, there is no reason why I should not die. Nothing prevents me from dying tomorrow. But as I am a member of the Gelede society, the witches will spare me."

Another dancer expressed it as follows: "God gave the world to the witches. They have permission to kill. In the olden days they did a great deal of harm to our fathers. But our fathers thought for a long time until they found a way to placate them and win their favour; thus the Gelede society was started. Fear of death made us join this society. Because the witches cannot harm anyone inside the society."

This is a good example of a culture-specific primitive ritual for the resolution of a culture-specific conflict about the threatening mother. Another dramatic illustration is the Zar cult, which is found in Ethiopia, Egypt and the Sudan. Describing this cult, Messing[51] has noted that:

Most patients (attending the cult for therapeutic purposes) are married women who feel neglected in a man's world in which they serve as hewers of wood and haulers of water, and where even the Coptic Abyssinian Church discriminates against females by closing the church building to them. Married women in the predominantly rural culture are often lonely for the warmth of kinship relations, for typical residence is in an exogamous patrilocal hamlet. Members of the lower classes, such as the Muslim (mostly Sudanese) minority, find social contact across religious barriers in the Zar cult. Ex-slaves, many of them descended from alien African tribes ([or] *Shanqalla*), are also admitted to full membership in the Zar cult. Finally, occupational and economic benefits are dispensed by the Zar doctor, who also functions as treasurer of the society, but does not render any financial accounting. Thus he has the opportunity, rare on the simple material level of traditional Abyssinia, to accumulate capital which he invests in economic enterprises (e.g., brewing honey-wine) and which further enhances the reputation of his special powers.

Cult membership mobilizes help for the patient and reenforces the group support given him. It is culture-specific when it meets special needs of patients in particular cultures and when it shares common features with other cultural activities that are familiar to members of the culture. The culture-specific characteristics of Cochiti Pueblo Clan cures, for example, have been noted by Fox:[52]

Our patient is now a member of the Water clan and a different lineage of the Oak: she is "little" Water, and is dependent on continuing membership in the Water clan for her continued good health. By becoming a member of this clan she is cured, and by continuing in membership she stays cured. She acquires a relationship of dependence with a previously unrelated set of people. What is more, her faith in the efficacy of the cure is reinforced when she goes along to participate herself in cures conducted by the Water people. Clan, or rather lineage, membership is also of practical importance in mobilizing help for the patient. Thus the clan system is an anchor on to which therapy can fasten and continuous reinforcement of treatment be assured.

What is the therapeutic significance of these symbolic acts and what can it tell us about matrilineal clanship? If we look at this cure, we can see that what was being cured was a neurosis stemming from dependency anxiety occasioned by traumatic loss of maternal nurturance. The psychosomatic symptoms began after the death of the patient's mother. The house, which should have "come from" the mother, was central to the patient's fantasies. It symbolized security and continuance of the lost nurturance. What was done to cure this? First the very practical measure of giving the patient the longed-for house. Secondly, giving her another clan, making her a "little Water" and a "little Oak" of another lineage. She was thus put into a relationship of dependence with the culturally defined set of people, who performed such symbolically nurturant acts as giving food, re-naming, and washing the head. The latter two, being symbols of rebirth into a new status, underline the ritual shedding of an undesirable state and the acquisition of a new and healthier personality.

I would argue that giving the patient clans is symbolically equivalent to giving her mothers. If we examine the actions outlined above in the light of what the Cochiti say about clans, they become meaningful. "We get our clans, like ourselves, from our mothers." "Our clans come from our mothers, like all good things." "My clan is my mother's name." "Why do we have clans? Because we have mothers." It would seem that the clan is thoroughly identified in Cochiti thought with the mother herself. The most popular idea by which the clan was explained to me was this one concerning uterine kinship: We come from our mother's body = we are the same clan. Linguistic clues to this conceptualization of the clan show in the following paradigm: /hanu/ = person (people); /hanu/ = female;

/hanuc/ = clan. Thus I would suggest that there are motivational reasons at the back of matrilineal clanship in Cochiti that have to do with a deep-rooted identification with the mother in both males and females, and a strong need for maternal nurturance (i.e., dependency need) in females. John W. M. Whiting has suggested that identification will occur with the sex-typed role of the parent who "mediates the major resources" in a child's early life, a resource being anything that a child wants (Whiting, 1959a). Studies carried out on the basis of this theory have borne out its fruitfulness. Two of these have found indices of strong maternal identification in initiation ceremonies for boys at puberty, and matrilocal residence. Both these characterize Cochiti and Keresan Western Pueblo society, or at least have done so until recently. If we take Steward's point (1937) that matrilineal organization in the pueblos grew out of matrilocal residence, then we can see that, with matrilocal residence, female house-ownership, female ownership of crops and produce, and the father away from the household a good deal of the time, either in hunting, ceremony, or attendance at his maternal home, the mother would indeed be in a position to mediate the major resources for the child.

The "psychodramatic" opportunities that are present in cult participation for expressing in socially approved ways impulses and desires that are ordinarily inhibited is well demonstrated in Wallace's[53] study of the Iroquois. At the height of their military power in the 1600's, the Iroquois idealized such traits as autonomy, emotional independence, courage, and indifference to pain. Their ritual therapies, by contrast, concentrated on providing opportunities, ritually insulated from contact with life, for the gratification of more passive-dependent, ordinarily repressed strivings. During the False Face medicine ceremonies, individuals wearing masks and impersonating the gods could cease to be independent, self-controlled, and self-sacrificing and could express "a longing to be passive, to beg, to be an irresponsible, demanding, rowdy infant, and to compete with the Creator himself—and to express it all in the name of the public good."

The interpretation of dreams was the nucleus of Iroquois treatment; this was based on the notion that it was the frustration of dream wishes that caused psychological illness. Thus it was necessary to interpret and to act symbolically upon dreams, in ceremonial context, in order to maintain community stability and prevent evil. According to Wallace:

The annual festival at Midwinter not merely permitted but required the guessing and fulfillment of the dreams of the whole community. There were probably several dozen special feasts, dances, or rites which might be called for at any time during the year by a sick dreamer: the *andacwander* rite, requiring sexual intercourse between partners who were not husband and wife; the *ohgiwe* ceremony, to relieve someone from persistent and troubling dreams about a dead relative or friend; the dream-guessing rite, in which the dreamer accumulated many gifts from unsuccessful guessers; the Striking Stick Dance, the Ghost Dance, and many other feasts, dances, and even games. The repertoire could at any time be extended by a new rite, if the dreamer saw a new rite or a nonsacred rite in a dream, or if his clairvoyant divined that such a rite was called for; normally social dances became curative when performed for someone at the instigation of his dream. Some rites were the property of "secret" medicine societies, membership in which was obtained by having received the ministrations of the society upon dream-diagnosis of its need. Visions of false faces called for the rituals of the False Face Society; visions of dwarf spirits indicated a need for the "dark dance" of the Little People's Society; dreams of bloody birds were properly diagnosed as wishes for membership in the Eagle Society; dreams of illness or physical violence and injury were evidence of need for the Medicine Men's Society Rite or for the Little Water Society. The relationship of dreams to ritual was such that the repertoire of any one community might differ from that of the next because of the accidents of dreams and visions, and any element might at any time be abstracted from the annual calendar of community rituals and performed for the benefit of an individual.

Healing was done by various members of the community known as "ceremonial friends." According to Wallace:

Sick persons often dreamed of someone (or a relative of the sick person dreamed), and the dream was interpreted to mean that the sick person "wants a friend." During the Eagle Society Ceremony, the sick person is given a ceremonial friend; thereafter the two treat one another as kinfolk, and the relationship of mutual helpfulness is lifelong. If a boy's friend, for instance, is an older man, he . . . must help the child to grow up to be a man. He must advise the boy, acting as his counsellor . . . When one is ill, they choose a friend for him from the other side (moiety). It is believed that the ceremony of making friends merges the relatives of the two principals into one kindred unit: the relatives of the man are linked with the relatives of the child. The older man must act as an example to his junior friend, the older man's conduct shall be observed by the younger boy, who considers the older friend a model of behavior. The creator has ordained that these two be friends and it is hoped the younger one will grow up to be the fine man his older partner is supposed to be. Whatever he observes the older man doing, he shall do it. The old man bears the onus of the child's future. As a reward he will see the Creator when he dies. When the two meet on the road, the older person speaks first. "Thanks, you are well, my friend?" The younger one answers, "Truly, thank you, I am well, my friend." Every time he sees me, he calls me "friend."

As noted in Chapter two, the Iroquois antedated Freud in their belief that the hidden desires motivating behavior could be determined by dream analysis. Wallace has noted the parallel with psychoanalytic formulations in Father Ragueneau's observations, made in 1649:

In addition to the desires which we generally have that are free, or at least voluntary in us, (and) which arise from a previous knowledge of some goodness that we imagine to exist in the thing desired, the Hurons (and, he might have added, the Seneca) believe that our souls have other desires, which are, as it were, inborn and concealed. These, they say, come from the depths of the soul, not through any knowledge, but by means of a certain blind transporting of the soul to certain objects; these transports might in the language of philosophy be called *Desideria innata,* to distinguish them from the former, which are called *Desideria elicita.*

Now they believe that our soul makes these natural desires known by means of dreams, which are its language. Accordingly, when these desires are accomplished, it is satisfied; but, on the contrary, if it be not granted what it desires, it becomes angry, and not only does not give its body the good and the happiness that it wished to procure for it, but often it also revolts against the body, causing various diseases, and even death. . . .

In consequence of these erroneous [so thought Father Ragueneau] ideas, most of the Hurons are very careful to note their dreams, and to provide the soul with what it has pictured to them during their sleep. If, for instance, they have seen a javelin in a dream, they try to get it; if they have dreamed that they gave a feast, they will give one on awakening, if they have the wherewithal; and so on with other things. And they call this *Ondinnok*—a secret desire of the soul manifested by a dream.

The cults are often made up of individuals who have themselves suffered from mental illness, and who now attain high status through their cult roles and their ability to become possessed. One such cult in Nigeria is the Sopono possession cult; its members are Yoruban women who have previously suffered from mental illness. Possession by their particular spirits during the annual festival is prophylactic for the members, and is believed to ward off illness throughout the rest of the year. Prince[54] has given a good description of the possession at one of these ceremonies:

A knot of younger women collected about one tall old woman with a pock-marked face, all singing and moving to the drum beat. One girl stood before the old woman with her arms about her neck. They placed one of the sacrificial bowls upon the girl's head, and the women began to sing louder, calling upon the spirit of the particular Sopono that habitually possessed this girl. The girl's face became vacant, and her eyes focused upon a distant place. Suddenly she fell forward in a kind of swoon; the "mother" supported her; someone else seized the calabash so that it wouldn't fall; others threw water on her feet. In a few seconds she revived a little; they guided her fingers up over the rim of the calabash, and she was drawn to one side, where she stood, somewhat dazed, the "wife" of the god.

Ten or twelve other girls were possessed in the same way. Then in single file, bearing the sacrifices upon their heads, they commenced a slow dance about a tree in the center of the clearing. Finally they moved out in a procession about the whole village. Each householder splashed a little water and palm oil on the ground, and the possessed girls each dipped her foot in the pool and moved on. When the bad luck and illness of the village had been collected in this way, the procession moved off, single file, to a place in the thick forest where sacrifices are deposited for Sopono beneath an ancient tree. The entire proceedings took about three hours.

Passive Techniques

Expressive cathartic rituals are usually associated with pre-scientific exorcism and with the personality traits that are characteristic of hysteria. More passive and relaxed techniques tend to be used by people and cultures with a preponderance of obsessional traits. It is quite clear that personality factors influence the form of therapy: obsessionals develop a structured treatment, hysterics a cathartic one. Indeed, therapy appears to be a projection of basic personality. What is needed for maturation, however, is often the very opposite of what is developed: the obsessional needs LSD and cathartic strategies; the hysteric, controls. Thus a therapy that is an extension of the self is likely to afford only temporary relief, so that the problem recurs.

The Navaho emphasis on quieter techniques has been vividly captured in Leighton's[55] description of a Navaho sing:

At the fire a pot is heating which contains an emetic composed of buckthorn, limberpine, bearberry, wild currant, juniper and Colorado blue spruce. Each person gets a portion of it and washes himself from the feet up, then drinks and vomits. The Singer takes a brush made of wing and tail feathers from an eagle, and an owl feather that fell out while the bird was flying, and brushes the patient, others, then the whole hut, making motions that sweep evil toward the door. The ends of the pokers are warmed and applied to the patient's body by the Singer. Then the others apply them to themselves, rubbing the warm wood to any part that hurts. The patient and the other participants walk around the fire sunwise, stepping over the pokers. Evil cannot cross the pokers and thus they leave evil behind. Then in succession everybody jumps over the fire, again with the idea of separating themselves from evil. The live coals represent lightning. Songs and prayers accompany each stage of the ritual. The heat is continuously very intense and all sweat profusely.

At the end the door-blanket is lifted with one of the pokers, the bull-roarer is made to thunder, and the patient steps out, followed by the others. After fire, ashes and vomitus have been disposed of, all return and the Singer, using the eagle feathers, sprinkles participants and hut with a fragrant lotion made of mint, horsemint, windodor and penny-royal, kept in an abalone shell. Glowing coals are placed before each participant and on these is sprinkled a fumigant made of a plant root, sulphur, corn meal, down from chickadee, titmouse, woodpecker, bluebird, and yellow warbler. These have been previously ground together by a virgin while the Singer sang special songs. Everyone breathes the fumes and rubs them into his body. After this the coals are thrown out the smoke hole, taking evil with them.

The culture-bound significance here is clearly delineated in Leighton's description of the aftermath of treatment:

Outside the patient stands facing the east, breathing in the dawn four times. A white man who stood beside him would see the yellow day coming up over miles and miles of sage, a copse of pinyon, three or four old yellow pines in the soft light, distant blue swells of mountains, with here and there a volcanic cone and very far away the snowy top of Mount Taylor, one of the tallest peaks in this portion of the Rockies.
Compare what the Navaho could see looking at the same landscape. The sage-covered earth is Changing Woman, one of the most benevolent of the gods, who grows old and young again with the cycle of each year's seasons. The rising sun is himself a god who with Changing Woman produced a warrior that rid the earth of most of its evil forces and who is still using his powers to help people. The first brightness is another god, Cow-boy, and to the north, south, east, and west the Navaho can see toward the homes of other deities. To the north is bitter, unhappy First Woman, who sends cold and sickness; to the

south is the Gila Monster, who helps reveal the unknown. The cone-shaped mountains have lava on their sides, which is the caked blood of a wicked giant killed by the Sun's warrior offspring, and lies as modern evidence of the truth of Navaho tradition. The white peak of Mount Taylor is the top of Turquoise Mountain, built and decorated by the House God, who later knocked its top off in a rage when he could not get the name for it he wanted, and forbade any living thing to try to reach the summit.

This contrast between white and Indian views of the same objects is a sample of what cultural differences mean, and the significance of value. It is true that all human beings have the same "dimensions, sense, affections and passions but they are not all roused by the same things, and there lie the seeds of misunderstanding, contempt and conflict imbedded in culture."

Treatment and Values

The connection of treatment with dominant values, by enlisting the support of the community, further reinforces the patient's faith in the treatment. This is well illustrated by the healing practices of the *hungans* or Voodoo priests and priestesses of Haiti. On the basis of much observation and training, they have developed a theory of disease causation, along with special techniques for diagnosis and treatment. Their categories of "natural" and "supernatural" psychiatric illnesses both conform to clinically recognizable syndromes. They believe that natural illnesses are depressive reactions and are caused by frustration, a weak brain, or excessive intellectual effort, whereas supernatural illnesses are schizophrenic in form and attributed to soul loss (through violation of taboos). Divination by watergazing, automatic handwriting, or card-reading is used to distinguish one from the other before treatment begins. Detailed histories are also obtained, in order to ascertain whether the patient has, by violating a taboo, offended someone who has sought revenge either through sorcery or through a *loa* (deity). Frequently, such a "diagnostic interview" is sufficient to induce the patient's recovery, probably as a result of the support and reassurance he derives from describing his difficulties to an interested listener.

Frequently, the *hungan* suggests more elaborate treatment. Thus, in order to banish a devil spirit, he counteracts the sorcerer's black magic with magic of his own. In one method, he beheads several white pigeons obtained by the patient, rubs the blood of the pigeons on the patient's head and their bodies over the patient's body. If this is ineffective, the patient may be given a foul-smelling concoction of leaves to drink, or he may have his face sprayed with mixtures of rum, spice, and leaves. Casting a *wanga* or spell over an enemy is another method for curing victims of sorcery.

If these methods fail, the patient may move into the *houn-fort,* or temple, for further observation and treatment. The treatments are conducted as religious ceremonials, and entire communities participate in them. The animated atmosphere, which is stimulated by rum and rhythmic drums in dimly lit shrines, crowded with excited dancers performing energetically while the *hungan* becomes possessed, offers a unique setting for treatment. Here, animals are sacrificed, patients are placed over hot flames, a variety of magic is performed, and exorcism is sometimes practiced by flogging and burning.

The *hungan* utilizes certain universal psychotherapeutic principles in his treatment: his faith in himself, his method, and his religion all foster hope and the expectation of relief. As one *hungan* said,[56] "In order to cure someone successfully, it is necessary for them to believe in me, in voodoo or in God." Community participation in a temple setting adds to the efficacy of his technique. The ritual and symbolic maneuvers are familiar to patients from early life. It is difficult for modern systems of treatment to compete with the established voodoo practices, not only because of the inclination people have to stick with the familiar, but also because of the *hungan*'s dominance over his followers. He is a community leader, a relative of many, and a high priest in the temple hierarchy.

The people have had little opportunity to develop reality-testing skills, being exposed from infancy to a system of beliefs that is focused on the *hungan*'s authority and the power he derives from the gods. As a result, he has the last word on all questions: success in business, health or love depends on the benevolence of the deities, and all must come to the *hungan* for advice, support, comfort and assistance. Submission to him and to the deities brings praise and reward. Thus do the religio-medical practices of voodoo at one and the same time reduce tensions and suppress ego development. It should be noted once again that individuals with severe depressions or obsessional tension states seem to be incapable of entering dissociative states. While psychopathic personality types, on the other hand, are capable of entering into these dissociative states, they are not as amenable to the suggestions or beliefs that are produced by the group ritual.

Sacrifice

Just as the observation of trances and dissociative states raises some questions about the psychophysiological mechanisms involved, so the phenomenon of sacrifice raises questions about the socially integrative effects of therapeutic practices. In sacrificial rites there is usually a god, a spirit or a supernatural being, who is either the victim or the recipient or beneficiary of some offering. Common to theories of sacrifice is the notion that such human problems as evil, sin, and illness can be transferred onto an animal. Thus, for Tylor,[57] sacrifice was based on the animistic principle of mistaking an ideal connection for a real one; as such, it constituted an effective procedure for injuring an enemy. Whatever one did to an effigy was expected to happen to one's enemy. Frazer[58] too recognized the existence of this same assumption among primitive groups who practiced vicarious sacrifice. He described numerous instances of this phenomenon, in which animals were employed as vehicles for the transfer of evil. Thus, when a Moor has a headache, he will sometimes take a lamb or a goat and beat it till it falls down. Among the Caffres of South Africa,

natives sometimes take a goat into the presence of a sick man and confess the sins of the kraal over the animal. Sometimes a few drops of blood from the man are put on the goat's head and it is turned out into the veldt, the sickness having been transferred to it. On a community level the public expulsion of evil, disease, or collected demons take the form of scheduled seasonal rituals, where a specific animal serves as a scapegoat. The custom was essentially a combination of the custom of killing the animal or human god to preserve his life from the inroads of age and the custom of the yearly expulsion of evils and sins.

For Freud,[59] sacrifice was originally "an act of fellowship" between the deity and his worshippers. The sacrificial community, the god and the sacrificial animal were of the same blood and members of one clan." Freud accepted Robertson Smith's idea that the sacramental killing and communal eating of the totem animal, which it was forbidden to consume on all other occasions, was an important feature of totemic religion. Like Tylor and Frazer before him, he too emphasized the transfer aspect of the sacrifice.

According to Freud, the totem animal is in reality a substitute for the father—a thesis that is compatible with the fact that the forbidden killing is at the same time a festive occasion, as well as the expression of an ambivalent attitude suggestive of the emotional attitude toward the father. This attitude persisted even after the animal lost its sacred character and became instead a simple offering to the deity, as shown in those rituals in which the god himself could be seen killing the animal, which was sacred to him and was in fact often himself. Here, according to Freud, was evidence of the most extreme denial of that original parricide that was the basis for the beginning of society and of the sense of guilt.

Money-Kyrle[60] in an extensive study of sacrifice, elaborated on this theory of sacrifice as a repetition and commemoration of the primal parricide. According to him, the sacrifice occurs because the god "excites the same ambivalent effects as the rival and protector (father) that each child learned to hate, love and fear. The father suggests that many unconscious fantasies are satisfied by the vicarious sacrifice of the totem animal—i.e. fantasies of killing the father, the mother, the self, of the father killing himself, or the mother killing the father, etc.

In Haitian voodoo, most of the gods are approached by way of the sacrifice of a barnyard animal, such as a chicken, a goat or a pig. Certain sacred powers, which are concentrated in the animal during the ceremony, are then liberated by the animal's death. The choice of victim depends on the ritualistic requirements of the *loa* or spirit deities. Sacrifices give strength to the gods; the more numerous and magnificent these sacrifices, the more powerful will the gods become. Although the pattern of sacrifice varies from god to god, from region to region and, most importantly, from priest to priest, there is a general conformation that suggests a similarity of origin for the different ceremonies, as well as the presence throughout Haiti, of a considerable degree of tradition, binding believers to voodoo.[61]

The *hungan* offers up a sacrificial goat that has been possessed by the same spirit that has conferred power on him. He offers the congregants the opportunity to participate in its death, and to identify with the god through the feast. In this way, they can express any resentments, or even murderous wishes, that they may hold toward the *hungan*. It seems essential that the *hungan* maintain control of the sacrifice, as well as of the aroused group, any of whom might, in the midst of the excitement, express the impulse to kill him more directly. He does this by asserting, at the very moment of the animal's death, that he is able to do the same thing to a man. Why this need to maintain power? For one thing, the disparity between the *hungan*'s style of life and that of his co-villagers is great, his only claim to this elevated position being his election by the spirit. He must therefore frequently demonstrate this election by the exercise of his "supernatural" capacities in the healing arts, in divination, and in such ceremonies as were just described. In addition, during ceremonials in which the congregants become possessed, he must maintain sufficient power and influence over the group to prevent injury, excessive violence or disruption from taking place.

In psychoanalytic terms, the sacrifice of the goat is, on one level, both the symbolic murder of, and identification by oral incorporation with, a divinely possessed animal, thus satisfying a number of different unconscious motives for everyone involved. In addition, the obvious release of tension and the emotional relief that follow the murder of the goat strongly suggest the group-solidifying aspects of the ceremonial in keeping with Freud's theory of the totem feast. The *hungan* reinforces the projection of irrational fantasy by encouraging controlled non-injurious "acting out." At the same time, however, by keeping the participants in a fear-dependent bind, he reinforces the destructive motivation in human relationships, and thereby prevents individuals from improving their ability to accept social responsibility.

Pentecostalism

Certain cults in the Caribbean are distinguished from what we know as religion by their incorporation of "pagan" or African beliefs and practices. The prevalence of these beliefs and practices is a direct result of the influx of African slaves during the sixteenth and seventeenth centuries. They vary in the extent of their similarity to conventional and established Christian denominations. In the Cumina cult of St. Thomas' parish in Southeastern Jamaica, for example, dancers importune the spirits to possess the dreamers, without making any mention of God or the Holy Ghost. Haitian voodoo, however, is an effective amalgam of African animism with the Catholicism of French missionaries. Pentecostal churches espouse the most fundamental form of Christian belief, so that possessions of the congregants are attributed to the Holy Ghost.

Increasingly, cults are becoming the focus of efforts to preserve traditional cultures in the face of modernization. There are a growing number of naturalistic movements in various urban centers in Africa, among them the Zionist churches of the South

African Bantu; the Healing Churches in West Africa; secret societies, such as the N'Jaijei of the Sierra Leonian Mende and the
Yassi of the Sherbro in Sierra Leone; the Zar cults of Ethiopia
and Sudan; and the voluntary associations in West Africa. There
is ample evidence that such movements are spreading throughout
Africa, to meet the special needs of tribesmen who are now living
in newly independent areas. This is undoubtedly a response to
the anxieties that are generated by urbanization, political freedom, and detribalization. Even though twenty million Africans
are nominally Protestant, and thirty million nominally Catholic,
the growth of these independent churches and sects continues.
There are an estimated 5,000 independent churches, with seven
million members. They focus on African renewal, or on protest
against the missionary founders and white colonialism, and they
are most numerous where oppression has been greatest. There are
over 3,000 such churches, with more than 3 million members, in
South Africa; the Congo has more than 500 such churches;
Ruwanda has none.

Like the Pentecostal churches, these sects combine tribal
superstitions with Christian concepts. Many have a decidedly
messianic tone. The Bantu churches, for example speak of themselves as the chosen race, for whom a black Christ will open the
gates of Heaven. This Heaven will be denied to the white
people, who have all the privileges in this life. Tribal elements
in the sect ceremonials include hand-clapping, dancing, drumming, whistling, and the use of bamboo flutes and tambourines.
The ceremonies permit baptism of polygamous wives, drinking,
and the use of masks, drugs, and drums to send spiritual messages.
Healing practices in these new independent churches rely on a
mixture of those modern and traditional customs that serve the
psychological needs of detribalized urban Africans.[62]

There have been instances of attempts on the part of the
established religions to accommodate the specifically African
needs that are reflected in these cults and churches. The Catholic
Church in Katanga has developed a special Baluba Mass, using
native drums along with Latin verses to accommodate the Yamaa
movement of 20,000 Baluba tribesmen. In Yaounde, Cameroons,
drumming and dancing are permitted in the Mass, so as to accommodate the revival movement of some 60,000 Fante tribesmen
from Cameroon and Gabon. In the 1960's, Sekou Touré deported
the white priests and nuns in Guinea, replacing them with African priests and nuns.

West Indian Pentecostal churches in London have similarly

provided a form of social integration for emotionally isolated immigrants, by supplying a structured world view and methods of attaining grace that are independent of particular personal qualities and require only a willingness to have faith. In the sect, healing is directed toward physical ills, emotional problems, and social difficulties. While some individuals come to meetings with the intention of being healed, others develop the desire to be healed only when the offer is made. Sometimes special healing meetings are held. Meetings are in general revivalistic, with much "hellfire and brimstone" preaching, Bible-quoting, and audience participation. The clergy are untrained charismatic leaders, who manifest such "gifts of the Spirit" as "tongues" and "healing." Meetings are opened by welcoming the Holy Ghost with a prayer. Extemporizing from the Bible, the leader then emphasizes the sinfulness of the world, by contrast with the members of the congregation, as well as the latter's indebtedness to Christ for His sacrifice. He employs a good deal of anecdotal material, the repetition of formulae, and exhortation of the congregation to participate, relying on these to stir up what is usually a very excited atmosphere. Audience participation includes exclamations of "Amen" and "Praise God," clapping, stamping, and responsive singing as well as the use of tambourines, and, occasionally, of cymbals, pianos, and guitars.

Those who are "there for healing" move to the front, kneel, and are prayed over by the leader, who places his hands on the heads of the sick or over the afflicted area, occasionally anointing their arms with holy oil. This technique derives from the literal interpretation of the Biblical command: "They shall lay hands on the sick and they shall recover and the Lord shall raise them up." The leader repeatedly invokes the help of God or the Holy Ghost, with shouts of "Deliver him, Lord," or "Heal him, Lord." Occasionally a member of the congregation who also has the power to heal assists in the ceremony, while all pray aloud. It is believed that the Holy Spirit will enter sick or troubled individuals, bringing strength to them as well as expelling the Devil, if he is present.

All West Indians, including those who are not members of the sect, are in agreement on the efficacy of these methods for those who believe in their value, emphasizing that belief in the healing ritual is crucial for successful results, even though outsiders can often find relief as well.[63] The healing takes place in a highly emotional and supportive setting, and is inextricably intertwined with themes and activities that promote religious conversion and participation in the sect. Having seen or heard of the workings of the Holy Spirit in previous meetings, participants are likely to have faith in the leader, as well as an expectation of positive results. Divine healing is not, however, completely confined to church meetings; visits to the home of the sick further emphasize that faith is the only necessary factor for invoking God's help. During the services, a reduction of self-identity and awareness, and a sense of merging with the group, are increased by the dogmatic preaching and the "testimonies," in an emotionally heightened atmosphere; this seems to contribute to an increase of positive good feeling, elation, and sometimes exaltation, such as may contribute to the therapeutic efficacy of the meetings.

TRADITIONAL SYSTEMS OF MEDICINE

There are a number of traditional systems of medicine in the East that are based on written tradition, scholarship, training, and the maintenance of strict professional standards. One in particular, Chinese traditional medicine, has experienced a resurgence since 1948. This system uses such techniques as acupuncture, ignipuncture, and breathing exercises. In acupuncture, the skin over the area involved is pricked with needles; in ignipuncture, heat is applied. These treatments are used in conjunction with modern medicine and pharmacologically active herbs for a variety of psychiatric disorders (especially the less severe neurotic and psychosomatic conditions), and occasionally for psychosis. According to Jan Cerny,[64]

Methods of Chinese traditional medicine have spread to other Asiatic countries and also to Europe. Acupuncture is practiced in Mongolia, Tibet, India, Korea, Vietnam and Japan. In 1954, 300,000 doctors in China graduated from universities of traditional medicine. In Shanghai there were 6,000 traditional doctors and only 300 doctors of "Western" medicine. In 1945 there were in Japan around 70,000 "acupunctural" doctors. After 1949 numerous research institutes of traditional Chinese medicine were built in China with a center in Peking. There are a few faculties of traditional medicine, e.g. in Peking, Shanghai, Canton, and other centers, and there exists a special hospital for treatment by traditional methods.

A form of traditional medicine in Kuwait has been described by Kline:[65]

A neuropsychiatric patient (including epileptic) when he becomes ill is usually first taken to a mullah (teacher), at whose home he may stay for two or three days, during which time the mullah reads to him from the Koran, blows on him in a prescribed ritualistic manner, or may write certain words on paper which are then wrapped in cloth and suspended on a string from the patient's neck or arms. The writing usually consists of magic symbols or words from the Koran, and is done with a special ink of characteristic colour and smell, made by mixing prescribed desert herbs.

Ja'Fai Hallaji[66] has described the use of hypnotherapy in Afghanistan:

After the patient had been assigned a bed, he lay on his back, with his eyes fixed upon one of a number of octagonal moldings. Set in the ceiling, these moldings were embellished with a nine-pointed diagram. The chief practitioner and his assistants now visited each bed in turn. While the rest of the group maintained a chant of the syllables "Ya HOO, Ya HUKK!", the chief passed his hands, held together with palms downward, horizontally over the patient. His hands were held about six inches over the patient's body and passed with a rhythmic movement from the eyes to the toes. The technique thus resembled that of the Mesmerists. An integral part of the proceedings was that the chief practitioner rhythmically blew upon the patient at a rate of about two breaths a second. It is this aspect of the procedure which is responsible for its name, "*Chuff*" (Breathing). The hypnogenic effect of this technique is probably facilitated by the relaxation of the body, the warmth of the room, the patient's concentration upon the diagram, and the occasional interruption of the light when the palms are passed across the face.

The subjects appeared to enter a hypnotic state in about six minutes. The induction, however, continued for an average of twelve minutes with younger patients; in the case of patients over forty, up to twenty minutes was usual. Not all of the patients closed their eyes. Rather, a sharp intake of breath and cessation of minor bodily movements generally signalled the onset of hypnosis for these patients. However, no attempt was made to test for the presence or depth of hypnosis.

One occasionally sees an interesting combination of the primitive and the highly complex. The magical treatment in Buddhistic and oriental religions is a special instance of such a mixture. According to Ames:[67]

The Sinhalese describe their healing rituals as practical sciences akin to Western and indigenous or Ayurvedic medical systems;

in fact the healing rites are occasionally referred to collectively as *bhuta, bidyava*, "the science of spirits." It is a science entirely concerned with misfortunes and untoward events in this life itself, whereas Buddhism, they say is mostly concerned with future lives and individuals. The Sinhalese call Buddhism an *agama* or moral community, the members of which are concerned about obeying certain ethical principles in order to attain salvation. Buddhism also has a formally organized institutional structure, composed of monks, holy books, temples, relics and laity, bound in loyalty to these sacred symbols.

Ames notes that the ambiguous relationship between theory and practice, text and context, is important:

Healing rituals, because they are ideologically profane but structurally fused with sacred activities, are therefore able to provide transition between the world of the profane and the world of the sacred. They do not provide formal rites of passage from profane to sacred roles, in the way described by van Gennep. They do not turn laymen into monks, they operate at quite a different level: they turn sick Buddhists (ones belabored by worldly desires) into healthy Buddhists (ones who can transcend these worldly interests). They work more to change people's attitudes and maintain motivational commitments to certain higher ideals. This is indicated by the fact that, in addition to removing psychological obstacles to mental development, magical rituals also reaffirm the supremacy of Buddhism: by definition only those who have not fully acquired Buddhist wisdom need rely on magical aids.

These spiritual change-oriented exercises are even closer than the more primitive therapeutic methods to contemporary dynamic psychotherapy, because of their emphasis on the ideal-ized human being, self-discipline and introspective techniques. The fact that such exercises occur within a religious or theologi-cal framework is less important than it would seem to be at first glance. These exercises have much in common with Zen Bud-dhism, Yoga and other techniques of personality-change through introspection.

Gaitonde[68] has noted that Hindu philosophy is based on some of the same premises as contemporary psychotherapy. Both are systems of anxiety-reduction, and seek to understand deeper psychological forces through introspection. The Hindu doctrine of Karma recognizes the tendency to project responsibility onto forces outside the self, and therefore focuses training on the development of individual responsibility. Hindu philosophy seeks to increase individual freedom by making the unconscious con-

scious and the irrational rational, much as the dynamic psycho-
therapies do. According to Gaitonde, "Both approaches strive to
help the individual tolerate pain and distress, but the deeper goal
is to expose people to an experience of growth in living relationships with others by understanding oneself as a person. The
objective of Hindu philosophy is to analyse the purpose and
meaning of human existence."

Such advanced introspective approaches generally place significance on the past as a determinant of the present, and on the
individual's responsibility for growth and development.

Morita therapy, which was developed in recent years in
Japan for what was considered to be a specific Japanese problem,
also has much in common with dynamic psychiatry.[69] It was
developed to treat *Schinkeishitsu,* the syndrome characterized by
neurasthenia, obsessions and anxiety that was discussed in Chapter Four. The aim of Morita therapy is to help the patient to
accept the symptoms rather than fighting them or trying to forget
them. The merit of this approach lies in its ability to reduce the
secondary symptoms that are generated when the patient tries the
impossible task of actively trying to control obsessive symptoms.
Since this effort is usually made through the use of obsessive
techniques, it is likely to produce more of the same symptoms.

This orientation is compatible with the Japanese focus on
present time, and their non-acceptance of the cause-and-effect
frame of reference that dominates Western psychotherapy. According to Morita therapy, one should follow the laws of nature,
accepting and enduring anxiety, and not trying to escape it or
avoid it. Since nature provides all that is needed for health, the
key is not to make any efforts to get rid of troublesome or obsessional thoughts. It takes the discipline of Zen to be able to relax
oneself so that cares flow from the mind. Morita therapy is an
elaborate formula for concentrating efforts on the present, and
adopting an attitude of "acceptance."

This attitude of "acceptance"—by which is meant a sense of
unity with one's self and one's surroundings—is usually expressed
in Morita therapy by the phrase *aru ga mama,* which may be
translated as "to take things as they are," or, more freely, "to
meet reality as it is." This state of mind, which is the main goal
of therapy, is often compared to *satori* (enlightenment) in Zen
Buddhism. Some Morita therapists make use of Zen literature in
their explanations, although Dr. Morita himself has specifically
disclaimed any special knowledge in that area.

It is evident that differences between the Eastern and

Western views of man are more ideological than behavioral—that is, they function more in terms of theory than of practice. Much of our tradition of transcendentalism concerns itself with techniques for self-realization, through escape from the constraints of the social self and social obligations. More than one hundred years ago, Emerson was advocating that the individual learn to maintain a degree of solitude or insulation from the group in order to be able to commune with his inner self.

This same ethic is fundamental to psychoanalysis, which advocates mastery of the self or ego, over the dictates of society or the superego and the dictates of the passions or id. Here the technique of free association and complete honesty, along with the neutrality of the analyst, all contribute to the individual's ability to develop an observing ego and to stand apart from himself in order to gain mastery over himself. The ethical and humanistic dimension in activities that focus on the development of self-interest is ensured by the belief that service to others is the highest form of self-interested individualism.

Recently, a number of new techniques have emerged for escaping the limits of the social self. Included among these are the LSD cults, new religious sects, sensitivity groups and a variety of self-help groups, all of which seem to be designed to shock the individual out of habitual ways of responding, so as to provide at least transient opportunity for him to view himself objectively, and thereby to facilitate his ability to become involved in the present.

More specifically, the idea of the attainment of peace of mind and the good society, as connoted by Nirvana, Tao, Satori, and Brahman, has not been inaccessible to the mainstream of Western intellectual tradition. The notion that such a religious or psychological goal is irrational, illogical or morbid is, I believe, inaccurate. Aside from the mystical strain to be found in the Judaeo-Christian tradition, one also finds more recently concepts of self-reliance, maturity, self-actualization, and self-realization in the writings of existentialist psychiatrists.

The Confucianist search for "true central self and harmony" is very much like the psychoanalytic balance between id and superego forces and the mastery of the ego. The Buddhist prescription of Bodhidharma, which emphasizes "no dependence upon words and letters," is remarkably like the limits we must set on obsessional personalities, whose fixation on a technique of anxiety reduction becomes for them a source of anxiety.

While the concepts of independence and freedom are central

to Western thought, they do not in any way rule out acceptance of man's link with nature and of his inability ultimately to escape from the "self." Those who do seek after this freedom come to recognize that it is at best a transient experience.

The Western emphasis on otherworldliness and transcendental being and the Oriental emphasis on the present and the harmony of nature represent differences in content only; the attainment of stability and peace of mind is the good that is common to both orientations. It is useful to emphasize that the East and West are at different stages of societal development, which is a crucial determinant of the various beliefs and practices pertaining to self-improvement. A sense of the harmony and the regularity of nature, such as is central to Oriental views, is certainly compatible with a tradition-oriented agricultural society. Our own seasonal holidays—Thanksgiving, Easter and the New Year—were undoubtedly more important moments in the lives of people when this country was an agrarian society. The Oriental concern for group welfare over individual welfare, for extended families, for elaborate hierarchical arrangements in interpersonal relationships, along with their placing special emphasis on maintaining a "respectful" distance, is very much related to traditionalism, and can be found in other tradition-oriented groups.

The individualistic orientation of Western culture, the nuclear family, and the stress on environmental mastery reflect the effects of industrialization and urbanization. The fact that these same patterns are now beginning to be seen throughout the developing world lends some support to the view that these factors are related to the stage of development and the nature of the society.

The distinctly conservative quality of the Asian orientation reflects much the same basic philosophical assumptions as the naturalistic forms of psychotherapy that are found in developing societies, and among acculturating groups in our own society. Similarities with some of the assumptions of the Mexican-American *curanderismo,* for example, include:

a. acceptance of life without attempting to change it—a view that encourages both passivity and security;

b. belief in a natural order or plan, in which illness is a natural part.

c. regarding an individual's plight as a community affair;

d. regarding the ability to suffer as a measure of faith;

e. emphasis on tradition, respect for elders, and living within the harmony of nature;

f. belief in the existence of evil and the divine side of man;

g. regarding health as the result of perfect equilibrium between man and his family, and between man and God (nature).

Oriental society is self-controlled, static, traditional, and agrarian; like other societies at the same stage of development, it emphasizes such values as authority, tradition, a philosophy of acceptance and resignation, form and role playing (as opposed to efficiency and practicality), group-centeredness (as opposed to an emphasis on individualism), the present (as opposed to the future), present obligations and social relationships (as opposed to personal goals), fatalism (as opposed to accepting personal responsibility for one's fate), belief in a cosmic cycle, indifference to death, and formalized social relationships.

THE VALUE OF PRE-SCIENTIFIC PSYCHIATRY

Freud[70] recognized that the various primitive methods of healing must be classed as examples of psychotherapy; that, in order to effect a cure, a "condition of 'expectant' faith was induced in sick persons, the same condition which answers a similar purpose for us today." Fenichel[71] has provided a cogent analysis of the therapeutic value of such techniques. He observed that a beneficial change in the conflict between undesirable impulses and the associated anxiety or guilt (the basis of neurosis) could be effected by way of the prohibition of symptoms by an authority, through suggestion or threats (symbolic castration). These methods, when they are too severe, may create an unwanted "substitute neurosis," in which the patient becomes afraid, introverted, rigid, and more dependent and may therefore lead to an increase of pressure on the repressed. Primitive methods may provide for emotional catharsis, which will diminish the inner pressure and at the same time serve to reinforce other repressions; or they may be accepted as a substitute for the spontaneous symptoms.

According to Fenichel, baths, exercises, or physical measures may substitute for conversion symptoms; prescribed diets and ritual penances for compulsive symptoms; and prohibitions for phobic symptoms. The efficacy of such methods then depends on whether the substitute fits the patient's personality; in other words, "a hysteric cannot accept 'artificial compulsions', nor a compulsive neurotic 'artificial conversions.'" To be acceptable, the substitute must also be pleasurable and sufficiently removed from the original instinctual meaning of the symptom. In addition, a "transference neurosis" develops, in which repressed conflicts are represented in the emotional tie to the doctor, thus reducing the number of expressive channels needed. As Fenichel has written: "The healing power of Lourdes or of a Catholic confession is still of a much higher order than that of the average psychotherapist for neurotics, who are persons who have failed in actively mastering their surroundings, and are always more or less looking out for passive-dependent protection, for a 'magic helper.' The more a psychotherapist succeeds in giving the im-pression of having magic powers, of still being the representative of God as the priest-doctors once were, the more he meets the longing of his patients for magic help."

While Fenichel's views have the merit of fitting a wide array of data into a single theory of human behavior, they fail to pay proper attention to social and cultural factors. Little regard is shown to the culture-bound nature of symptoms and conflicts, or to the specific cultural applicability of therapeutic maneuvers. Devereux[72] has recently modified these psychoanalytic explana-tions, suggesting that the shaman provides his patient with a whole set of "ethnopsychologically suitable," congenial, and cul-turally recognized defenses against his idiosyncratic conflicts. Ac-cording to Devereux, what the shaman provides, strictly speaking, is not a "psychiatric cure" but a kind of "corrective emotional experience"; this leads to a repatterning of defenses without real curative insight. Such a repatterning involves changing from idiosyncratic conflicts and defenses to culturally conventional conflicts and ritualized symptoms. Devereux underlines the fact that such "remission without insight," while it is not a "cure" (because the patient remains vulnerable), is nevertheless a "social remission" and therefore sufficiently valuable to the patient and the community to warrant recognition.

This last point is of special importance because it demon-strates the relative merits of varying therapeutic ends, a view emphasized by Frank,[73] who has distinguished between two dis-tant effects of psychotherapy: symptom relief and improved func-tioning. Symptom relief is rapid, independent of the type of therapy, and dependent mainly on the expectation of help. Im-proved functioning appears to be related to the type of therapy an individual receives—whether minimal, individual, or group—and is dependent not only on a learning process that has been accelerated by the therapist but also on extratherapeutic social interactions. This view has the merit of recognizing the value that is inherent in a variety of techniques, and of refocusing attention on those forms of therapy that may most profitably be utilized for the handling of the vast numbers of patients who are in need of rapid treatment.

More recently, Sargant[74] suggested that methods of thought reform ("brainwashing"), religious conversion, and psychotherapy all facilitate change by producing excessive cortical excitation, emotional exhaustion, and states of reduced resistance to change or hypersuggestibility; these in turn increase the patient's chances of being converted to new points of view. In other words, such emotionally arousing activity can free individuals from their neurotic symptoms while introducing new ideals.

Frank (see [73]) says that in faith healing, psychotherapy, and thought reform, the person who acts as a cultural or group mediator genuinely cares about the welfare of the supplicant, sufferer, or prisoner, and is committed to producing a desirable change in him. It is by virtue of this ascendancy of role and status, as well as through his control of the means of coercion and his ability to inspire the sufferer's expectation of relief, that he can exert pressures on the sufferer. Since he impresses the latter with the importance of a particular procedure, through the use of symbols, a knowledgeable manner, and a systematic approach, he is able to increase the expectation of relief even further, thereby enhancing the probability of success.

In most societies, as we have seen, treatment procedures are governed by particular rules and follow prescribed patterns of relationship among the healer, the patient, and the group. The mysteries of illness and of healing procedures are rationalized and made understandable. Accuracy of diagnosis and efficacy of treatment count for less than does the simple fact that anxiety, fear, and doubt—all of which may contribute to an illness by way of complicating symptoms and reactions—are dispelled. The prospect of help and a sense of hope contribute directly to the patient's improvement. In all instances, the healer can exert a tremendous amount of personal influence and arouse a multitude of emotions in the patient, as well as in the group, during the course of a healing situation. This use of influence to arouse emotion may have therapeutic value. In addition, the healer's ability in most instances to utilize the beliefs and ideas of the group as a fulcrum for influencing treatment increases the chances for the successful reintegration of the patient into the community. Such basic features of all modes of psychological treatment may be more important than the features that differentiate them.[75]

Although many have pointed to the psychological benefits

afforded by religious activity and participation in healing cults, several have cautioned against the occasional adverse effects of such participation. In one clinical study of three individuals, for instance, participation produced increased feelings of guilt, fear, and depression, as well as a progressive loss of interest in old ties, old interests, and realistic issues of life; in the absence of an acknowledged leader, who was also able to recognize the progressing symptoms and discourage participation, the process of participation culminated in hospitalization.[76]

It should be emphasized again that, while some treatments strengthen the individual's capacity to deal with reality, others seem to do no more than relieve him temporarily, by providing an opportunity for catharsis or "acting out." La Barre[77] felt this to be the case with snake-handling cults, which attracted people with repressive anti-sexual tendencies, primarily hysterical women and men with paranoid trends. This seems to be true also for cults that maintain their membership through weekly or monthly participation. Although this kind of cult participation may be very supportive for chronic schizophrenics, it may not be useful in the resolution of more basic conflicts.

Systems of psychotherapy can be viewed in terms of the placebo phenomenon. Insofar as the structural features of most systems of psychotherapy include a characteristic pattern of interaction between a designated healer and the patient, as well as an ideology or theory that explains the distress of the individual, usually in terms that are understandable to the group which is lending its support to the interaction, they may be viewed as essentially support systems. Systems of psychotherapy differ in terms of factors pertaining to the healer, the patient, the procedure, the ideology, and the tasks, and also in the role of the group or community. These non-specific factors, which enhance the therapeutic value of the interaction, contribute to the "placebo" value of the therapy. Factors that increase the healer's authority or the patient's faith in the procedure are crucial elements of the placebo phenomenon. For example, the patient's faith in the healer and his consequent willingness to accept advice, suggestions and orders may be increased by the skillful communication of the healer's psychodynamic insights, by the use of LSD or other potent substances (the effects of which are attributed to the power of the healer or the powers he represents), or by the induction of strong emotions, both positive and negative. Whatever it is that increases the patient's faith in the healer and his expectation of help intensifies his involvement in the present; at the same time, it reduces his dependency both on past cues and future fantasies, and increases his dependency on present situational cues. It is this that enables the individual to give up neurotic, unrewarding or distressing patterns of behavior; or, at the very least, it reduces the distress that is associated with these old patterns. Most new patterns must be continually reinforced, if they are to be lasting, and cult leaders are usually aware of this.

In the more complex systems designed to produce maturation and growth, such as dynamic psychotherapy, Zen, Yoga, and certain religious procedures, the factors involved in increasing the therapist's authority and the patient's faith are supplemented by techniques for introducing modulated or titrated amounts of anxiety. These techniques de-emphasize the supportive aspect of the healer-patient relationship and emphasize its educative aspect. They are designed to produce maturity, objectivity, humility and self-reliance, without at the same time producing alienation from the social system. Occasionally, too much anxiety is produced and the individual requires supportive therapy; at other times, too much dependency develops, and more pressure is required if progress is to occur.

To the extent that indigenous forms of treatment are effective, the extent of psychiatric illness in any given community will tend to be underestimated. Some individuals who receive help within a religious context will not be identified as cases, even in the most rigorous of community surveys. Others, satisfied with the results of the indigenous healer, have little urge to consult modern medical facilities. For these and other reasons, it is difficult, when one is assessing the community's needs, to make rational provisions for extending the delivery of health care. It is here that the epidemiological approach becomes an important tool, since it asks and tries to answer those questions that have broader social implications, in terms of the management of illness and its complications. These and other issues are considered in the next chapter.

CHAPTER 6   THE EPIDEMIOLOGY
OF PSYCHIATRIC
DISORDER IN
DEVELOPING
COUNTRIES

EPIDEMIOLOGY, THE STUDY OF THE MASS
aspects of disease, concerns itself with the frequency and distribution of phenomena of illness in a given society and with the factors that contribute to that pattern. In that regard, epidemiological inquiry is fundamental to an investigation of the various psychopathological patterns and culture-bound disorders that have been described in earlier chapters as well as the social and cultural factors accounting for changes in the patterning and frequency of these phenomena.

There is an extensive literature connecting prevalence and incidence patterns with cultural factors. In the eighteenth century, Esquirol[1] and his colleague, Georget,[2] attributed an increase in the rate of mental disorders to the progress of industry, commerce, and civilization in general. Others have placed the blame on civilization for the physical, intellectual and moral degeneration of mankind: Kraepelin[3], for example, suggested that the stresses of civilization have led to an increase in psychiatric disorder. Some, noting that rates of disorders were lower among less developed people, arrived at the conclusion that the primitive is extraordinarily free from those life stresses that cause psychiatric illness. Many have believed that the "savage," who lives in nature, is content and free of illness—an idealized view, used to support the notion that civilization is pathogenic.

We now know that such views are inaccurate, and that

Notes for Chapter 6 will be found on pages 206–209.

psychiatric disorders do indeed occur, with varying frequencies, in pre-literate and developing societies—even though they do so at lower rates than in developed societies. The data that have been gathered—while they are often inexact, inadequate, and unnecessary for the purposes to which they have been put—are nevertheless interesting and suggestive of areas of study.

THE PROBLEM OF METHOD

The complexity of efforts to study prevalence and incidence patterns of psychiatric disorders in the underdeveloped and developing societies is underlined by the diversity of the conclusions that have been reached by various investigators about the effects on the development of mental illness of such social changes as detribalization, migration, acculturation, urbanization, and industrialization. Studies have ranged from reports of a complete absence of psychoses in underdeveloped areas to reports of its increased incidence as the result of Westernization.

Schizophrenia has been reported as absent among the forest Bantu in New Guinea, in the Brazilian interior, and among Okinawans. In 1932, Faris[4] reported on the rarity of psychoses among the Bantu in the Congo. Laubscher,[5] on the other hand, found the rates of psychosis among the tribal Bantu in South Africa to be similar to those in Western nations. Tooth's[6] 1950 Gold Coast survey "provided no evidence in support of the hypothesis that psychosis is commoner in the Westernized group than in the rest of the population . . . However, it may be that, among the neurotic and minor forms of personality disorder, the exposure to Western culture has a more unsettling influence." Carothers, in 1947, reported a low incidence of insanity among tribal Africans in Kenya,[7] while an increase in psychiatric disorders in Africa has been attributed to detribalization in Kenya, alphabetization and industrialization in Ghana,[8] rapid economic development and urbanization in Lagos,[9] and culture change in Nigeria.[10]

Different incidence rates of schizophrenia have been variously explained in terms of: the accumulation of hereditary factors in isolated areas in Japan,[11] high population density in Formosa,[12] the lack of social contacts in Chicago business districts,[13] and contact with Western civilization in India,[14] Brazil[15] and Hawaii.[16]

Rate differences for manic-depressive psychosis have been

attributed to constitutional factors, social class and education, an attitude of self-responsibility, differences in diagnostic criteria among manic-depressive disorders, and failure to distinguish psychotic from neurotic disorders.[17,18]

Depression has been reported as extremely rare in Java, Kenya, South Africa, and on the Gold Coast.[19] Incidence rates of psychiatric disorders have invariably been reported as being higher among Westernized portions of the same population or cultural group. Okinawans in Okinawa had less than the average rate of psychosis, whereas Okinawans in Hawaii had a high rate of hospitalization.[20] Western-trained Javanese doctors had higher psychosis rates than Javanese in the Army;[21] in another study English-trained Chinese males, 20-49, had a much greater hospitalization rate for all disorders than did Chinese-educated males at the same age;[22] Papuans and Melanesians associated with missions had higher psychoses rates than villagers.[23] Similar observations have been made about acculturating Indian groups, as in Hallowell's study of the Ojibwa.[24] On the other hand, a study[25] made in Israel has reported that both European and African/ Asian immigrant groups, who are most exposed to the forces of development and social change, have lower rates of mental hospitalization than the native-born Israelis. Murphy[26] found native rates for first admissions to mental hospitals in Singapore to be higher for most age groups than for immigrant groups. Hispano-Americans acculturating to American culture have been found to show lower rates than Anglo-Americans.[27] The mental hospitalization rates for Cape Coloured in Cape Province are lower than for the local whites.[28]

The reported differences in the kinds of disorders most commonly found in different parts of the world reflect diagnostic customs, as much as they do the actual presence of specific conditions. Arteriosclerotic psychoses and general paralysis of the insane are much more common in East Asia and Southwest Asia than in the West; schizophrenia, however, still accounts most frequently for hospitalization, just as it does in the West. Postpartum psychoses and conversion hysterias are also common. Obsessive compulsive neuroses, pre-senile and senile psychoses, manic depressive psychoses and alcoholism are reported infrequently—although alcoholism is on the increase, especially in Japan. Opium addiction, while presumably declining in China, still remains a problem there.

Hospital admission data, on which most of these studies and consequent conclusions have been based, simply do not provide the kind of incidence data that are needed to determine anything about social causes. They are limited, moreover, by their dependence on such factors as the number of beds, the administrative arrangements for getting people to use the hospitals, and the attitudes of the healing professions and the community. Because unacculturated groups often have a greater tolerance for unusual mental states and for psychiatric symptomatology than those that are acculturating, many psychiatric disorders may never come to outside attention or they may be treated by native doctors, who do not report their findings to public health authorities. While most hospital studies have drawn attention to a number of important epidemiological questions, they have, in the main, been inconclusive because of methodological inadequacies. Without knowing such things as patterns of hospital use, the number of untreated cases and the kinds of alternative facilities or treatment methods that are available to the population, they have perforce been unable to draw definitive conclusions about the actual number of cases in the society at a given time (prevalence) or the rate of inception of new cases during a given period (incidence).

In addition, there has been a paucity of prospective and longitudinal studies such as might provide information on the incidence of spontaneous recovery, recurrence, mortality and individual risk, as well as on the time lag between the start of an illness and its recognition by the community. Comparability of most studies has also been limited by the use of different criteria and divergent definitions of psychological and demographic variables, along with differing methods of investigation. The risk of error is very high.

Deciding on *what constitutes a case* is often a difficult matter. If only illnesses with conspicuous clinical manifestations are counted, many cases are omitted—for example, those of simple schizophrenia. Further problems arise when one has to decide which cases to include on the basis of the *time of occurrence of the symptoms*—that is, whether to count people who have improved or recovered. Diagnostic criteria are rarely based on objective measures; this renders clinical diagnosis unreliable and makes for much disagreement among psychiatrists. The data in most studies focus on the incidence of hospitalization, rather than on the incidence of disorder in the community. While such data are useful in planning services, real incidence data are needed in order to determine the frequency of occurrence of cases being produced, so as to be able to establish:

1. the extent of the public health problems, and
2. clues to the etiology of psychiatric disorders.

It is possible to utilize prevalence data that have been gathered in community surveys for estimates of incidence, by using Weinberg's correlation for mortality; but that method is limited by the fact that the estimated length of illnesses is not certain.

Even when some of these problems are worked out, the complexities involved in investigations in this area of study are tremendous. Thus, for example, if one posits that social change or development leads to an increase in mental illness and the increase does not seem to occur, that does not necessarily mean that there is none. Similarly, an increase can be attributed to a change in the manifestation of the disorder, as a result of the fact that new conditions have emerged that reward, suppress or punish a different kind of behavior. This is seen most clearly in relation to exotic disorders.

It is probable that some of the so-called exotic disorders are variations of the major Western psychoses and that, with social change, their obvious manifestations will be so changed that they can be recognized as such. Other cases may subsequently prove to have been caused by organic factors, as Tooth discovered with trypanosomiasis.

While changing social conditions lead to the solution of such problems as infectious diseases, one may encounter an increase in the number of cases of mental disorder as these disorders come to be recognized and to attract the attention of those people who were previously concerned with infectious diseases. It is also possible that one may encounter an increase in the number of cases, even though not in the actual scope of the disease, as the result of new diagnostic techniques, new diagnostic categories, new treatments and improved case-finding methods. Rates may also remain the same, when an actual increase in number of cases is the reflection of a population increase.

One must examine the data carefully before drawing definitive conclusions from them. It is possible to obtain an increase in rate, or prevalence, without there being any increase in incidence. Better treatment methods of both psychiatric and non-psychiatric conditions can increase the number of survivors, and therefore the number of current cases, even though the incidence rate has not changed.

The essential weakness of studies that are based on hospital data is that hospital admissions are not representative of the population at large. Laubscher[29] reported on 555 patients in the

Queensland Hospital, but without characterizing the non-hospital population. Carothers,[30] reporting on 558 natives of Kenya who had been admitted to the Mathari Mental Hospital over a five-year period, indicated an annual admission rate of 3.4 per 100,000; this accorded with Tooth's[31] figure of 3.3 per 100,000 for the Accra Asylum in the Gold Coast. Beaglehole[32] found that, for a ten-year period, the weighted incidence for hospitalization (corrected for age) was 8.37 per 10,000 for Europeans and 4.19 per 10,000 for Maori in New Zealand. Winston[33] reported six cases of psychiatric illness in Samoa, and Joseph and Murray[34] nine cases for Saipan. So few cases, however, make it very difficult to formulate adequate incidence or prevalence estimates.

Rates ultimately depend on good denominator data—that is, on census information about the larger population at risk. In most underdeveloped areas, this is difficult to ascertain. Without such simple census information as age and sex distribution, it is extremely difficult to know what the actual rates are for a given population; it is therefore impossible to make an adequate comparison of rates for two different groups, even within the same country and the same hospital. Since mental illnesses are differentially distributed among different age and sex groups, comparisons are impossible in the absence of such information. In many underdeveloped areas, life expectancy is limited, so that the disorders of middle and later life are rarely seen.

It is important also to recognize the limitations of age-specific rates. Since the number of people in a particular age group in one given society may account for a disproportionate percentage of the entire population, comparison of age-specific rates between two populations does not tell us very much about the amount of disorder in the particular group, relative to the rest of that society. It is important to standardize in terms of a normal population, or a larger population, or to use indirect standardization procedures, which yield a picture of differences relative to particular age-sex groups.

Another major methodological obstacle is the difficulty of keeping count of cases that migrate out of or into an area. This is particularly important if one is to determine, for example, whether schizophrenics are originally from the area in which they are counted or have simply drifted into it. The distinction is crucial if one is to assign any etiological significance to the social context in which the cases are counted. High rates of schizophrenic disorder have been reported for densely crowded urban areas, which are characterized by social isolation and by the absence of primary group ties and social organizations. There is, however, some evidence that schizophrenic patients first develop their disorders and then move into the areas in which they are picked up in surveys. High-density urban areas may be able to tolerate such patients better than do rural or tribal settings, and may therefore have a cushioning effect on the progression of the illness. It is necessary to avoid the ecological fallacy, which often attributes causation to environmental variables, but without providing any evidence that the cases are under the influence of these variables more often than non-cases are. Differing criteria of mental disorder, differences in age distribution of population, and differences in the computational procedures that are used to examine the data are among the methodological factors that account for rate differences and for the difficulties involved in doing comparative studies.

Accessibility to population subgroups also differs from society to society. In industrial societies, for example, men are less accessible than women because of their work obligations, while in Asia and the Middle East, for various sociocultural reasons, it is the women who are not accessible. Comparisons between surveys are thus rarely feasible. It is also difficult to develop instruments for cross-cultural studies, because of the different meanings that concepts have. There may be differences in response styles—that is, in the conscious or unconscious need to respond affirmatively, so as to meet the expectations of the interviewer.[35] Similarly, cultural attitudes may influence the willingness to answer straightforward questions, as opposed to open-ended ones. In some cultures, there is a reluctance to be interviewed in the absence of a third party, or by women interviewers, or to have women interviewed at all. This limits the kind of data that can be obtained in some settings, and thus prevents the collection of comparative data from every culture.

Comparative studies of the incidence and prevalence of nonpsychotic mental disorders (mental deficiencies, psychoneurosis, alcoholism and psychopathy) are even more difficult to make than studies of the major psychoses and epilepsy; the latter generally require in-patient treatment at some time during the course of the illness and, as a result, are more readily enumerated. Because the less severe disorders are more significant indicators of social change and problems than are the psychotic disorders, however, it is necessary to develop adequate techniques for case identification and a universally applicable set of diagnostic criteria. Crucial to these are the cultural definitions of illness, and the criteria for entry into the sick or disabled role, that we have been examining throughout this book. For example, work performance, which is so often used in Western culture as a criterion of impairment, may not apply in most of the developing societies. There is also the question of whether to regard behavior disorders of children, situational reactions, juvenile delinquency and mental deficiency as diagnostic entities, or to treat them as patterns of deviance. Furthermore, since the majority of non-psychiatric mental disorders do not appear in psychiatric clinics or hospitals, they have to be identified by household-survey methods.

The relevance of surveys of non-psychiatric disorders to the prevalence of all psychiatric disorders is questionable; the belief that a continuum exists between non-psychotic and psychotic disorders has not been proven. One cannot be sure that reports of an increasing frequency of non-psychotic disorders reflect an increasing frequency of the more severe disorders; in the same way, the characteristics of the hospital population do not reflect the character of disorder in the population at large. One's expectations are to some extent based on whether one subscribes to a view that both kinds of disorders derive from the same etiological factors, or to the idea that parallel rate-increases, where they exist, are simply the result of improved diagnostic skills and treatment facilities.

PREVALENCE STUDIES

Prevalence studies are both more feasible and more useful than incidence studies, because they do not rely on the inadequate data that are routinely collected in hospitals. In most prevalence surveys, however, it is difficult to obtain an unbiased sample, such as would permit every person in the population to have an equal chance of being included in that sample. Contact with respondents can be facilitated, in developing societies, through key informants, such as tribal chieftains and village heads. When Tooth[36] was sampling Gold Coast districts for cases, he found a higher rate in one district, with four large towns; he attributed this to the ease of case ascertainment, and concluded that psychoses were not more common in the Westernized group. In his survey of non-hospitalized cases, however, he had asked census enumerators and local chiefs to supply lists of names of "mad" persons; their reactions to his request were "erratic and unpredictable": in only 173 of the 400 cases was a satisfactory record of illness obtained from friends and relatives. It was impossible to estimate rates from tribe to tribe and area to area.

The efficiency of field or prevalence surveys in case-finding is well illustrated by Lin's[37] Taiwan study. In the first stage, key informants (officials, general practitioners, teachers), census registers, and police records were used to identify suspected cases. Information was collected on family size, age, sex, education, occupation, and social class. Personal histories of these cases were next obtained from the family and from neighbors. Finally, small psychiatric teams interviewed all the inhabitants and examined the suspected cases. As Lin has noted:[38]

. . . prospective longitudinal studies of a general population may be regarded as an ideal method of obtaining epidemiological data on mental disorder, provided the sample remains reasonably stable and the research design constant throughout the whole period. One great advantage of prospective studies is that they permit the collection of accurate and objective information on uniform materials, independent of histories based on personal recollection. Moreover, they diminish the risk that the observer may interpret past histories in the light of the hypothesis the study is designed to test. Prospective studies of this type can provide accurate information not only on the onset and evolution of mental illness, but also on the little-explored question of spontaneous recovery. In other words, this type of study may clarify the natural history of mental disorder. The well-designed prospective study can yield the true incidence rate of a disease as well as the estimate of the risk of developing a given disease when a particular characteristic is present (Lilienfeld, 1957). Since the sample is under observation over a period, a better understanding is possible of the roles of predisposition and environmental factors in determining the onset of mental disorder. The time-lag between the onset of the illness and the discovery by the community can also be observed more accurately. A greater awareness of social changes and attitudes in relation to mental disorder becomes possible.

Baseline data on the duration and spontaneous recovery rate of untreated patients can be very useful in evaluating new treatments. In Lin's study of the Malay-Polynesian aborigines in Taiwan, forty-five percent (3.9 per thousand) of those who were diagnosed were classified as psychotic. None had received medical or psychiatric treatment. While the symptomatology of the mental disorders encountered differed little from that of other ethnic groups, there were certain characteristic clinical features. An acute onset was recorded in 84.5% of the cases; further, the psychotic episode tended to be of short duration: within three months, 46.2% had recovered; 53.8% within six months; 65.4% within a year, and 84.6% within two years; only 12.5% remained ill for more than two years. Half the cases had only one psychotic episode; one-third had multiple episodes; the remainder ran a chronic course. Few of the chronic cases suffered severe deterioration. Most cases made adequate social adjustments.

These findings differ significantly from those of psychotic patients treated in state hospitals, who have a high rate of severe chronic social breakdown. The Taiwan data suggest that deterioration in psychiatric patients may be the result of treatment rather than an inherent part of the process of the illness. The opportunity to identify and follow cohorts of patients with the same disorder, but in different cultures, may clarify some of the causes of disability and deterioration. Here one would focus on such environmental factors as the expectations and role requirements of different ages and sex groups.

Large-scale prevalence surveys are easier to carry through in small traditional societies than in large developed ones. Opportunities to study such etiological factors as nutritional disorders and birth traumas are also numerous, because obstetrical and hospital facilities are so scarce. The homogeneous and limited size of the various populations affords a unique opportunity to test out psychodynamic hypotheses about specific child-training practices and later personality and illness patterns. This has been demonstrated with particular effectiveness by Lin's survey in Taiwan and by the Cornell-Aro[39] social and psychiatric survey of the Yoruba in Nigeria.

The survey team in Taiwan comprised about 15 medical students and several psychiatrists; each team was made up of one physician, with one or more years of experience in psychiatry, and two or three 4th-year medical students, accompanied by the elder official of the village. The entire study took four months in Baksa, six months in Simpo and six months in Ampeng.

The Yoruba study in Nigeria covered an area of one hundred square miles around Abeokuta, with a population of eighty thousand. Most of these people were Yoruba of the Egba subtribe. Fifteen villages of differing size, modernization and degree of social integration were selected for study. The interviews were done on a random selected group of mental patients at the Aro hospital, by a staff that consisted of four full-time and two part-time psychiatrists, and three social scientists. Within three months, they were able to collect data on 262 villages, 64 residents of Abeokuta, 59 mental hospital patients, and 12 patients of native healers. They found greater similarities than differences, with regard to prevalence pattern and quality of psychiatric symptoms, between the Yorubans and the Nova Scotians who were studied in the Stirling County study[40]—a significant finding, in view of the generally held belief that cultural differences are likely to produce major differences in the prevalence of specific psychiatric disorders.

INCIDENCE STUDIES

In order to specify the incidence of specific abnormalities in a culture, one has to determine exactly when an illness begins. This requires close observation, over a long period of time, so that incidence is not easy to study. It is difficult, for example, to divide the population in developing societies into homogeneous sub-groups; it is also difficult to design etiological studies that hold constant all factors but the one under study. Ideally, etiological factors should be differentiated from those that perpetuate and influence the natural history of the diease; but this differentiation is difficult to make experimentally. It is more feasible to compare patients who have specific diagnoses with matched individuals who do not have the disorder, so as to determine how they differ in terms of etiological characteristics. It is often useful to investigate a cohort that was formed in the past, in terms of present functioning; one might thereby assess what happened to a known group of patients in terms of community acceptance, secondary syndromes, recurrent episodes. The natural history of the illness can be more illuminating than the mere determination of frequency distribution; it would also make better use of the kind of data that is presently available. There is, in addition, a greater chance of finding other cases of psychiatric disorder in the families of index cases than in the population at large. In this type of study, one can also assess the burden of the community.

Another useful epidemiological approach would be to study the relationship between environmental variables and individual susceptibility. The spread of rumors, fear of witchcraft, and the development of Cargo cults may follow quite distinct patterns, which can be studied independently of individual susceptibility. The size, nature, stability, and cohesion of the community may have a significant effect on the development of panic.

The absence of rigorous methods of epidemiological research

is even more true of developing societies than of developed ones. Accurate recording of census data, morbidity and mortality figures must be developed. The distribution of infectious, parasitic and nutritional diseases in these countries differs from that found in the more developed countries. The population also differ: they are predominantly youthful, below the age of greatest risk for schizophrenia, manic-depressive psychosis, and diseases of the senium, which account for most of the disorders in the Western world. Unless these patterns are known, cross-cultural comparisons cannot be adequately performed. More must be known about occupational factors, social factors, the availability of cultural defense systems, and the availability of native pharmacopea. Psychiatric case registers would also facilitate studies of the inception of new cases, the duration of illness, and the frequency of prior episodes.

RESEARCH GOALS AND OBJECTIVES

Recent efforts to develop casefinding techniques for the study of incidence and prevalence have often gone aground, through becoming overinvolved in issues of methodological accuracy. Much of the work has had little bearing on the immediate task of bringing treatment to the psychiatric populations of the developing countries. What is needed is practical research on such questions as: why do patients with recognizable disorders fail to obtain available treatment? what makes indigenous treatments so effective? how can programs be introduced without rousing excessive resistance from the people involved? It is curious that researchers in the developing countries have not been as circumspect in determining feasible priorities of research directions as have those who are in the business of providing aid. Certainly, if one were to pose these questions to the society itself, studies of child-training practices and dream patterns would be given a lower priority than questions of the delivery of services. The measurement of the pupillary reflex, in order to improve diagnostic methods, is clearly less crucial at this time than is a study of the impact of illness in general on the family and the community.

There are other important questions to ask. What relationship is there between various disorders in the community? What social factors can be differentiated from the clinical syndromes and studied systematically in their own right? Can changes be introduced? How can cooperation and collaboration with native healers be developed? How can people be persuaded to take medicine, and to visit clinics? How can doctors be trained to differentiate between psychiatric disorders and the normal life styles of particular groups?

Within a service-oriented framework, it is possible to focus on the relationship between social stresses and social changes in particular groups. It is also possible to use standardized instruments and case registers to assess the incidence of new disorders and the prevalence of all disorders. Within such a framework, one is able to examine the full range of psychiatric disorders and, where altered states of consciousness are encouraged by cultural institutions, the culture-bound disorders in particular. At the same time, indigenous treatment methods can be studied and compared with more modern methods. It is also possible to examine the obstacles to the introduction of new programs.

Implementing such a research strategy in the developing societies requires the skills of sociologists, anthropologists, hospital administrators, public health specialists and those with experience in program development. Epidemiologists and biostatisticians would also be able to recognize those research techniques that are applicable and relevant to particular substantive issues. Since no single technique or theoretical approach is sufficient, various approaches must be brought to bear on the specific problems of psychiatric illness and treatment.

Mental disorders are often but some of the consequences of physical disease. Research into such etiologically defined diseases is particularly relevant to the developing countries, where parasitic, infectious and nutritional diseases are so prevalent; it can be supplemented by investigations into the consequences of exposure to certain toxic or noxious situations.

Etiological hypotheses can be made that distinguish between groups with differential exposure to particular factors, such as maternal deprivation and pregnancy complication.[41,42] This is particularly valuable if the specific causes are known, because it is then possible to follow those cases that do develop and in that way to study the natural history of the disease. Supplementary investigations may also be carried out to determine how groups of people are exposed to these causative factors and how those factors are distributed in the population.

The distribution and frequency of such entities as schizophrenia, manic-depressive psychosis and obsessional neurosis, which are defined in descriptive rather than etiological terms, can also be examined. Cross-cultural comparisons are eminently suited for the study of specific symptom-entities, many of which are learned patterns of response to a specific cultural milieu. Many symptoms, such as epilepsy, can be disabling. Juvenile delinquency, alcoholism, school failure, low IQ test performances, paranoid thinking and phobias are among the multi-determined syndromes. In the case of suicide, the relevance of such studies is apparent. As Gruenberg[43] has said, "It is well-known, for example, that there is a vast range of diagnoses, etiological as well as descriptive, associated with suicide. Yet suicide is a vitally important symptom and many studies attest to the fact that this symptom has epidemiological characteristics rather independent of the distribution of psychiatric diagnosis."

Symptoms are not only medically important; they are perhaps the phenomena *par excellence* to be investigated cross-culturally, since many symptoms are learned, in much the same way as behavioral patterns, attitudes and beliefs are. Many symptoms occur in individuals who are not suffering from illness, and it may be possible to compare their experiences with those of others who develop specific illnesses, by clarifying in only one group the mechanism involved in the development of the disorder.

By examining one particular symptom in a population consisting of people both with and without that symptom, it may be possible to determine the underlying connections between cases. Thus it may be, for example, that phobic symptoms occur in family patterns or follow ethnic lines. One may also be able to study epidemics of symptoms. Thus one can study the distribution of causative factors, after which it may become possible to determine the characteristics of the causative factors and the forms of exposure to them, as well as methods of control.

The psychological mechanisms of individuals who break down must be examined by comparison with those of individuals who do not. Inferences about psychological causes or mechanisms cannot be made on the basis of correlations arrived at between ecological and prevalence data, because mental illnesses are not all caused in the same way. Sometimes it is a combination of factors that converts a potential case into an actual one. Not everyone with a positive tuberculin test has tuberculosis, although no one who does not show a positive test can have it. Some psychiatric illnesses develop as a result of the fact that multiple factors interact with a specific etiological agent. Some have the quality of syndromes (for example, cardiac decompensation); these illnesses develop from deficiencies that have been produced by nutritional, noxious, infectious, or metabolic factors.

Epidemics of psychiatric disorders can be studied with the same methods as those that are used to study infectious diseases. One can track down cases in specific areas, establish the common factors to which they were exposed as a way of figuring out the attack rate, and ultimately determine both the distribution of the causative agent in the population and the conditions that account for its development and spread—after which one can isolate the causative agent and prevent its development. Vulnerable groups can be isolated and clinically examined. Social change provides the opportunity to study not only these conditions, but others, such as juvenile delinquency and alcoholism, which have reached epidemic proportions in the modern and developing world.

Epidemics of psychiatric disorders may occur; they are shown by the fact that there is an increase in the number of cases of the disease that is greater than can be explained in terms of chance alone. This may happen when there is an increase in the number of pathogenic factors, increased susceptibility on the part of the relevant individuals, or a general change in the character of the environment. While a conceptual model for infectious diseases is applicable to psychiatric disorders, delineation of the specific factors involved is obviously much less easy, particularly when the pathogenic agent causing the illness is not known.

There are a number of important questions and issues for which data can be gathered during the course of routine service or treatment programs. To facilitate such investigative efforts and the systems analysis of the treatment program itself, it is important to establish certain standardized data-gathering procedures.

The Case Register

Standardized pre-coded questionnaires are particularly useful. The regular recording of information on the age, sex, race, residence, diagnosis, and mental state of patients admitted to psychiatric facilities provides a "case register," with which the social and psychiatric characteristics of the patient population in different cultures can be compared. Case registers can be developed readily with the present availability of computers that can process and store great quantities of data.

From such a register one can determine patterns of admission and re-admission to hospitals and out-patient departments;

the characteristics of patients with recurrent hospitalizations; unduplicated hospital and patient utilization rates, and resource needs in the community for particular diagnostic and population subgroups. One can also evaluate the characteristics of the patient population and in that way better plan facilities. Such information can aid in retrospective studies of the demographic and social factors that have led to psychiatric treatment, as well as in prospective studies of the community adjustment of those individuals who are drawn into the psychiatric network. Where good census data are available, it is possible to compare samples of patients with the non-patient population, in terms of household composition, employment, medical care and child care. A register can also provide information on the kinds of patients that psychiatric facilities may expect to receive from selected geographic areas in the community, on the basis of the kinds of cases they are already receiving from these areas. The establishment of this kind of standardized bookkeeping, both on demographic-social characteristics and on mental status and clinical conditions, will also facilitate and encourage the development of record-linkage systems among the various medical and social agencies in the community, thus making it possible ultimately to examine the range of the facilities that are used by selected groups of patients and to make more comprehensive studies of the natural histories of various psychiatric illnesses.

A register will also facilitate the selection and follow-up of population subgroups, in order to determine the prevalence and the characteristics of specific disability syndromes in individuals with different psychic histories. It will make it more possible to determine which cases do not go to hospital or out-patient facilities in different countries, and to investigate what alternative systems of care are sought by these patients. Information obtained in a standardized way in one particular area will make possible the initiation of standardized studies throughout the world. The presence of urgent needs, coupled with the availability of an improved technology, makes it especially worthwhile at the present time to pursue this kind of epidemiological research in the planning of services.

Procedures might be established along the following lines: As each patient arrives at a clinic for his initial visit, he is assigned a computer-identification number. The professional staff completes a number of standardized social and psychiatric forms, in interviews with the patient; additional forms, chosen in accordance with the patient's specific diagnosis, may also be completed. Depression scales are used for depressive patients, other scales on schizophrenic symptomatology or acting-out behavior for schizophrenic patients. Forms are then scored for presence or absence, as well as for degree of intensity; they are pre-coded for computer-usage with 80-column data cards, or arranged for optical scanning. Information can also be recorded with regard to medication, dosage and frequency of administration, as prescribed on the initial visit. On subsequent visits, patients can be evaluated and rated on symptom forms. Global evaluations of change can be made, and the fate of medication—that is, change in dosage, frequency, kind, etc.—as well as the reasons for this, can be entered on a medication record sheet.

All the information from standardized forms on patients in various participating countries would be available in the computer memory for comparisons, thus making possible frequency counts of the incidence of specific alternatives to an item of background information, as well as comparisons, using chi-square techniques, of the relative frequencies for any or all patient groups. Register information may also be matched with information from the census, the courts and other agencies, to ascertain the relationship among various psychiatric disorders and such factors as economic status, marital stability, unemployment, education, overcrowding, crime rates, juvenile delinquency rates, school drop-out rates, absenteeism and so on.

It is most important to develop a register that provides unduplicated counts of patients, rather than admissions, and which obtains its information from as many psychiatric and medical facilities in the network as possible—including outpatient facilities. A cumulative record of the psychiatric service received by each patient in the community is especially valuable when one is assessing the resources and the needs of the community. In addition, the selection biases that are inherent in collecting data from a single facility are eliminated.

Case registers can facilitate studies of the relationships between early life disorders and those that occur in later life; between specific family patterns and disorders; and between behavioral abnormalities and subsequent social and psychiatric disorders. They can aid studies of special groups, such as children from disturbed or broken homes or from orphanages, who are subjected to specific social and physical stress and are at great risk of developing psychiatric disorders. Population data on alcohol consumption, family patterns, school performance and other variables may form the basis of cohorts for follow-up studies, to determine which individuals are more likely to develop disorders of a specific nature and what kinds of early events correlate with them. Tests of these etiological hypotheses have rarely been possible, since the necessary data have generally not been recorded with the aim of future testing.

It is, of course, essential to determine what information should be put into the computer, how to insure that the information is incorporated into the computer files, and what research and administrative questions may be asked. Computer centers in the developed countries can be linked with those in the developing countries for information processing.

Other Tools

QUESTIONNAIRE SURVEYS. Comparative international data can also be collected through mail-survey questionnaires, as Murphy and his colleagues[44] have shown, although it is important to be aware of the limitations of this approach. Problems of question reliability and data comparability are inevitable. Questions elicit responses of different quality, so that many of them are not adequate for statistical analysis. There are no objective or independent methods for assessing the validity of respondent reports, which may be influenced by different theories, case materials, languages, national sentiments, bureaucratic controls, respondent experiences and statistical reporting systems.

The rate of return in such surveys is often low. Ultimately, it has to depend on the investigator's relationship with his informants, and this in turn usually makes for selected samples. A cadre of participants using standardized techniques should hopefully develop over time, thus reducing the problems of sampling bias, reliability and validity.

SURVEY INSTRUMENTS. The Cornell Medical Index has been used in a number of surveys in Nigeria, St. Lawrence Island, Peru and elsewhere. It is readily translated and applied in other countries. In that it focuses on symptom patterns rather than diagnostic entities, it is useful for studying the distribution of symptoms in a population and avoids the problems of standardizing diagnoses cross-culturally. The Cornell Medical Index, and screening instruments like it, are useful for establishing a general profile of a population's health, to be used in planning services. These questionnaires, however, produce limited information. Definitive statements about the distribution of specific diseases, or about their relationship to specific social factors, are more difficult to make from data that have been collected solely by the use of such instruments. They do not contain items for psychotic, psychopathic and organic conditions, and are instead generally weighted for psychosomatic, psychoneurotic and depressive items. An additional weakness of instruments such as the Cornell Medical Index is the uncertain validity of the questions and the uncertain reliability of responses to them—particularly in different cultural settings, where meanings may differ, or where some items become totally irrelevant because of the differences in culture.

CLINICAL TECHNIQUES. Standardized instruments, controlled observations, standardized diagnostic criteria and a uniform nomenclature are all important in reducing the variation between different studies. Clinical investigators must routinely utilize rating scales that impose order on the information obtained. Comparability of rating scales can be accomplished by standardizing interview techniques and questionnaires. This will increase the certainty that the differences observed are due to actual differences between patients, rather than to differences in the technique or terminology used. Standardized psychiatric interview schedules are useful for obtaining comparable data on patient populations: such interview schedules provide scaled judgments on the severity and intensity of various aspetcs of psychopathology. It is possible to study differences in diagnostic approach by comparing the conclusions arrived at by different interviewers, as they assess the same taped patient interviews.

Another approach to comparable data involves the use of standard checklists of variables that have universal applicability.[45] Psychological tests are generally regarded as being objective instruments and, as such, little influenced by the interviewer's bias. It is sometimes difficult, however, to distinguish cultural from psychopathological factors in the responses to projective techniques.

The use of motion pictures has enabled some investigators to examine repeatedly various aspects of the same bits of data.[46] This is important in assessing the validity and improving the reliability of judgments. Such recording devices enable the investigator to reaffirm his original insights, as well as to study the data from different viewpoints. Another useful instrument is the interaction chronograph; this is used for measuring interaction between individuals in a form that can be reduced to simple units, coded, and quantified, so as to establish reliable patterns of behavior that are characteristic of specific individuals, groups or situations.[47] An additional tool is slow-motion film microanalysis, in which small bits of data are examined by microanalysis.

Reference should also be made to the Piblokto research program, because it utilized multiple techniques.[48] To determine whether Piblokto (i.e., Arctic hysteria) is a form of hypocalcemia, psychomotor epilepsy, spontaneous functional hypoglycemia, psychogenic hysterical fit, food poisoning or a form of encephalitis, data were obtained on: serum calcium, serum potassium, diet, ultraviolet radiation, food distribution, kinship patterns, genealogy, electroencephalography, blood sugar, liver function, adrenocortical function, life histories, psychocultural factors, the toxicology of shark meat, and the presence of viruses from individuals living in crowded quarters. This model for investigating a culture-bound syndrome is of relevance to other developing countries because of its all-inclusive approach to a psychiatric disorder. Such a broad etiological inquiry may be especially illuminating, in that the same clinical syndrome may be a common final pathway for several different disorders. If these can be differentiated by means of such careful etiological study, effective treatment may be possible in a portion of the cases. By extending the study of clinical phenomena into the developing societies, it is possible to study variations of the most common syndrome that may stem from different etiological factors, thereby extending our concept of the origin of these psychiatric disorders.

STATISTICAL TECHNIQUES. Data analysis techniques must be developed for analyzing a variety of variables from a given population. Until now, the Pearson Product-Moment Correlation has been used for problems with one variable. Theoretical statisticians are now trying to fractionate mixtures of the modulate populations,[49] so as to compare more than one group of people in large-scale populations. In 1938, Zubin[50] developed the method of "like-mindedness analysis," which was suitable for finding individuals clustered on qualitative variables, such as responses to dichotomous items. Lazarsfeld[51] later developed the method of "latent-structure analysis," which attempted to locate subgroups of a population of such a character that within the subgroups the items were uncorrelated among themselves. Continuous measurements and a number of clustering procedures have also been developed. More recently Fleiss developed a system of analysis for isolating homogeneous groups. This takes as its point of departure the definition of homogeneity as a multivariant normal distribution within each subgroup (see [49]).

PHYSIOLOGICAL TECHNIQUES. Culture-dependent techniques such as the interview, while controlled, rely on cultural norms in the assessment of individual patterns or behavior. Thus, we inquire as to whether individuals talk spontaneously, handle their own finances, and are gainfully employed—questions that stem from our own culturally based concepts of "normal functioning." In another setting with different norms, analogous bits of behavior would have to be examined in any effort to assess social performance. It is also possible that, in some cultures, the social performance of the psychiatrically ill may not be altered.

Along these lines, Zubin[52] has suggested a useful distinction between "culture-bound indicators," in which diagnoses are based on observed deviations from sociocultural norms; "culture-fair" indicators, which are the cross-cultural invariant deviations from expectation that characterize mental disorders; and such "culture-free indicators" as can be provided by biochemical, neurophysiological, and behavioral measures. Zubin has suggested that the first 1000 milliseconds of a patient's response to stimulation in various sense modalities can be a suitable testing ground for "culture-free" or "culture-fair" indicators; this is based on the assumption that the effects of learning may not be expressed quickly enough to influence the response in this phase. Although culture undoubtedly influences an individual's attitude to the taking of tests, these tests are less readily influenced by cultural factors than are such conceptual tests as the IQ.

The rationale for differentiating culture-specific from culture-free divisions has been well stated by Burdock and Zubin:[53]

In dealing with culturally determined or symbolic behavior, it is well to recognize that such behavior is dependent on well-established patterns which are deeply ingrained and not readily alterable. Because it is so completely overlearned, such behavior can be extracted from the organism's repertory with a minimum of attentive effort. Altered brain function, psychosurgery, shock therapy, and mental disease itself may leave these functions relatively intact. They may be so distorted as to assume bizarre forms in mental illness, but the basic elements involved in such behavior—vocabulary, speech patterns, old association, etc.,—are relatively immune even to radical alterations in brain functions. . . . For these reasons, physiological activities and those psychological activities which do not draw exclusively upon socially overlearned behaviors are likely to provide more accurate measures of the current state of the organism, while conceptual activities give a better estimate of its past history. Both types of measure are useful, especially if they are contrasted or viewed as a pattern.

The detection of differences in mental illness in different cultures, therefore, requires a greater reliance on physiological indicators, which are more likely to get at the basic biological vulnerability, than on social performance indicators. Ideally, we must use culture-free measures, which remain immune to environmental influences: for example, the initial components of response to specific stimulation in various sense modalities may be culture-free. Zubin has noted that culture may only indirectly affect responses to light stimuli, while it would directly affect conceptual processes.

Culture may influence "culture-fair" tests, by affecting the individual's attitude and approach to test situations. Insofar as cultural influences are minimized in both "culture-free" and "culture-fair" measures, findings may truly reflect vulnerability, or the invariant characteristics of mental illness. Having identified individuals with the same vulnerability, one can assess the effects of culture by comparing those among these individuals who show different clinical manifestations.

The various "culture-fair" tests have been constructed, according to Zubin, to minimize contamination by variables such as the subject's understanding of the test, his motivation, attention and cooperation. Such variables contaminate not only the testing itself, but also comparisons of schizophrenics and normals from the same culture. As Zubin[54] has noted: "Such designs include obtaining complete functions rather than isolated points of measurement for each individual, comparisons of slopes of functions rather than level, the measurement of functions under idling state conditions and under load conditions and finally the use of the range of variation within a population as a basis for assessing observed deviation."

Insofar as conceptual and therefore cultural elements appear to enter into most physiological responses—as is to be seen in conditioning, perceptual, placebo and other studies—there are a number of kinds of study that may succeed in minimizing them. The techniques that have been developed that are little dependent on sociocultural norms include pupillography, cross-modality reaction time, and measures of temporal resolution in vision and audition. In one well-documented study, schizophrenic subjects displayed longer and more variable reaction times than did normal subjects. Venables[55] in 1960 reported on the periodicity of reaction times, in which both normals and schizophrenics demonstrated 100-millisecond periodicities that were out of phase with each other by 10 milliseconds. In 1962, King[56] demonstrated that schizophrenic and normal subjects differ in their ability to tap in synchrony with a repetitive click that is presented 1–3 seconds apart. Normal subjects tend to anticipate—that is, to respond before the synchronizing stimulus is given. Other behavioral studies of phenomena which occur in the 1000 milliseconds range include critical flicker frequency, apparent movement, two pulse thresholds, auditory localizations and masking. The culture-free indicators derived from laboratory experiments appear to be more objective than culture-dependent techniques such as systematic interviewing schedules and accompanying inventories for evaluating mental status and social adaptation. In addition the results obtained from them are not dependent on the trained judgment of the operator or technician as in culture-dependent techniques but only on his skill at operating the apparatus. In these indicators according to Zubin: "The speed, accuracy and temporal or spatial integration of responses to specified types of stimuli can be measured and contrasted in patients and controls."

Zubin has been particularly interested in the response occurring a thousand milliseconds or less subsequent to a stimulus. Schizophrenic patients have been shown experimentally, for example, to display longer and more variable types of response than normal subjects.

Johnassen, Dureman, and Salde[57] in 1955 demonstrated a technique that successfully differentiated normal subjects from psychiatric patients who were autistic and socially isolated. Their technique, according to Zubin, "was based upon the observation that two objects moving in opposite directions are perceived as moving much faster than their actual speeds. Under these conditions, autistic subjects seem to be less influenced by the illusion of the two moving objects, since they judged their objective velocity more accurately than normal subjects."

Studies of apparent motion have shown that schizophrenics require longer periods of time between light impulses, and longer exposure to stimuli, for recognition and for the correct differentiation of a group of dots that are spatially ordered (Fesanaro;[58] Kaswan[59]). Shagass and Schwartz[60] recorded evoked potentials to two discrete electrical stimuli presented to the wrist and separated by brief periods of time. They plotted the resulting "recovery" functions, with regard to the effect of the first stimulus upon the amplitude of the evoked potential to the second stimulus. Schizophrenic subjects were found to require a longer temporal separation between pulses than normal subjects; the amplitude of the second-evoked potential to return to its baseline suggested that these schizophrenics displayed less cortical excitability and responsiveness than normals.

On the basis of these considerations, Zubin has suggested that such behavioral phenomena as critical flicker frequency, apparent movement, two-pulse thresholds, auditory localization and masking can all be characterized as temporal, environmental manipulations in the thousand-millisecond domain.[61] Patients have been found to differ from non-patients, by way of the psychophysical investigations of these effects. Adequate methodological precautions must be taken to minimize the non-sensory contributions to the determinations.

Such investigations will enable us to separate out groups of people with psychophysical vulnerability, who can then be compared from culture to culture, so as to determine the effects of different cultural stresses. It would be of particular interest to find that people with specific physiological vulnerabilities have the same risk of developing psychiatric disorders in different cultures, irrespective of the complexity of the culture. Identification of these biological factors will assist in the delineation of the psychological and social factors that might contribute to the emergence of mental illness in those for whom it is not possible to demonstrate any psychophysiological vulnerabilities.

CONCLUSIONS

In the determination and the study of the epidemiology of psychiatric disorders, cultural factors influence case-finding methods, criteria for entry into treatment, diagnosis as well as prognosis, and the possibility for follow-up study. They also influence popular attitudes toward the mentally ill and toward treatment institutions, native as well as modern. Their impact is of particular relevance to developing societies, which have limited resources to allocate to these problems, and which must not only assess the kinds of disorders they must provide for—many of which are inextricably linked with the development process—but must also determine ways in which to introduce programs to overcome specific cultural resistances in particular societies. How this can best be done is considered in the next and final chapter.

CHAPTER 7   INTRODUCING
PSYCHIATRIC
PROGRAMS TO
DEVELOPING
COUNTRIES

MEDICAL PROGRAMS IN DEVELOPING COUN-
tries generally have a much lower priority than programs for industrialization, rural development and food production; of the
medical programs, psychiatric programs usually have the lowest
priority. Widespread malnutrition, high infant and child mortality rates, and the shortening of life expectancies because of
infectious diseases are usually given much greater attention.

The cost to society of untreated psychiatric disorders is
obviously underestimated. Unlike other illnesses, the extent of
which can be readily calculated from morbidity and mortality
statistics, psychiatric illnesses, and particularly the less severe
disorders, do not lend themselves so readily to enumeration.
Often they manifest themselves in ways that are not easily recognized. Much of the absenteeism that so seriously affects the manpower pools of the developing nations is frequently due to
psychiatric illness. Similarly, high rates of social disorders, such
as narcotic addiction, alcoholism, prostitution, and child ex-
ploitation, are in large measure related to the presence of psychiatric disorders. Of even greater importance is their presence
in persons in crucial positions of leadership, who may as a result
cause irreparable harm to the development of their societies.

If the development of human resources is to be encouraged,
psychiatric programs must receive more attention. Psychiatric
illness must be recognized, in terms of such effects on the social
system as unemployability, absenteeism, lack of motivation, de-

Notes for Chapter 7 will be found on pages 209–210.

linquency, crime, drug addiction and alcoholism, as well as susceptibility to revolution, violence and social turmoil.

Psychiatric disorders are chronic conditions, which reduce the work force, swell the welfare rolls, and produce social and economic burdens far greater than is suggested by the hospital admission data on severe disorders alone. Psychiatric disorders may also have serious consequences for the mental, physical and social well-being of other family members—in particular, the children. This may ultimately be reflected in social performance.

The high cost of caring for patients in poorly staffed custodial institutions, filled with chronic long-term patients, is also insufficiently considered when priorities are being determined. Maintenance of these large institutions often costs more than community treatment. Oftentimes, government agencies or charitable institutions construct new facilities as visible evidence of their commitment to the psychiatric needs of the community, with little or no regard for the rationality of such capital expenditures. In 1967, I visited an empty 200-bed hospital in Baranquilla, Colombia, which had been built by a national charitable organization, the Beneficiencia, without determining whether sufficient staff could be found to operate it, and without any consideration of alternative ways to upgrade existing facilities at a considerably lower cost.

Considerable thought must go into the expenditures of funds. Representatives of both donor and recipient agencies must carefully assess priorities before plunging into programs that may lend themselves to the techniques of cost accounting, yet may have little relevance for long-term needs. Given limited financial resources, educational and training programs should, in the long run, prove to be more profitable investments than buildings.

Furthermore the traditional one-to-one psychiatrist-patient model of modern psychiatry is not applicable to the developing societies, where there is an insufficient number of psychiatrists for the number of patients. The rationale that the "successful analysis" of a single individual can significantly affect many others does not justify the intensive time investment required by dynamic psychotherapeutic treatment. Developing countries must recognize that the public health model already being used is relevant for psychiatric problems, and can be adapted in such a way as to incorporate a psychiatric approach. Paramedical personnel, technical specialists, and large-scale treatment programs are ideally suited for introducing the most modern psychiatric programs into the developing world.[1]

It is always less expensive to treat individuals in the early stages of their illness than to wait until complications have developed, and psychiatric hospitalization is required. Early recognition and treatment, by preventing the development of secondary handicaps and disability, reduces the numbers of unproductive and unemployed persons. It is now economically possible, through the use of psychopharmaceuticals, to develop large-scale out-patient treatment programs. Much as penicillin and anti-malarial drugs have facilitated nationwide campaigns to eradicate yaws and malaria, the psychopharmaceuticals can be used in a public-health approach to psychiatric disorders. In India, for example, there are a million epileptics and over a million ambulatory psychotics, who could be receiving anti-epileptic or tranquilizing drugs. The psychopharmaceutical agents reduce the amount of time that psychiatrists must spend with patients; overcome previously formidable language barriers; and facilitate programs for training paramedical personnel to monitor patient responses to drugs. All these factors contribute to the expansion of effective health personnel.

To the extent, then, that psychiatry is concerned with fundamental human issues that are central to the political and economic stability of developing societies, it is imperative that such programs be established as a first and major priority.

ADMINISTRATIVE COOPERATION

The introduction of modern medical programs into the developing countries requires considerable effort, if the inertia on the part of government and local administrations is to be overcome. Cooperation must be established between those who introduce the program and the government, university and/or local organizations that have initiated the project. Protocol must not be minimized. The international specialist must know who are the responsible authorities in the developing country, and to whom he is responsible; he has to make every effort not to cross administrative boundaries without proper consultation. He must determine which programs are most feasible, given the nature of existing conditions. It is often easier to provide direct aid than it is to implement a training program; the latter requires attention to the follow-through, and the establishment of appropriate procedures by the international agency. Attitudes towards the helping nation or individual, previous experiences with receiving foreign aid, and the availability of specialists from the developing country—all these have considerable influence on the ease with which relationships can be established and programs implemented.

As a consultant, the international specialist must be fully aware of his role in his own organization, and the extent to which he can make firm commitments to the developing country with regard to the initiation of a program. He is likely to find that he is under strong internal pressure to demonstrate his willingness to help. Constraint and patience must be consciously exercised here. If the consultant's authority is unclear or unspecified, conflict may develop of the sort that may undermine any further efforts. If the key contact person is not in a position of influence in his own government or organization, or has to rely on others to initiate activity and implement the program, or if the bureaucratic machinery impedes efforts, frustration and, ultimately, abandonment of the project may be the consequence.

Here, of course, the foreign specialist must be sensitive to the felt needs of the recipient society; he must not seek to impose his own priorities, irrespective of their merits. He must not ignore the desires of recipients to develop self-reliance by assuming the responsibility for developing projects themselves, as well as by participating in decisions as to what they will be receiving. All interaction with other cultures should recognize the importance of providing people with an opportunity of returning gifts and grants, in some manner that is traditional to their culture. This will reduce power and status differences that are likely to interfere with working collaborations.

The international expert must be flexible and willing to alter preconceived plans, in order to fit existing limitations that often do not become apparent until a project is well under way. He must also discourage expectations that cannot be met. Serious conflicts may develop unless he is as explicit as possible, at all stages of transactions, about the limits of planned activities. When the overseas specialist promises something that he is unable to deliver, because of limitations in the system of the developing country, the faults of that system will not be accepted as a satisfactory explanation for his failure. He or the country he represents will be expected to "pick up the tab and deliver." To this end, the expert must also recognize any incompatibility between his own idealistic aims of helping the impoverished peasants and the more cynical and negative attitudes of the upper classes in those same countries. Indeed, it may take some time before he can find those in the developing countries who are genuinely interested in helping the disadvantaged groups. It is important to remember here that individuals who have had contact with Western psychiatrists are often not in the most appropriate position to implement programs that ultimately depend on government policy and priorities.

Foreign experts must also avoid being used to implement the aims of one particular group, in opposition to those of others. A sponsoring organization has the obligation to ensure that its program is developed in accordance with standards that it has established in its other programs. This requires continual consultation and supervision in the developing countries, and underscores once again the importance of establishing a working relationship with the most qualified people in any given country.

Pilot projects are often useful in training local personnel. Differences between groups, despite their ostensible similarities, and the different kinds of interpersonal relationships in different subcultures may influence the acceptance of care. Communication about the facility may be better achieved through local leaders than by way of public health ministers, if the population ignores or reacts negatively to government personnel. Thus a tribal chieftain or local faith healer may be essential for establishing contact with the people.

Here the foreign specialist will benefit from a broad, comprehensive view of the meaning and significance of cultural beliefs and behavior patterns, as well as from a recognition of his own ethnocentric biases about native superstitions and magic. In particular, he is well-advised to recognize the complexities of native institutions, and the enormous extent to which the functions of the native healer integrate a diverse group of institutional values and customs. Unfortunately, the path to making such discoveries usually requires official approval, which is often difficult to obtain because of the unwillingness of established groups to acknowledge the validity of the native healer's role. Foreign experts must therefore be alert to the disparity among social statuses that exists in developing countries; the structural antagonisms between elite groups and native groups within a given society; and the need to proceed cautiously, without alienating either the elite sources of power or those native leaders who can facilitate communication with the disadvantaged majority.

Foreign specialists must realize that influencing policy is a key part of their work in the developing countries, since ultimately they are dealng with issues of public health. At times, one must persuade the ministries of the need to provide or purchase sufficient drugs, and of the value of various coordinating community agencies. In particular, people in government must be convinced of the cost effectiveness of putting money into preventing psychiatric morbidity, rather than concentrating solely on preventing diseases with a high mortality rate.

Finally, the consultant must face the question of his involvement in matters of education, welfare, social services and politics. In the pursuit of some specific projects, such involvement is unavoidable. As a matter of course, however, it is wise to remain as neutral as possible regarding political matters, focusing as much as possible on the practical problems at hand. This not only clarifies the consultant's position in a society, but also delimits his responsibilities and obligations and facilitates his acceptance.

A related issue concerns the extent to which the consultant is familiar with the native development processes, in their most general sense. A broad philosophical and historical perspective of the often dialectical nature of development is a valuable guideline for anyone who is involved in international efforts. Recognition of this basic dialectical process helps underscore the fact that development is not a uniform, unilinear, evolutionary phenomenon, but a continually changing, unpredictable vital process; it will assist the expert in understanding the conflicts, resistances, and unplanned events that may often result from the impact of new ideas or techniques. It will restrain overplanning, and encourage broad developmental strategies that are based on generic principals and goals.

CULTURAL COOPERATION

Psychiatric programs should probably not be introduced until the appropriate infrastructure has been established. Where no medical programs exist, it is sometimes desirable first to introduce certain measures that are not directly related to disease. Roads, dams, bridges and sanitation measures can have a dramatic effect on general health, and thereby facilitate the introduction of other health development programs. Simple steps are often quite effective in the first stages of introducing care. As simple a step as the cessation of the practice of sealing the severed umbilical cord of the newborn with animal dung can significantly reduce the death rate from neonatal tetanus. Improved nutrition can also yield significant benefits. Purification of water, drainage of swamps, and the use of insecticides are useful second-stage steps, while immunization can be introduced in the third stage.

These stages are a reflection of the ease with which various programs can be applied. In the first stage, the cessation of a customary practice is sufficient to effect a change. Next changes in technology might be accomplished; and only after demonstrable results have been effected can one begin to do things to people such as inoculating them.

Read[2] has described how a health-education project in Ceylon was facilitated by first helping people with their agricultural problems. The program was initially introduced through a mass rally of villages. A survey was made the occasion for music and dancing. The villagers then discussed their needs for a road, for bus service, for post office and bathing facilities; these needs were later classified into self-help problems and those requiring government assistance. The organization of work camps and the implementation of the project followed. Within one year, the village leadership changed, as young men became committee members.

Visible success is also a desirable attribute of any new program. The World Health Organization has demonstrated, for example, that campaigns to eliminate yaws, malaria and trachoma are useful for stimulating general health services, because these diseases are relatively easy to diagnose and to treat successfully, and as such demonstrate dramatically the value of large-scale health programs. Within such a framework, psychiatric services might most appropriately be initiated in the third stage, at a time when more sophisticated techniques and concepts, which have some direct impact on people, are being introduced. It should also be emphasized that immunization, sanitation, and nutrition programs will themselves reduce the incidence of the organic psychiatric disorders.

New programs must take into account cultural beliefs, as well as traditional theories of illness and methods of treatment. A direct attack on the prevalent theory of disease will rarely facilitate the acceptance of new programs; more often, it will encourage resistance. Health customs are integrally related to religious beliefs and values, and cannot readily be changed without evoking marked resistance. Demonstrable results are the most effective phenomena for producing attitude changes. Where it is not possible to demonstrate rapidly the value of a new technique, it may be useful to introduce it in close conjunction with native concepts and practices. Ascorbic acid, for example, might be introduced into the diet in India by suggesting that "hot" honey should be added to "cold" orange juice so as to get rid of the "coldness" of the latter; in that way, one makes use of already accepted notions of hot and cold humors.

New practices can also be reinforced by new ideas or new values that may be accepted for reasons irrelevant to health. Foster[3] has described an experience in Pakistan, where the construction of latrines was facilitated by an interest among the men in using earth-augers for boring holes. A change in ideology, or the acceptance of new ideas, generally takes longer than do changes in practice. Fortunately, many modern practices may be adopted without any change in ideology; indeed, they may even be conceptualized in native terms. Margetts[4] has noted that, insofar as East African patients were accustomed to receiving colored water injections from native healers, the acceptance of modern injections was relatively easy. Such customs may facilitate acceptance of the new psychopharmaceuticals, and this in turn will assist in avoiding the hospital era that was until recently predominant in psychiatric care in the Western world.

Acceptance of modern medical treatments thus does not require acceptance of scientific theories of disease. Successful treatment can be explained in terms of native beliefs, along with the concurrent use of indigenous therapies. Where these are not counterproductive, it is good sense not to oppose them. Indeed, certain existing native practices may be useful: taboos against eating diseased animals or uncooked food, or drinking unboiled water are quite clearly of value in disease prevention. Discarding the clothes of the dead may also serve to prevent the spread of contagious diseases.

Gluckman[5] has pointed out that science functions to explain *how* a given process occurs, while witchcraft explains *why* the process occurs, or why it occurs in one individual and not another. According to him, "the difficulty of destroying beliefs in witchcraft is that they form a system which can absorb and explain many failures and apparently contradictory evidence."* Caution, however, must be exercised in this regard. The model of psychiatric illness, which assigns etiological significance to childhood experiences or family conflicts, for example, is related to the witchcraft belief that an individual can both consciously and unconsciously influence the health and welfare of other individuals.

* The same thing may be said for many quasi-scientific belief systems in Western culture, which are readily adaptable to any set of data.

Should this psychodynamic notion be communicated in settings in which a belief in witchcraft and black magic exists, there is a risk of reinforcing witchcraft fears, which may in turn encourage the initiation of witch hunts. Introduction of the concept of contagious diseases, such as tuberculosis, may similarly provoke earlier anxieties about witchcraft; it must therefore be done cautiously.

Native ritual practices can be highly complex; they must be carefully assessed before any attempt is made to eradicate those that are considered to be medically unsound. Betel-nut chewing, for example, is generally opposed by public health authorities because, like many other stimulants, it is habit-forming, and may lead to addiction, withdrawal syndromes and symptomatic psychotic states. What these authorities underestimate, however, is its larger social and cultural significance.[6] Betel nuts are used in betrothal ceremonies; in religious ceremonies, as propitiatory offerings to spirits; in magic, to ward off sickness; and for the purpose of seeing spirits. In southeast Asia, the sharing and chewing of betel mixture are standard acts for formalized greetings, for selecting partnerships, for concluding negotiations, and for restoring peace and ending controversy and conflict. One cannot simply abolish the use of the betel nut, without affecting the stability of individuals, of their interpersonal relationship, and of the social system. Substitutes for the socially integrative activities that surround the utilization of the betel nut must be introduced simultaneously—an almost impossible task, since public health officials tend to follow a scientific and medical ethic, and thus have no legitimate way for incorporating symbol and ritual in their activities. When new practices are consonant with existing values, customs, and institutions, they are more likely to develop effectively than when they represent a disruption of tradition.

The introduction of modern medicine into developing countries produces numerous social changes that may, in turn, produce new problems unless they are adequately anticipated. Improved care increases the life expectancy not only of the general population, but also of those with hereditary defects and their offspring; there is thus a concomitant likelihood that mutation rates will also increase. Expanding populations are likely to strain agricultural and technological resources and to create new social and medical problems. Indeed, some have argued against the introduction of change unless provision is made for these consequences. Dubos,[7] for example, has underscored the fact that solutions at one end of the life cycle are offset by the development of problems such as cardiovascular and chronic conditions in the older age groups. To the extent that there is likely to be a geometric increase in the need for medical facilities, going beyond the capacity to provide such care, new social conflicts may be generated.

There may be limits to the number of opportunities that can be introduced into the developing nations. Max Millikan[8] has pointed to the unsettling effects of alternative opportunities: "People who have been brought up in a society where their alternatives were very narrowly restricted, where they had to make only very few choices, find that suddenly when their choices are enormously broadened this is a somewhat disorienting experience." One must also consider the speed and extent of the changes that are introduced, as well as the form of care. As we have seen, the Western model of the patient-doctor relationship may not fit the patterning of roles and values in some developing countries. A public-health emphasis on control and prevention, and treatment at a community clinic, is not only more suited to the needs of traditional societies, but more feasible as well, given their limited resources and personnel.

The cultural and social environment is intricately related to adaptation. Health is related not only to agents of disease, animal hosts and environmental conditions, but also to cultural values and attitudes toward illness. If modern medical programs ignore established religious customs, for example, disruption and resistance may follow. The introduction of change must also take into account established lines of communication and traditional patterns of authority. The fact that the new nations of Africa have been formed with little regard for tribal groupings has accounted for much of the civil and political strife in these countries. Medical projects are more likely to succeed in Africa when they can be established along tribal lines. It is particularly important to remember that social structure and social relationships change more slowly than do other aspects of culture, and that behavior may change before attitudes and beliefs are able to.

PSYCHIATRIC PROGRAMS AND COMMUNITY HEALTH CENTERS

In some developing countries, psychiatric institutions modeled on those in Europe and America either already exist or are being brought into existence. At times, some of the anachronistic and least applicable elements of modern psychiatry are being introduced into the developing countries. According to the 7th report of the WHO Expert Committee:[9]

In the societies that have been more profoundly affected by the industrialization and concomitant social changes of the last 150 years, there is one common feature which is of fundamental importance in considering the goals of social psychiatry: in nearly all these countries the mentally ill patient has been increasingly excluded from society during the period of his illness. Thus in the countries that first experienced the massive social changes of the industrial revolution, the population movements and social upheavals of the mid-nineteenth century led to the creation of enormous mental hospitals, situated remotely from big cities, in which the patients and staff lived a life of their own, cut off from the community. It required a legal certificate either to get a patient into or out of these institutions; and significantly the doctor empowered to sign such certificates was termed an "alienist." This social rejection of the mentally sick has created an extraordinary set of artificial conditions. The mentally sick individual, having been excluded from the community for the duration of his illness, then had to be reintegrated into the social community. This, broadly speaking, has been the goal of social psychiatry in these countries. Advances have been made in introducing easier certification proceedings; voluntary admission to hospital without certificate; the open-door principle; day hospitals; night hospitals; and therapeutic social clubs. But this is still insufficient. Psychiatrists now see that their therapeutic aims can be achieved only by getting right away from the practice of excluding the psychiatric patient from society. However, they also realize that this exclusion is not just a matter of certificates and locked hospital doors, but depends to a very large extent on the attitude of the ordinary man and woman to psychiatric illness and psychiatric practice.

The psychiatrist is nowadays often able to place a person at the door through which he can step out into normal life, but this action will not have the desired effect if outside that door there is only empty space. If society is to reap the full benefit of the advance of modern psychiatry, it must learn to collaborate in the prevention of mental disorder and in the rehabilitation of the mentally ill. In other words, further progress now largely depends on the attitudes of the community towards mental patients and towards social psychiatry itself.

Thus must the introduction of psychiatry to the developing countries by-pass the kinds of problems that have arisen in the more developed countries. It must avoid the traditional emphasis on asylum treatment for the psychotic, and intensive, time-consuming, and costly psychotherapy for the motivated neurotic, which has characterized the development of psychiatry in the West. This is now possible with the psychopharmaceuticals.

Psychopharmaceuticals

Since World War II, the care and treatment of the mentally ill have undergone radical changes as a result of the introduction of psychopharmaceuticals. The tranquilizing drugs (resperine, chlorpromazine) and the psychic energizers have revolutionized the care of state-mental-hospital patients. In the last decade in the United States, they have accounted for an unprecedented sustained annual reduction in state hospital population, the total number of patients having been decreased by twenty percent despite a sharp rise in hospital admission. This dramatic reduction has resulted in enormous savings in both construction and treatment costs; most important, patients formerly regarded as lost to society are now able to function as responsible and productive members of it.

Pharmaceuticals have opened up new possibilities for treating patients outside the hospital setting. For some time it had been recognized that isolation of the mentally ill impeded their recovery more often than it helped it; but until the development of drugs, little could be done about this. Today, automatic referral to hospitals no longer occurs, and care is increasingly being entrusted to community health clinics. The community health centers relieve the pressure at the two points where it hurts most: first, they save money, because they obviate the need to build huge, costly hospitals for the mentally ill; second, they maximize the use of existing manpower. Experience has shown that large hospitals make for more patients, require more doctors and personnel, and tend at greater costs to perpetuate the same chronic patterns as are already in motion. Furthermore, large-scale expansions of hospital programs tend to lead to the neglect of more feasible community-oriented treatment clinics, designed to avoid hospitalization, as well as to create a hopeful outlook in the community as to the treatment possibilities of psychiatry. The increasing referral rate over several years to one such clinic program in Haiti is evidence of positive feedback to an active treatment-oriented program.

The introduction of a psychiatric clinic in Haiti is a significant demonstration of the value of the psychopharmaceuticals in facilitating the establishment of a modern psychiatric treatment program in a very underdeveloped society. The 20-bed clinic was established in 1959. Emphasis was put on ambulatory treatment, with the 18–22 hospital beds being used for short periods in acute stages of illness. In the first year, the 244 patients who were treated in this way avoided the harmful experience of incarceration at the Pont Boudet Asylum, an abandoned marine barracks, which provided only custodial care. Four hundred and thirty patients were treated in the second year, 123 of whom (including 28 readmissions) were admitted as in-patients. During the first year, twenty percent of the patients were referred by physicians; thirty percent of them were referred by physicans during the second year, as more and more people in the community came to see the value of the clinic. The volume of new cases continued to grow over the years. By 1969, some 8,000 patients had been treated at the Centre. In 1968–69, 846 new cases were treated: 283 as in-patients and 563 as out-patients.[10] The utilization of the major tranquilizers, such as Thorazine, Trilafon, Mellaril and other phenothiazines, enabled the acutely disturbed schizophrenic patient to be brought rapidly under control and returned to the community, thereby avoiding the detrimental effects of long-term hospitalization. The anti-depressant drugs improved the prospect for out-patient treatment of recurrent depressive disorders and thus reduced the necessity of shock treatments. The psychopharmaceuticals had thus made it possible for many more patients to be treated than before.

The availability of effective drugs reduces the need for large hospitals and asylums, and facilitates the development of various community programs. The dramatic effect of the medicines also does much to reinforce the acceptance of new programs, in that the physician may even be viewed as a magician. The successful treatment of patients and their rapid return to community life visibly demonstrates the value of the clinic, and does much to dispel the mystery and stigma that had developed in the days when patients were isolated in asylums. The community is more likely to accept the emotionally and mentally disturbed, and this encourages those who are less disturbed to seek help. Nurses and psychiatric social workers can be readily trained to assess clinical symptomatology and social functioning, to recognize side effects and to administer drugs to counteract them. In this way, the effects of limited numbers of professional personnel become multiplied.

The crisis-intervention clinic developed by the Cornell Program in Social Psychiatry (at Cornell University Medical College–New York Hospital Medical Center) for patients who have attempted suicide is another relevant model for developing societies. It has been fostered and made possible because of drugs.

It takes what might be described as a very "activist" position. Where symptoms are present, medication begins almost immediately, the patient's symptoms being explicitly attributed to a medical illness or syndrome. The latter is tentatively related to biological or biochemical factores that have not as yet been elucidated, but which develop in much the same way as ulcers—that is, as an automonous process, sometimes precipitated by external stress. A distinction is made between the symptoms from which the patient is suffering—for these, medicine is given and he is not held responsible—and the suicidal behavior or other behaviors that he has been engaged in, which are regarded as his responsibility. Thus the symptoms that are considered to be controllable by medicine are put outside the realm of the patient's responsibility, and the patient is put into the sick role, in the traditional medical sense and as Parsons has defined it. The patient is then obligated to follow the instructions of the technically competent person who has been called to attend to his problems. The symptom relief brought about by the drugs, and by absolving the patient of responsibility for his symptoms, appears useful in relieving guilt and anxiety, increasing faith in the treatment, and facilitating the start of a more dynamic psychotherapeutic approach. This distinction between symptoms and areas of behavior under the patient's control is comparable to the distinction some native healers make, when they attribute symptoms not to the patient but to supernatural agencies, yet require that the patient take full responsibility for his behavior.

In addition, this approach adheres to the medical model of psychiatry that is so prominent in England and Europe, and which lends itself so well to the developing countries. The key assumptions of this model are best underscored by an examination of differences between it and the American psychological model. The belief is not correct that the British hypothesize an organic etiology for all psychiatric illnesses—an impression that is associated with the denigration of British psychiatry as descriptive and Kraepelinian. What is key is that the British differentiate between the personality, the illness, and the environment. Each of these, while they are all interdependent, can thus be examined independently, because the illness is viewed as *occurring* to an individual, rather than being *synonymous with* him—that is, a patient has a schizophrenic illness, but is not "a schizophrenic." American psychiatry, by contrast, is inclined to see the illness as part of the personality.

This distinction has significance for diagnosis, for attitudes towards psychiatric illness, for the integration of psychiatry into the National Health Services, for psychiatric training programs for physicians, and particularly for the delivery of public health services. The conceptual separation of illness, personality, and social factors, and therefore the opportunity to study their integration in terms of social factors, makes possible a more vigorous approach to diagnosis and to research in epidemiology, and a much more thorough and scientific comparative investigation of the prevalence and incidence of psychiatric disorders. By contrast with the American inclination to view psychodynamic theory as a fundamental core of contemporary psychiatry, the British are inclined to view psychodynamics as but one theoretical model, hard to test empirically and relevant to but one dimension of treatment. Thus at the University of London's Institute of Psychiatry at Maudsley Hospital, for example, patients are assigned to special "firms" or units for psychotherapy, when this is indicated. Psychotherapy is not applied across the board, and it is only rarely that one will find someone who feels that schizophrenia can or should be treated with psychotherapy.

The use of the medical model in England seems to produce a greater tolerance of psychiatric abnormality in the community, as well as an inclination to differentiate between psychiatric disorder and social functioning. Thus a diagnosis of schizophrenia does not automatically confer a poor prognosis on the individual, in terms of his capacity to be trained to work. At the same time, the presence of life difficulties or eccentric personality traits do not necessitate the rendering of a diagnosis or recommendation for treatment, as so often happens in the United States. Diagnostic criteria and the indications for treatment are more rigorous in England. This goes along with the greater concentration of personnel in the management of the more seriously ill in England.

The availability of psychopharmaceuticals, the already existing medical model, and the National Health Service have all facilitated the delivery of psychiatric care to the population, to a much greater extent in Great Britain than in the United States. They have even facilitated programs, such as Balint's, to train general practitioners in the practice of psychodynamically oriented psychotherapy with both psychiatric and medical patients.

The emphasis on psychopharmaceutical treatment is not, of course, without its problems. Can such an approach be accepted by the population and by the medical profession, as well as by psychiatrists? What about the pharmacological reactivity of patients from diverse cultures who differ in race and in constitutional type? Recent literature on this subject reinforces earlier observations that cultural factors influence the secondary (compensatory or pathoplastic) features of most clinical syndromes. Thus international comparisons are hazardous, because clinical behavior does not directly reflect the underlying clinical disorder. To the extent that some manifestations of disturbance reflect instead personality patterns, cultural attitudes and patterns of behavior, dosages received by patients may be different even though their underlying condition is the same. Similarly, differences in expectation of treatment, diagnosis and the criteria for assessment will account for differences in drug use. Denber and his colleagues, for example, found that psychotic patients in New York required ten times the mean dose of Haloperidol that was required by a similar group of Belgian patients.

Such problems and questions do not mean that active programs based on psychopharmaceuticals should not be established at the earliest possible moment in the developing countries. This is the only realistic hope—at this stage of our knowledge of mental illness—of bringing relief to vast numbers of psychiatric patients. Once a pharmaceutical program is established, patients who pose no danger to themselves or others should be released from existing asylums to the care of their families and at the same time directed to the clinic for further treatment. This will encourage patients to assume a productive role in the community and will also release hospital beds for the care of others. In addition, it will have the long-range advantage of convincing the community that the mentally ill can be rehabilitated.[12]

Maximization of Resources

Community-oriented clinics can be run by a few professionals, with the aid of a well-trained core of paramedical personnel. Such facilities can initiate community programs for those with less severe disorders. The treatment of these disorders is crucial for the developing nations, in terms of providing a healthy and motivated populace from whom will come the leaders of the future. The 40-bed Catherine Mills Clinic in Monrovia, Liberia, built in 1961, is one example of such a facility. The staff consists of 15 nurses, 12 nurses' aides, 20 maintenance workers, a laboratory technician, hospital administrator, tailor and dietician. Maintenance facilities, staff quarters, and an out-patient clinic are also located in the compound. Occupational therapy, market gardening and poultry-raising projects are available. Twenty admissions and discharges occur each month. Five hundred patients were treated at the center in 1961.

While such facilities have only limited bed space, they can serve as the basis for more comprehensive programs. In 1964, the Liberian Red Cross created a mental health center in Monrovia, at which one hundred patients were seen each month. Wintrob was able to establish a follow-up clinic for the continued treatment of discharged patients and to see one hundred patients each month. Thirty nurses were able to participate, for a period of six to twelve weeks, in a newly established training program. In addition, special training programs were established for aides and attendants from the hospital. Wintrob was also able to make use of personnel and dependents from AID and other international missions. In a two-year period, more than one hundred nurses and nurses aides were in training, many of whom learned of the possibilities of combining native therapies with the modern chemotherapy they were exposed to in the hospital. To the extent that these people return to a range of outposts throughout the country, such a training center can have a significant impact on the mental patients at most points in the country.[13]

Between 1961 and 1968, there were 656 in-patient admissions and 365 new out-patient admissions to the Catherine Mills facility. Only 228 of the 656 admitted to the in-patient facility were re-admissions. In the year 1967–1968, there were 122 in-patient admissions, 124 discharges, 4 deaths, 46 re-admissions and 47 patients who remained at the end of the year.

The linking of mental health centers with hospitals, community organizations, and welfare and social agencies facilitates the establishment of a comprehensive treatment network, as well as the early identification of cases, and early treatment. These latter are crucial for preventing the development of more severe secondary reactions to mental illness, such as the social breakdown syndrome, long-term hospitalization, alcoholism and suicide.

At the Catherine Mills Hospital, a nurse conducts the pre-admission screening, remains in contact with the family during hospitalization, and visits with them and the patient periodically during the year following discharge. The maintenance of contact with the family during the hospitalization is effective in reducing the abandonment of patients—a common consequence of hospitalization, insofar as the removal of the patient from home may free food and living space for others. Such abandonment results in the accumulation of many long-staying patients in custodial settings.

The use of existing programs and personnel is most desirable. Jayasundera has noted that midwives and public-health nurses can be employed to educate the population in the principles of mental health, and to detect early psychiatric disturbances, through the use of various screening programs. He has also emphasized the usefulness of school teachers in the detection, treatment and management of emotionally disturbed children and defectives. In Ceylon, he has developed a system of intensive health drives in restricted areas. These drives are staffed by health officers who are skilled in obtaining community cooperation for the introduction of new schemes that tread on traditional beliefs and activities. The immediate access to the community that they provide is particularly important in countries such as Ceylon and India, where traditionally the extended family has cared for patients and has resisted the institutionalization of the mentally ill.[14]

We are increasingly aware of the skills that are contributed by people from various fields; this strengthens the health team. The social worker now does social psychotherapy, while nurses do administration. In some areas, these people are more useful than psychiatrists. Lectures for community leaders and caretakers, such as priests and teachers, adolescent clubs, and other community-oriented programs, can also be initiated so as to involve these various groups in useful psychiatric activities. Aftercare programs require community cooperation, the absence of hostility and suspicion, and a positive accepting attitude toward the mentally ill.

Some programs have recognized the therapeutic value of the family as a treatment resource. The family in China controls behavior through tolerance of deviance and care of the deviant person. Lin,[15] at the National Taiwan University Hospital, has utilized the mother or the wife to nurse the patient during hospitalization, and has found this to benefit both recovery and re-adjustment after discharge. The family is an integral part of the treatment team in this setting,[16] thus providing additional personnel for patient care. The traditional extended family in India, for example, actively supports and undertakes responsibility for mental patients. At the Christian Medical College in Bellore, a relative must remain with the patient throughout treatment. Responsibility for the patient's safety and care is given to the family, which is provided with a small living unit; they are also informed about treatment at all stages. The program at the Aro Mental Hospital in Abeokuta, Nigeria is similar:[17] a therapeutic unit for 200 to 300 patients is located amidst four large traditional villages, and patients are required to bring a relative to cook, wash and escort them to the hospital. Family participation not only provides additional personnel; it also diminishes resistance to treatment, and creates a favorable therapeutic milieu, by maintaining the well-defined kin groups, the traditional roles and the culturally prescribed mutual obligations.

In 1964, at the University of Indonesia, a training program for general practitioners was initiated in the Municipal Polyclinic of Djakarta.[18] The focus of the course was on elementary psychiatric diagnosis and psychopharmaceutical treatment, with the aim of reducing the need for hospitalization. This project convincingly demonstrated that general practitioners working in polyclinics could be adequately trained to treat psychiatric patients with psychopharmaceuticals. It is essential that general practitioners learn more about the psychiatric significance of physical illnesses, and in particular the psychiatric consequences of infectious parasitic and nutritional diseases. This increased knowledge ought to lead, among other things, to more favorable attitudes toward psychiatric programs and the management of the mentally ill.

Another approach for maximizing existing resources in countries at the first stage of development is to utilize native healers. At the Aro Mental Hospital in Abeokuta, Nigeria, village chiefs and elders participate in monthly hospital meetings, at which treatment programs are planned. Native healers assist in community surveys and supervise group activities. Confession, native rituals and therapeutic cults are also encouraged as supplemental treatment.[19] The integration of indigenous healing practices with Western psychiatric techniques has been effective in British Guiana, where there is one psychiatrist for 500–800 in-patients and 2,000 monthly out-patient visits per month in the mental hospital. Since 90% of these patients are East Indian, and suffer from the less severe neurotic disorders, somaticized depressions and hysteria, cooperation with East Indian native healing cults is particularly useful in treatment and greatly reduces the pressure of manpower shortages.

The use of traditional healers in modern programs is very difficult for many to accept, since it may bring into question the legitimacy of their own "scientific" beliefs and practices. An anthropological perspective, however, can enable one to grasp some of the similarities and the parallels between modern and traditional forms of healing, as well as their common therapeutic value. Ideally, there should be some way of monitoring the qualifications, training and practice of native doctors. In East and West Africa, traditional healers are organized into guilds, which ensures the maintenance of standards and provides the opportunity to formalize cooperative relationships. The Nyanga in Rhodesia, Zambia and Malawi are organized into the Nyanga Association.[20] In Nigeria, several associations of traditional doctors hold examinations and give certificates.[21] Shrine priests in Ghana pay local councils several guineas a year to practice.[22]

Native healers, as we have seen, can have a great influence on the acceptance of modern practices. Describing his experience in Togoland, where he was able to arrange three-day meetings with influential herbalists, diviners, shrine priests, and witch doctors, Spens[23] reported in 1960: "While many of them were prepared to accept the germ theory of infection, they showed of course familiar preoccupation with 'why' does a particular man get sick, rather than 'how.' . . . What is clear is that resort to these practitioners serves as an outlet for anxieties not confined to those created by the belief complex itself. My impression amongst those I met was that they were not unwilling to permit and even recommend modern medical treatment at the same time that they were providing advice and therapy on the supernatural level."

The same people may thus visit both modern medical practitioners and native healers. Indeed, it is likely that the seeking of help itself is itself the factor that is common to those who go to the physician and those who go to the healer. Many physicians working in the developing countries are cognizant of the propensity of patients to seek help from several sources. Amara[24] has indicated that when patients in Liberia asked him whether he could help them as much as the native doctors, he always recommended that they visit the native healers first, so as to avoid entering into competition with them. When they were not helped and then returned to him, he was in a better position to demonstrate the value of modern medicine over traditional forms, in those instances in which it was indeed apparent.

It is important to establish some ground rules as to how one will work with native healers. Where they are organized into guilds, it may be possible to establish formal working relationships. However, where a charismatic personality is sufficient for maintaining an individual in the role, charlatanism and quackery frequently prevail; and it is not only difficult but unwise to establish formal relationships. The value of native healers lies in their knowledge of the members of the community and of the culture; this facili-

tates diagnosis and prognosis, as well as the resolution of interpersonal difficulties through indigenous forms of crisis intervention. According to Beaubrun:[25]

It is possible that the type of collaboration arranged by Lambo in
Nigeria . . . might be feasible in Haiti, where such healers enjoy
some prestige and official status. In the other territories, they are banned
by law, and any collaboration with them by medical men is fraught
with legal hazards. Moreover, they seldom enjoy sufficient prestige
to make such collaboration worthwhile. Western medicine already has
the greater prestige, and to incorporate the obeah man in any sort
of community psychiatry, even in a subsidiary role, would be to give
him status. One might well ask, "who is using whom?"

In limited communities, such as the Rada and Shango communities in Trinidad, there is some genuine traditional status
accorded to the healer; but most of the other *obeah* practitioners
in the Caribbean, outside of Haiti, are resorted to surreptitiously
and in a shame-faced manner, and more for the purpose of casting evil spells on enemies than for healing. Nevertheless, there is
real faith in such methods, as in the religious healing of the
Pentecostal Churches of Jamaica, and psychiatrists have sometimes invoked their help in isolated cases.

The native healer may in fact be better equipped to deal
with a variety of behavioral disorders that have become the
domain of psychiatry, but which are not in fact mental illnesses.
This assortment includes untreatable psychosomatic conditions
which might just as reasonably be handled by internists, and also
marital problems (see [25]). Native healers in Ghana are unionized,
have a training scheme, and are recognized by the government. In
Liberia, agitated psychosis is in many instances treated successfully with rauwolfia by native healers, who also assist in reinte-
grating the patient back into the community.

It is crucial to determine with which types of patients native
healers can deal effectively. My own experience suggests they are
best for neurotic and borderline disturbances and for the secondary syndromes associated with schizophrenia. "Boufée delirante,
aigüe," the six-day schizophreniform illness discussed in Chapter
4, and characterized by Wintrob as an intense belief in bewitchment as the result of the projection of anxiety, is amenable to
the native healer's intuitive and manipulative skills. In essence
the native healer is dealing with compensatory or pathoplastic
symptomatology. He is good at calming down the patient, even
though he does not necessarily affect the basic process; but how a

patient is treated, and what is expected of him, is of course important.

According to Amara (see [24]), most traditional healers are part of the culture they operate in; they have won the esteem and admiration of their community, and, except for the charlatans, they are able to collaborate with the psychiatrist in a naturally beneficial relationship. The alleviation of symptoms depends on drugs, psychotherapy and the patient's recuperative powers—the last of which can be influenced by the native practitioner. If the patient feels that his cure lies with the native healer, the psychiatrist will be doing the patient a disservice to refuse the patient his right to choose. Because of our advantage as trained doctors, we ought, however, to advise the patient as to the merits of both systems.

The psychotherapeutic values of a wide range of native beliefs and practices has been examined extensively in Chapter 5. Those who are engaged in introducing programs into a developing country should be familiar with the specific customs of the culture, and with certain general principles pertaining to the various roles that native healers can play in different societies. Knowledge of these general principles will assist the expert in assessing the potential usefulness of the native healer in the development of modern programs in a particular country.

If the native healers have psychiatric problems well in hand, it may be possible to devote efforts to other kinds of community projects or scientific surveys, or to the establishment of programs for those population subgroups that are not being reached by the native healers. Where the native healers devote all their efforts to rehabilitative cult groups, it may be advisable to avoid duplication of such a program, and instead to focus energies on acute problems or child-training programs, relying on the native cult as an after-care program to which improving patients may be referred. In other instances, the modern psychiatrists may want to draw on the community contacts of native healers by employing them as key informants, liaison personnel or field interviewers.

Most important, the modern psychiatrist can learn from the native healer, whose beliefs and practices have not developed willy-nilly, but in response to specific problems of the members of the culture. Study of these beliefs and practices may reveal much about the culture. Most useful are the therapeutic techniques that have been developed to assist people in coping with the characteristic stresses of the culture. Certain roles—for example,

those of mother-in-law or unmarried women—feature promi-
nently in some indigenous etiological theories of disease causation,
pointing to certain high-frequency stresses in some social systems.
One can learn about patient expectations with regard to treatment—for example, as to the extent to which family members are
expected to participate in the treatment program—which may
help to develop ways of educating the populace to new health
practices and objectives. One can also learn about the limits of
the treatment relationship—for example, the extent to which the
healer is expected to assume an authority role in relationship to
the patient.

A Model for Developing Countries with Some Facilities

Not all developing countries are handicapped by a subsist-
ence economy and a total lack of facilities and trained personnel
Some do in fact have a developing industrial base and modern
medical public health systems, and are in a position to implement
more sophisticated strategies for psychiatric programs, with the
help of already trained psychiatric professionals. What is in great
need, however, is a coordinated approach to the planning and
operation of a program, so as to make better use of available
talent for the public good.

Steps should be taken to set up a State or Community Mental Health Board, with representatives from all sectors of the
community—both governmental and non-governmental—that are
concerned with mental health. Such a board would, in addition,
ensure the most effective use of the financial and manpower resources of the State and the community.

It is also highly desirable to carry through a two-to-three-
month survey of questions that have to be answered before a
community-oriented psychiatric program is established in any
urban area. Experience has shown that a carefully planned survey will ultimately save valuable effort, time and money. The
survey might be carried out either under the supervision of a
university psychiatrist, or by the World Health Organization,
which has the resources to conduct such an inquiry.*

Psychiatric care, in most of the countries with some programs, has been restricted to confinement of the seriously disturbed, and psychotherapy-oriented private-practice treatment of

---

* A request for a consultant should be addressed by the Ministry of Health
to WHO Director General in Geneva, Switzerland. The consultant should
then be asked to undertake the survey and recommend steps to set up the
psychiatric program.

a small percentage of wealthier patients, who are suffering from less severe disorders. The character of these custodial institutions tends to follow a general pattern: patients arrive at the mental hospital as a consequence of court orders, which are usually issued for violence, unmanageability, or the commission of nuisances. Schizophrenics most often comprise fifty to eighty-five percent of the patient population, with varying numbers of cases of manic-depressive psychosis, alcoholic psychosis, marijuana psychosis, addiction, epilepsy and mental retardation. The number of chronic cases usually exceeds the number of new admissions, since discharge is in many instances a rare occurrence. Because of space limitations in the homes of patients, families are often reluctant to take patients back home; the longer patients remain in the hospital, the less their chances of discharge.

As a result of the lack of facilities, patients reside together in the same cramped quarters. It is not unusual to find criminals mixed in with cases of chronic psychosis and mental retardation. Patients are usually poorly clothed, occasionally nude, and sometimes soiling. Foul odors may be mixed with the smell of food being cooked on open stoves in the living area. Plumbing is frequently inadequate, and running water a luxury. Treatment consists of custodial care, although electric shock therapy is used freely—when the apparatus is available. Chemotherapy can occasionally be found, although short supplies result in the fact that patients rarely receive adequate doses, and occasionally none. Occupational and recreational therapy are employed systematically only when special or imaginative personnel are able to create tasks from limiting resources.

While centers must of course be prepared for all sorts of situations, they should ideally provide six essential elements of service: in-patient, out-patient, partial hospitalization (on a day or night care basis), emergency, educational, and consultative. Many of the following recommendations can be put into practice immediately, while others must await the resources as they become available.

A 10–20 bed unit in a general hospital should be selected as the basis for the psychiatric program. Ideally, if a free-standing separate building exists, it should be selected as the site for the program.

The center should serve a multipurpose function:

a. diagnosis of all psychiatric patients;

b. treatment of the vast majority of mentally ill, who do not require hospitalization;

c. intensive short-term treatment of patients who require brief hospitalization;

d. research and development of new ideas and methods of treatment;

e. training of medical students and residents;

f. training of community workers as psychiatric paramedical aides;

g. education of the community about mental illness;

h. demonstration projects.

In addition, the center should include ancillary activities. Residents and medical students should work in the center part-time to gain practical experience in the treatment of psychiatric patients, and cooperation should be established with the general physicians in the community. Efforts should be made to establish special programs, such as custodial farm programs for geriatric, chronic psychiatric and mentally retarded cases. In-service training programs for psychiatric nurses, and special programs for psychiatric social workers and public health nurses, should be initiated. Both psychiatric and student nurses can be used to assist in follow-up programs in the outlying districts, as part of a district hospital program when such a program exists. A qualified psychiatrist must be found to organize these activities, and to establish a psychiatric case register, an out-patient program at the general hospital, and a day program for the mentally retarded at other community agencies. It would also be desirable to build a day/night school for the retarded, for manageable in-patients and for out-patients who can live at home. The size of this school would depend on the need, which could be determined by survey.

In countries with limited resources, active effort should be made to establish links with all community resources that are in any way involved with the physical and mental well-being of the population. Too often, suspicion and distrust, as well as competition for what is incorrectly perceived as a limited number of patients, escalates into ideological conflict, with neither side recognizing the legitimacy of the other side's view. Visiting experts should be aware of this all-too-common occurrence, and make active efforts to initiate friendly non-threatening relationships with native doctors, rather than withdraw behind the defense of "scientific" medicine. Where sound medicine points to the need for modification of certain harmful native practices, the foreign expert must recognize the necessity of establishing a relationship of trust, and demonstrating to the native healers the beneficial effects that will result from the suggested modification of their approach.

The expert is well-advised to learn about the healer's lore and techniques. Over time, as mutual trust grows, mutual distortions and misconceptions will be corrected; in time it may be possible for experts and native healers to learn to make appropriate referrals to each other.

A Model for Developing Countries with Considerable Facilities

In Latin America, facilities, personnel, and training programs for ancillary personnel are available to a much greater extent than in other developing areas; they provide an infrastructure onto which new programs can be grafted. Colombia, for example, has 140 psychiatrists: sixteen in Cali, ninety in Bogota, nineteen in Medellin, and fifteen scattered in other cities. While these psychiatrists serve eighteen million people and are, moreover, in the urban centers, they nevertheless represent a considerable advance beyond the least developed societies and afford a foundation for developing new programs. There are also a number of psychiatric hospitals in these cities, from which expanded efforts could begin. In Bogota, there are eight psychiatric hospitals, one state hospital and one facility at the university level. In Cali, there is a university psychiatric hospital with 250 beds, along with two other mental-health clinics, which have 40 beds. In Medellin, there are 1454 beds, four hospitals and one university hospital.

A primary objective is to maximize the existing facilities and personnel, so as to bring more people into the treatment network at earlier periods in their illness, and to coordinate social welfare and follow-up programs, so as to reduce the need for subsequent hospitalization. Strategy should include:

1. A case register of all patients and programs for systematic follow-ups, utilizing public health nurses, midwives, welfare workers and others who are already in touch with these patients in their communities.

2. A program of comprehensive family medical care, whereby a case worker will be assigned to entire families in a given community, to facilitate early case identification, reduce the fragmentation of services and agencies, and diminish the frequently encountered resistance to psychiatric care among the poor.

3. A national health scheme for assigning people to particular clinics by districts, so as to ensure comprehensive coverage of the entire population, whether or not they are in treatment.

4. Expansion of the traditional role of the psychiatrist and other professionals in the education and training of others. New programs should start at the level of existing needs. Paramedical

personnel must be trained to replace physicians wherever possible, thereby allowing physicians more time to supervise and develop new programs. Health teams make it possible to delegate treatment responsibilities to people of different skills at different phases in treatment. This amplifies the effectiveness of the physician and at the same time increases the number of patients who can be seen. The "team model" for delivering care is especially applicable to drug-oriented community psychiatric programs; it is feasible in countries where a range of experts exists.

The health team should include physicians, psychiatrists, sanitary engineers, population control experts, and behavioral scientists—all of whom can contribute to mental health programs, not only in traditional ways but through the control of sanitation, the improvement of nutrition, and the management of population movements, all of which have significant pathogenic significance in the developing countries.

The major task in a country as advanced as Columbia is thus not the development of a primary facility, or the training of a basic core team, but the allocation of resources in the most useful fashion. The opportunity exists in such countries to develop new models for delivering care, in line with geographic and residential patterns. The major cities have low income *barrios,* with medical clinics that maintain nutritional, birth control, antituberculosis and sanitation programs. Contact with the population of the *barrio* makes it a particularly useful place to introduce mental health programs. At this level, patients can be seen early in their illness, thereby preventing the need for hospitalization. The clinics are particularly useful for training residents and medical students, who are assigned to them on a rotating basis. Universities can establish contact with them and thus form the vanguard in community mental health programs. Leading citizens, as well as general practitioners and specialists in internal medicine, can form community mental health boards to help implement the programs. The *barrio* clinic offers the psychiatrist direct access to the population, in that way enabling him to initiate a variety of anthropological, sociological, and transcultural psychiatric studies. Methodologically adequate epidemiological studies can be carried out, because of the existence of comprehensive information on the population at risk.

In 1967, such a program was developed through the Universidad del Valle in Cali, Colombia.[26] Utilizing local medical personnel, it was established in three public health centers, in two *barrios*, Guabal and Villa Nueva, and in the rural area of Candelaria. The objective was to treat in the community and thus avoid unnecessary hospitalization. The main task of the resident psychiatrist was to spend one day a week in each clinic, training the non-psychiatric physicians and senior medical students in psychiatric diagnosis and treatment, as well as running meetings for various community groups and engaging the participation of community leaders. During the first year at the clinic in Guabal, 75 patients were seen, 205 consultations were carried out, 19 classes were held, 10 public lectures for patients were held, and 20 doctors and 10 school teachers were trained in the rudiments of psychiatric diagnosis and treatment. From its inception in August 1967 to June 1969, the clinic in Guabal (population 17,500) provided extra-mural care to 184 adults and 143 children.

This sort of program is feasible in countries, like Colombia, where long-term follow-up of psychiatric patients can be carried out by public health nurses and non-psychiatric personnel in remote provincial clinics. The maintenance of drug therapy for specified periods, and the early identification of recurrent episodes, are essential to its success. In addition, periodic examinations have the added features of reducing unnecessary referrals to overcrowded central facilities, and facilitating the combined medical and psychiatric management of patients who are suffering from both physical and emotional illnesses. With such a scheme, it is possible to identify problem families, with various physical and mental disorders, who can be treated by a team, thus avoiding the fragmentation of services and preventing the accumulation of large cohorts of custodial cases.

Multiplication of Manpower

Because of the frequent lack of educational facilities, there are often few trained technicians and teachers to assist in developing the necessary personnel. Occasionally, one will find lectures and courses in health education for nurses and other ancillary personnel; developing countries that were once colonies often have a cadre of expatriate physicians staffing the general medical hospital or running private clinics. But nurses, technicians and other personnel are usually in short supply, and the number of interns and residents is negligible.

Educational programs in the developing countries also suffer from lack of funds, low priorities, inadequate facilities and limited training personnel. While exchange programs are not difficult to establish, they should take place in countries at similar stages of development, so that training can occur in a context that is as close as possible to the level of subsequent practice. Psychiatrists trained in European or American centers are over-qualified for the problems they will have to handle. Skilled in the methods of psychotherapy, but not in adjusting to the needs of the population in the developing country, they often create tension, resentment, or apathy. This problem can be avoided by limiting the amount of training people might have had in Europe or the United States, and instead emphasizing advanced training in social and community psychiatry. It makes more sense, for example, for an individual from Brazil to train at the Universidad del Valle, which is actively involved in community psychiatry, than in the United States. Medical education programs must be integrated with the specific problems of the country, preferably through a central planning or government agency, so as to avoid the overtraining of some specialists and the inadequate training of others.

It may even be desirable to develop an educational system in which all health services personnel are able to attend the same faculty. This would increase the quality of education for the paramedical personnel, reduce duplicated educational efforts, foster an integrated approach to treatment, and establish working relationships early in professional careers. The present type of autonomous training center, which is unrelated to the ongoing service needs of a country, tends to isolate the various professionals and to foster stratification among groups. It also creates political conflict and reduces the effective integration of health services.

New communication techniques can also counteract manpower shortage. A television referral hospital program could link regional hospitals to rural health centers by way of closed-circuit microwave television, thus bringing medical and psychiatric care to areas that would not otherwise be served. Such a system would maximize the use of existing facilities and personnel, and encourage the integration of medicine and social welfare programs. It is quickly rendered operational and relatively cheap, and it would also serve as an emergency communication network and a public educational medium. Patients can be examined in front of the television camera, in accordance with an established procedure. The doctor or nurse at the monitor end in the regional hospital can observe and direct this examination by two-way voice channel. In this way, the patient can receive minor medical treatment or advice, without having to travel long distances to the urban centers. Serious cases, on the other hand, can be transferred to the regional hospital via helicopters, airplanes, or ambulances. This system can bring medical attention to areas not yet served, and relieve regional hospitals of the flow of thousands of minor cases each year, thus freeing bed space for the more serious cases. It can be installed at a cost of $1,000 per rural health station; cables can be installed at a cost of $2,000 per mile. Such a system can serve the medical needs of many more people than is possible in a single regional hospital, and it is a far more effective way to spend a given sum of money allocated for medical programs.

In such settings, the psychiatrist may also be able to capitalize on the native healer's special access to certain population sub-groups for the collection of survey and follow-up data. To the extent that native or folk healers in these more advanced societies often operate in clandestine ways, it may be necessary first to educate the country's physicians and psychiatrists to the view that native practices can have pragmatic and instrumental value, in addition to the by now usually recognized ethnographic folkloric value.

Where development has advanced to a stage of self-sufficient autonomy and economic viability (e.g. Mexico, Brazil, Argentina, Venezuela, and Colombia), it is also feasible to consider programs for the paraprofessional training of native healers. This can have particular value in reducing manpower shortages. Such educational programs make little sense in the small disintegrating regions of Latin America, or in the tribal pre-literate areas of Africa, whose very existence and evolution remains uncertain. In these poorly developed countries, it is more advisable to deal with native healers without trying to change them; in the more advanced countries with some resources, however, it may make more sense to try to incorporate native healers into some parallel or collaborative system of treatment.

CONCLUSIONS

The introduction of psychiatric programs into the developing countries is a complex and difficult phenomenon, as this chapter has emphasized. Unlike medical programs, which are often accepted because of the high visibility of both problems and results, psychiatry deals in a borderline area, in which the problems as well as the solutions are intangible and unfamiliar. This makes it much more difficult for such programs to be accepted, since it is hard to justify the need in terms of hard facts of mortality and morbidity. Of equal significance is the necessity to adapt newly introduced programs to the stage of development of the society, both in terms of resistance to psychiatric programs in general, and in terms of available resources and personnel. It is not possible to introduce the same kind of program in each situation. One can, however, follow certain general guidelines, as suggested in this chapter. Particular effort should be made to avoid trying to introduce a program that is in advance of the capacity of the country to accommodate it.

It is also important to recognize the impact on other areas of society that may be affected by the introduction of any type of psychiatric program. In particular, competition for scarce resources, and an unwillingness to coordinate with other agencies and activities, can generate much interdepartmental friction and embroil important social measures in political turmoil. Sensitivity to existing rivalries, as well as an awareness of the legitimate boundaries of responsibility, pertain not only to the development of a program within the country, but to the first contacts made by the consulting agency. There is much that the developed nations can contribute to the developing nations; the task remains, however, to determine the best ways of helping, so as to avoid failure, as a result of overly ambitious projects, or lack of communication, and inattention to the complex needs of those being helped.

The issues considered in this book must be understood by those who are involved in planning to introduce change. We have seen how a given culture's concept of health may significantly influence its acceptance of new programs. Ill health may be attributed to supernatural forces, taboo violations, poor diet, or failure to follow the group's customs. It may be fatalistically accepted as part of life and therefore as not requiring medical attention. The modern use of complex scientific methods and equipment by experts in hospitals, while it is highly valued in Western culture, may in other cultures be viewed as evidence of the group's rejection of the patient and the physician's disregard for the strategic role of the extended family. We must understand the standards by which a culture judges well-being and illness, since the patient may or may not cooperate, depending on these standards. Treatment goals must be formulated in line with cultural expectations. The incentive to recover, for example, and to return home, may not be very great for those who must return to abject poverty, slums and special reservations.

In sum, certain imperatives ought to be followed in establishing collaborative programs in developing countries:

a. Avoid concepts of treatment of research that have little immediate application to the overriding service needs.

b. Fit the program into existing practices. This will often lead to the development of new ways for delivering services, which may be suitable for use in other countries.

c. Insist on active commitment by the host country, with the ultimate goal of assumption of complete responsibility for the project. Unless this is done, there is always a high risk that the project will cease, once international support is stopped. Participation by the host country can include matching funds, commitment of space and personnel, and assistance in fund-raising.

d. Establish priorities that are relevant to the needs of the developing country. Costly epidemiological studies seeking to establish the etiology of psychiatric disorders deserve a lower priority than studies of the factors pertaining to the delivery of services.

e. Recognize the potential psychotherapeutic value of non-medical native beliefs and practices, and seek to avoid the usual error of trying to suppress such native treatment systems. Instead, explore ways in which their beneficial elements may be incorporated into comprehensive modern treatment programs.

NOTES

Chapter 1   Notes to Pages 1–15

1. Pavlov, Ivan P., *Lectures on Conditioned Reflexes*. Translated and edited by W. H. Gantt. New York: International Publishing, 1941. 2 Volumes.
2. Montagu, Ashley, "Culture and Mental Illness," *American Journal of P.ychiatry* 118:15–23, 1961.
3. Murphy, Jane M. and Leighton, A. H. eds., *Approaches to Cross Cultural Psychiatry*. New York: Cornell University Press, 1965.
4. Hughes, Charles C., "Psychocultural Dimensions of Social Change" in Finney, Joseph C. (ed.), *Culture, Change, Mental Health and Poverty*. Lexington: University of Kentucky Press, 1969, pp. 173–202.
5. Lambo, T. A., "Malignant Anxiety: A Syndrome Associated With Criminal Conduct in Africans," *Journal of Mental Science* 108:256–264, 1964.
6. Amara, I. B. "Psychiatric Problems—Observations In Sierra Leone and Liberia," Paper presented at Roundtable Conference On Psychiatry in Underdeveloped Countries, held in New York in 1967, Eastern Regional Meeting, American Psychiatric Association.
7. Reusch, J., Jacobson, A., and Loeb, M. B., "Acculturation and Illness," *Psychological Monographs* 62:5:1–40, 1948.
8. Mead, Margaret, "The Implications of Culture Change for Personality Development," *American Journal of Orthopsychiatry* 17:663–645, 1947.
9. Seguin, Alberto, "Migration and Psychosomatic Disadaption," *Psychosomatic Medicine* 18:404–409, 1956.
10. Tyhurst, Libuse, "Psychosomatic and Allied Disorders" in Murphy, H. B. M. (ed.), *Flight and Resettlement*. Paris, UNESCO, 1955, pp. 202–213.
11. Kiev, A., *Curanderismo*. New York: Free Press, 1968.

Chapter 2   Notes to Pages 16–19

1. Benedict, Ruth, *Patterns of Culture*. Boston: Houghton Mifflin, 1934.
2. Benedict, Ruth, "Configurations of Culture in North America," *American Anthropologist* 34:1–27, 1932.

3. Braum, Joseph, "Spirits, Mediums, and Believers in Contemporary Puerto Rico," *Transactions*. New York Academy of Sciences, Ser. 2, Vol. 20: 340–347, February 1958.

4. Devereux, G., "Cultural Thought Models in Primitive and Modern Psychiatric Theories," *Psychiatry* 21:359–374, 1958.

5. Devereux, G., "Primitive Psychiatric Diagnosis," in Galdston, I. (ed.), *Man's Image in Anthropology and Medicine*. New York: International Universities Press, 1963.

6. Linton, R., *Culture and Mental Disorders*, Devereux, G. (ed.). Springfield, Ill: Thomas, 1956.

7. Kraepelin, E., *Psychiatrie*, 1:8th Ed., 1909. Leipzig: Barth.

8. Kaplan, Bert and Johnson, Dale, "The Social Meaning of Navaho Psychopathology and Psychotherapy" in Kiev, A. (ed.), *Magic, Faith, and Healing: Studies in Primitive Psychiatry Today*. New York: Free Press, 1964, pp. 203–229.

9. Carstairs, G. M.. "Cultural Differences in Sexual Deviation," in Rosen, Ismond (ed.), *The Pathology and Treatment of Sexual Deviation*, London: Oxford University Press, 1964, pp. 419–34.

10. Bohannon, Paul (ed.), *African Homicide and Suicide*. Princeton: Princeton University Press, 1960.

11. Sechrest, Lee, "Philippine Culture, Stress and Psychopathology" in Caudill, William and Lin, Tsung-Yi (eds.), *Mental Health Research in Asia and the Pacific*. Honolulu: East-West Center Press, 1969, pp. 306–334.

12. Kinzel, August, "Toward an Understanding of Violence," *Attitude* 1: No. 1 13–18, November/December 1969.

13. Driver, Edwin D., "Interaction and Criminal Homicide in India," *Social Forces* 46:2, 154–58, 1961.

14. Wolfgang, Marvin, E. and Ferracuti, Franco, *Subculture of Violence: An Interpretative Analysis of Homicide*. Philadelphia, Penna. and Rome, Italy, Typescript 14 pp.

15. Sasaki, Yuji, "Psychiatric Study of the Shaman in Japan" in Caudill, William and Lin, Tsung-Yi (eds.), *Mental Health Research in Asia and the Pacific*. Honolulu: East-West Center Press, 1969, pp. 223–241.

16. Sargant, William. Introductory remarks to *Trance and Possession States*, 1968, R. M. Bucke Memorial Society.

17. Douyon, E., "L'Examen Au Rorschach Des Vaudouisants Haitens." *Trance and Possession States*, Proceedings of the Second Annual Conference of R. M. Bucke Memorial Society, edited by Raymond Prince.

18. Wallace, Anthony, "Mazeway Disintegration: The Individual's Perception of Socio-Cultural Disorganization" in Demerath, Nicholas J. and Wallace, Anthony (eds.), *Human Organization* 16: No. 2, 23–27, Summer, 1957.

19. Laubscher, B., *Sex, Custom and Psychopathology*. London: Routledge and Kegan Paul, 1937.

20. Sargant, William, *Battle for the Mind: A Physiology of Conversion and Brainwashing*. London: William Heinemann, Ltd., 1957.

21. Bleuler, E., *Textbook of Psychiatry*. London: Macmillan, 1924.

22. James, W., *The Varieties of Religious Experience*. New York: Longmans Green, 1902.

23. Anderson, E. W., "A Clinical Study of States of 'Ecstasy' Occurring in Affective Disorders," *Journal of Neurological Psychiatry*, 1:80, 1938.

24. Janet, P., *De L'Angoisse a L'Extase*. Paris: Librairie Felix Alcan, 1928.

25. Kiev, A., "SUBUD and Mental Illness," *American Journal of Psychotherapy*, Vol. XVIII: No. 1, January, 1964, pp. 66–78.

26. Leiris, Michel, "La Possession Par Le Zar Chez Les Chretiens Du Nord De L'Ethiopie," *Mental Disorders and Mental Health in Africa South of the Sahara, Bukavu.* Paris: C.S.A. Publication No. 35:168–175, 1958.

27. Merton, Thomas, Comments on Dr. Prince's and Dr. Savage's Paper on Mystical States and Regression. *The A. M. Bucke Memorial Society Newsletter* Vol. I: No. 1, 4, January 1966.

28. Lee, S. G., "Social Influences in Zulu Dreaming," *The Journal of Social Psychology* 47:265–283, 1958.

29. Stewart, Kilton, *A Cross-Cultural Study of Dreams.* Original Article. An extended version of this paper was to be published in *Mental Hygiene.*

30. Devereux, George, Mohave Culture and Personality. Paper read before the Annual Meeting of the American Anthropological Association, New York City, December 1938.

31. Devereux, G., "Dream Learning and Individual Ritual Differences in Mohave Shamanism," *American Anthropologist* 59:1036–1045, 1957.

32. Wallace, Anthony, "Dreams and the Wishes of the Soul: A type of Psychoanalytic Theory Among the Seventeenth Century Iroquois," *American Anthropologist* 60:234–248, 1958.

Chapter 3

1. Kraepelin, E., *Psychiatrie*, I: 8th Ed., 1909. Leipzig: Barth.

2. Bleuler, E., *Dementia Praecox or The Group of Schizophrenias.* New York: International Universities Press, 1950.

3. Van Loon, H. G., "Protopathic Instinctive Phenomena in Normal and Pathological Malay Life," *British Journal of Medical Psychology* 9:264–276, 1928; Cooper, J. M., "Mental Disease Situations in Certain Cultures," *Journal of Abnormal and Social Psychology* 29:10–17, 1934; Hallowell, A. I., "Culture and Mental Disorder," *Journal of Abnormal and Social Psychology* 29:1–9, 1934; Landes, Ruth, "The Abnormal Among the Ojibwa Indians," *Journal of Abnormal and Social Psychology* 33:14–33, 1938; Yap, P. M., "The Latah Reaction," *Journal of Mental Science* 98:515–564, 1952 and Yap, "Mental Diseases Peculiar to Certain Cultures: A Survey of Comparative Psychiatry," *Journal of Mental Science* 97:313–327, 1951.

4. Tooth, G., *Studies in Mental Illness in the Gold Coast,* Colonial Research Publication No. 6. London: H. M. Stationary Office, 1950.

5. Carothers, J. C., "The African Mind in Health and Disease, A Study in Ethnopsychiatry," *WHO,* Monograph Series, Geneva, 1953.

6. Seligman, C. G., *British Journal of Medical Psychology* 9:187–202, 1929.

7. Berne, E., *American Journal of Psychiatry* 106:367–383, 1950.

8. Carothers, J. C., "The African Mind in Health and Disease, A Study in Ethnopsychiatry," *WHO,* Monograph Series, Geneva, 1953.

9. Spiro, M. E., *American Anthropologist* 54:497–503, 1952.

10. Slotkin, J. S., *The Peyote Religion: A Study in Indian-White Relations.* New York: The Free Press of Glencoe, 1956.

11. Opler, M. K., *Culture, Psychiatry and Human Values—The Methods and Values of a Social Psychiatry.* Springfield, Ill.: C. C. Thomas, 1956.

12. Carothers, J. C., "The African Mind in Health and Disease, A Study in Ethnopsychiatry," *WHO,* Monograph Series, Geneva, 1953.

13. Tooth, G., *Studies in Mental Illness in the Gold Coast,* Colonial Research Publication No. 6. London: H. M. Stationary Office, 1950.

14. Laubscher, B., *Sex, Custom and Psychopathology*. London: Routledge and Kegan Paul, 1937.

15. Tooth, G., *Studies in Mental Illness in the Gold Coast,* Colonial Research Publication No. 6. London: H. M. Stationary Office, 1950.

16. Stainbrook, E., "Some Characteristics of the Psychopathology of Schizophrenic Behavior in Bahian Society," *American Journal of Psychiatry* 109:330–335, 1952.

17. Lambo, T. A., *Journal of Mental Science* 101:239, 1955.

18. Ibid. "Role of Cultural Factors in Paranoid Psychosis among Yoruba Tribe."

19. Carothers, J. C., "The African Mind in Health and Disease, A Study in Ethnopsychiatry," *WHO,* Monograph Series, Geneva, 1953.

20. Enright, J. B. and Jaekle, W. B., "Psychiatric Symptoms and Diagnosis in Two Subcultures," *International Journal of Social Psychiatry* 9:12–17, 1963.

21. Meadow, Arnold and Stoker, David, "Symptomatic Behavior of Hospitalized Patients. A Study of Mexican-American and Anglo-American Patients," *Archives General Psychiatry* 12:267–277, March 1965.

22. Lin, H. and Lin, Tsung-Yi, "Mental Illness Among Formosan Aborigines as Compared with the Chinese in Taiwan," *Journal of Mental Science* 108:134–146, 1962.

23. Carothers: see ref. 19.

24. Amara, I. B., "Psychiatric Problems—Observations in Sierra Leon and Liberia," Paper presented at Roundtable Conference on Psychiatry in Underdeveloped Countries, held in New York in 1967, Eastern Regional Meeting, American Psychiatric Association.

25. Tooth, G. *Studies in Mental Illness in the Gold Coast,* Colonial Research Publication No. 6. London: H. M. Stationary Office, 1950.

26. Collis, Robert, "Physical Health and Psychiatric Disorder in Nigeria," *Transactions of the American Philosophical Study,* New Series Vol. 56: Part 4, 1–45, May 1966.

27. Lambo, T. A., "A Form of Social Psychiatry in Africa," *World Mental Health* 13: No. 4, 190, 1961.

28. Vahia, N. S., Cultural Differences in the Clinical Picture of Schizophrenia and Hysteria in India and the United States. Presented at the Postgraduate Center for Psychotherapy. New York City, Nov. 27, 1962, p. 16.

29. Kiev, A., *Curanderismo.* New York: Free Press, 1968.

30. Wittkower, E. C., "Cultural Psychiatric Research in Asia" in Caudill, William and Lin, Tsung-Yi (eds.), *Mental Health Research in Asia and the Pacific.* Honolulu: East-West Center Press, 1969, pp. 433–447.

31. Lenz, H., *Vergleichende Psychiatrie. Eine Studie Uber Die Beziehung Von Kultur, Soziologie Und Psychopathologie.* Wilhelm Maudrich Verlag, Vienna, 1964, p. 175.

32. Vahia: see ref. 28.

33. Parker, S., "Eskimo Psychopathology in the Context of Eskimo Personality and Culture," *American Anthropologist* 64:76–96, 1962.

34. Yap, P. M. "Mental Diseases Peculiar to Certain Cultures: A Survey of Comparative Psychiatry," *Journal of Mental Science* 97:313–327, 1951.

35. Kagwa, Benjamin H. "The Problem of Mass Hysteria in East Africa," *East African Medical Journal* 41: No. 12 December 1964.

36. Parker, S., "The Wittiko Psychosis in the Context of Ojibwa Personality and Culture," *American Anthropologist* 62:603–623, 1960.

37. Murphy, H. B. M., Wittkower, E. D., Chance, N. A. et al., "Cross-Cultural Inquiry into the Symptomatology of Depression: A Preliminary Report and Critical Evaluations," *International Journal of Psychiatry* 3:1–22, 1967.

38. Lambo, T. A., "The Concept and Practice of Mental Health in African Cultures," *East African Medical Journal* 37:464–472, 1960.

39. Asuni, T., "Suicide in Western Nigeria," *British Medical Journal* vol. ii:1091–1097, Oct. 27, 1962.

40. Baasher. T. A., "Observations from the Sudan" in Lambo, T. A. (ed.), *First Pan-African Psychiatric Conference Abeokuta Nigeria.* Conference Report Ibadan: Government Printer, Nov. 1961, pp. 238–240.

41. Amara, I. B. "Psychiatric Problems—Observations in Sierra Leone and Liberia," Paper presented at Roundtable Conference On Psychiatry in Under-developed Countries, held in New York in 1967, Eastern Regional Meeting, American Psychiatric Association.

42. Benedict, P. and Jacks, I., *Mental Illness in Primitive Societies* 17:377–389, 1954.

Chapter 4

1. Yap, P. M., "Suk-Yeon or Koro—A Culture-Bound Depersonalization Syndrome," *The Bulletin of the Hong Kong Chinese Medical Association* 16:1, 31–47, 1964.

2. Rin, Hsien, "A Study of the Aetiology of Koro in Respect to the Chinese Concept of Illness," *The International Journal of Social Psychiatry* XI: No. 1, 1965.

3. Carstairs, G. M., "Hinjra and Jiryan," *British Journal of Medical Psychology* 29:128, 1956.

4. Rubel, A. J., "The Epidemiology of a Folk Illness Susto in Hispanic America," *Ethnology* 3:268–283, 1964.

5. Prince, R., "The Yoruba Image of the Witch," *Journal of Mental Science* 107:795–805, 1961.

6. Yap, P. M., "Mental Illness Peculiar to Certain Cultures: A Survey of Comparative Psychiatry," *Journal of Mental Science* 97:313–327, 1951.

7. Doi, Takeo L., "Morita Therapy and Psychoanalysis," *Psychologia*, Vol. V, No. 3, September 1962.

8. Yap, P. M., "Mental Illness Peculiar to Certain Cultures: A Survey of Comparative Psychiatry, *Journal of Mental Science* 97:313–327, 1951.

9. Ibid.

10. Uchimura, Y., "Imu, eine psychoreacktive Erscheinung der Ainu-Frauen," *Nervenarzt* 27:535–540, 1956.

11. Yap, "Mental Illness," 97:313–327.

12. Hunter, M., *Canadian Wilds.* St. Louis: A. R. Harding, 1907.

13. Castellani, A. and Chalmers, A. J., *Manual of Tropical Medicine.* London: Bailliere, 1919.

14. Rubel, A. J., "Concept of Disease in Mexican-American Culture," *American Anthropologist* 62:795–814, October 1960.

15. Sauna, Victor, E., Healing Practices and Prevention of Illness Among the Egyptian Fellahin. New York: Typescript 18 pp.

16. Hes, Jozef, "The Changing Social Role of the Yemenite Mori," in Kiev, A. (ed.), *Magic, Faith and Healing: Studies in Primitive Psychiatry Today.* New York: Free Press, 1964, pp. 364–383.

17. Rubel, Arthur, J., "The Epidemiology of a Folk Illness: Susto in Hispanic America," *Ethnology* Vol. III: No. 3, 268–283, July 1964.

18. Prince, R., "Patterns of Curse," *Canadian Psychiatric Association Journal* Vol. 5: No. 2, 68, April 1960; and Prince, "Curse, Invocation and Mental Health," *Canadian Psychiatric Association Journal* Vol. 5: No. 2, 71, April 1960.

19. Cannon, W. B., "Voodoo Death," *Psychosomatic Medicine* 19:182–90, 1957.

20. Richter, C. P., "On the Phenomenon of Sudden Death in Animals and Man," *Psychosomatic Medicine* 19:191–8, 1957.

21. Prince, "The Yoruba Image of the Witch," 107:795–805.

22. Collomb, H., Boufées Delirantes en Psychiatrie Africaine, Mimeograph, 1965, 87 pp.

23. Ibid.

24. Devereux, G., "Mohave Ethnopsychiatry and Suicide: The Psychiatric Knowledge and the Psychic Disturbance of an Indian Tribe," Bureau of American Ethnology No. 175, Washington, D.C.; The Smithsonian Institution, 1961.

25. Parker, S., "The Wittiko Psychosis in the Context of Ojiwba Personality and Culture," *American Anthropologist* 62:603–623, 1960.

26. Lambo, T. A., "Malignant Anxiety," *The Journal of Mental Science* 108:454, 256–264, May 1962.

27. Yap, P. M., "The Culture-Bound Reactive Syndromes" in Caudill, William and Lin, Tsung-Yi (eds.), *Mental Health Research in Asia and the Pacific.* Honolulu: East-West Center Press, 1969, pp. 33–53.

28. Krapelin, E., *Psychiatrie*, Vol. 1, 8th Ed., 1909. Leipzig: Barth.

29. Van Loon, F. H. G., "Amok and Latah," *Journal of Abnormal and Social Psychology* 21:434–444, 1927.

30. Carothers, J. C., "The African Mind in Health and Disease: A Study in Ethnopsychiatry," *WHO,* Monograph Series, Geneva, 1953.

31. Van Loon, "Amok and Latah," 21:434–444.

32. Van Wuefften-Palthe, P. M., "Psychiatry and Neurology in the Tropics," in de Laugan, C. D. and Lichtenstein, A., *A Clinical Textbook of Tropical Medicine.* Batavia G. Kloff and Co., 1936.

33. Pfeiffer, Wolfgang, Sichen Volksstammen (Meditation and Trance States in Indonesian Tribes). Erlangen, Germany. Typescript 31 pp.

34. Lin, Tsung-Yi, "A Study of the Incidence of Mental Disorder in Chinese and Other Cultures," *Psychiatry* 16:313–336, November 1953.

35. Gussow, Zachary, "A Preliminary Report of Kayak-Angst Among the Eskimo of West Greenland: A Study in Sensory Deprivation," *The International Journal of Social Psychiatry* Vol. IX: No. 1, 1963.

36. Sanseigne, A. and Desrosiers, M., "Evaluation of Psychopharmaceuticals in an Undeveloped Country" in Kline, N. S. (ed.), Psychiatry in the Underdeveloped Countries: Report of a Roundtable Meeting. A.P.A. Annual Meeting Atlantic City, May 12, 1960, pp. 52–58.

37. Kiev, Ari, "Spirit Possession in Haiti," *American Journal of Psychiatry* 118:133–8, 1961 and Kiev, "Folk Psychiatry in Haiti," *Journal of Nervous and Mental Disease* 132:260–5, 1961.

38. Devereux, G., "Normal and Abnormal: The Key Problem of Psychiatric Anthropology," in Casagrande, J. B. and Gladwin, T. (eds.), *Some Uses of Anthropology: Theoretical and Applied.* Washington: Anthropological Society of Washington, 1956 pp. 3–48.

Chapter 5

1. Tylor, E. B., "The Origins of Culture," *Primitive Culture* Vol. I. New York: Harper and Bros., 1958.

2. Clements, F. E., "Primitive Concepts of Disease," *University of California Publications in American Archaeology and Ethnology* 32:185–252, 1932.

3. Frazer, James G., *The Golden Bough: A Study in Magic and Religion.* New York: The Macmillan Co., 1922.

4. Burstein, S. R., "Public Health and Prevention of Disease in Primitive Communities," *The Advancement of Science* 9:5, 1952.

5. Sigerist, H. E., *A History of Medicine (Vol. I).* New York: Oxford University Press, 1951, p. 148.

6. Erasmus, C. J., "Changing Folk Beliefs and the Relativity of Empirical Knowledge," *Southwest Journal of Anthropology* 8:411–428, 1952.

7. Abraham, R. G., African Concepts of Health and Disease. Paper presented at the Institute of Social Research in December 1959—(for a one-day symposium on Health and Disease Attitudes).

8. Gerlack, L. P., Some Basic Digo Conceptions of Health and Disease. Paper presented at the Institute of Social Research in December 1959 (for a one-day symposium on Health and Disease Attitudes).

9. Ackerknecht, E. H., "Medical Practices" in Steward, J. (ed.), *Handbook of South American Indians* Vol. 5, Bureau of American Ethnology, Bulletin 143, 1949.

10. Ackerknecht, E. H., "Problems of Primitive Medicine," *Bulletin of the History of Medicine:* 11, 1952.

11. Harley, G. W., *Native African Medicine.* Cambridge: Harvard University Press, 1941.

12. Ibid., pp. 73–74.

13. Gillin, J., "Moche: A Peruvian Coastal Community." Washington, D.C.: Smithsonian Institution, Institute of Social Anthropology, Publication No. 3, 1945.

14. Polgar, Steven, "Evolution and the Thermodynamic Imperative," *Human Biology* 33:99–109, May 1961.

15. Leighton, A. H. and Leighton, D. C., *The Navaho Door.* Cambridge: Harvard University Press, 1944, p. 63.

16. Marriott, McKim, "Western Medicine in a Village of Northern India" in Paul, Benjamin (ed.), *Health, Culture and Community.* New York: Russell Sage Foundation, 1955.

17. Kiev, A., "Ritual Goat Sacrifice," *The American Imago,* Vol. 19 No. 4, 1962.

18. Sasaki, Yuji, "Psychiatric Study of the Shaman in Japan," in Caudill, William and Lin, Tsung-Yi (eds.), *Mental Health Research in Asia and the Pacific.* Honolulu: East-West Center Press, 1969, pp. 223–241.

19. Marriott: see ref. 16.

20. Clements, F. E., "Primitive Concepts of Disease," *University of California Publications in American Archaeology and Ethnology* 32:185–252, 1932.

21. Kiev: see ref. 17.

22. Field, M. J., *Search for Security: An Ethnopsychiatric Study of Rural Ghana.* Evanston, Ill.: Northwestern University Press, 1960.

23. Evans-Pritchard, E. E., *Witchcraft, Oracles and Magic Among the Azande.* London: Oxford University Press, 1937.

24. Prince, Raymond, "The Yoruba Image of the Witch," *Journal of Mental Science* 107:795–805, 1961.

25. Kiev, Ari, "Primitive Therapy: A Cross-Cultural Study of the Relationship Between Child Training and Therapeutic Practices Related to Illness," in Axelrod, Muensterberger and Sidney (eds.), *Psychoanalytic Study of Society* Vol. I: 185–217. New York: International Universities Press, 1961.

26. Kligfeld, B. and Krupp, G. R., "The Bereavement Reaction," *Journal of Religion and Health* 1:222–242, 1962.

27. Nadel, S. F., Social Control and Self Regulation," *Social Forces* Vol. 31: 265–273, 1953.

28. Field, M. J., *Search for Security: An Ethnopsychiatric Study of Rural Ghana.* Evanston, Ill.: Northwestern University Press, 1960.

29. Spiro, Melford E., "The Psychological Function of Witchcraft Belief: The Burmese Case," in Caudill, William and Lin, Tsung-Yi (eds.), *Mental Health Research in Asia and the Pacific.* Honolulu: East-West Center Press, 1969, pp. 245–258.

30. Norbeck, Edward, *Religion in Primitive Society.* New York: Harper and Row, 1961.

31. Rogler, L. H. and Hollingshead, August, B., "The Puerto Rican Spiritualist as Psychiatrist," *American Journal of Sociology* 67:17–21, 1961.

32. Sigerist, Henry E., *A History of Medicine, Vol I: Primitive and Archaic Medicine.* London: Oxford University Press, 1951.

33. Devereux, George, "Cultural Thought Models in Primitive and Modern Psychiatric Theories," *Psychiatry* 21:359–374, 1958.

34. Devereux, George, "Primitive Psychiatric Diagnosis—A General Theory of the Diagnostic Process" in Gadston, I. (ed.), *Man's Image in Medicine and Anthropology.* New York: New York Academy of Medicine and International Universities Press, 1963.

35. Margetts, Edward L., "Traditional Yoruba Healers in Nigeria," *Man* No. 102, 115–118, July–August 1965.

36. Sigerist, Henry E., "The Story of Tarantism" in Schullian, Dorothy and Schoen, Max (eds.), *Music and Medicine.* New York: Henry Schuman, 1948, pp. 96–116.

37. Kaplan, Bert and Johnson, Dale, "The Social Meaning of Navaho Psychopathology and Psychotherapy" in Kiev, A. (ed.), *Magic, Faith, and Healing: Studies in Primitive Psychiatry Today.* New York: Free Press, 1964.

38. Yonebayashi, T., "Kitsunetsuki (Possession by Foxes)." *Transcultural Review Newsletter,* October 1964.

39. Rubel, A. J., "Concept of Disease in Mexican-American Culture," *American Anthropologist* 62:62, Oct. 1960.

40. Senanayake, I. A., Exorcism: The Art of Curing by Suggestion in Ceylon. Unpublished manuscript presented at the Third World Congress of Psychiatry, Montreal, 1961.

41. Lewin, Louis, *Phantastica, Narcotic and Stimulating Drugs.* London: Routledge and Kegan Paul, 1964.

42. Efron, Daniel, H., Holmstedt, Bo, and Kline, Nathan, S. (eds.), "Ethnopharmacologic Search for Psychoactive Drugs," *Public Health Service Publication No. 1645,* 1967.

43. Burton-Bradley, B. C., "Some Implications of Betal Chewing," *Papua and New Guinea Transcultural Psychiatry Medical Journal of Australia* Vol. 2:744–746, 1966.

44. Sahagun, Bernadino, "Historia General de las Coas de Nueva Espana

Editorial Nueva Espana," S. A. Mexico 1:472–77. Cited in Laurette Sejourne, *Burning Water, Thought and Religion in Ancient Mexico*. New York: The Vanguard Press, 1956.

45. Lewin, Louis, *Phantastica, Narcotic and Stimulating Drugs*. London: Routledge and Kegan Paul, 1964, p. 100.

46. Boyer, Bryce L., "Psychological Problems of a Group of Apaches. Alcoholic Hallucinosis and Latent Homosexuality Among Typical Men," *Psychoanalytic Study of Sociology* Vol III:203–277.

47. Kaplan and Johnson: see ref. 37.

48. Akstein, David, Les Trances Rituelles Brasilienness et Les Perspectives de Leur Application à La Psychiatrie et à La Médécine Psychosomatique. Rio de Janeiro, Brazil. Typescript 15 pp.

49. Prince, R., "Indigenous Yoruba Psychiatry," in Kiev, A. (ed.), *Magic, Faith, and Healing: Studies in Primitive Psychiatry Today*. New York: Free Press, 1964, pp. 84–119.

50. Beier, U., "Gelede Masks, Odu, A Journal of Yoruba and Related Studies," *Ministry of Education* No. 6, 5–18, 1958.

51. Messing, S., "Group Therapy and Social Status in the Zar Cult of Ethiopia," *American Anthropology* 60:1120–1126, 1958.

52. Fox, J. Robin, "Witchcraft and Clanship in Cochiti Therapy," in Kiev, A. (ed.), *Magic, Faith, and Healing: Studies in Primitive Psychiatry Today*. New York: Free Press, 1964, pp. 174–199.

53. Wallace, A. F. C., "Dream Wishes of the Soul: A Type of Psychoanalytic Theory Among the Seventeenth Century Iroquois," *American Anthropologist* 60:235–242, 1958.

54. Prince, Raymond, "Indigenous Yoruba Psychiatry," in Kiev, A. (ed.), *Magic, Faith, and Healing: Studies in Primitive Psychiatry Today*. New York: Free Press, 1964, p. 108.

55. Leighton, A. H. and Leighton, D. C., "Elements of Psychotherapy in Navaho Religion," *Psychiatry* 4, 1941.

56. Kiev: see ref. 17.

57. Tylor, Edward B., *Religion in Primitive Culture*. New York: Harpers, 1958.

58. Frazer, James G., *The Golden Bough*. New York: The Macmillan Co., 1948, p. 576.

59. Freud, Sigmund, *Totem and Taboo* in *The Basic Writings of Sigmund Freud*, edited by A. A. Brill. New York: The Modern Library, 1938, p. 133.

60. Money-Kyrle, R., *The Meaning of Sacrifice*. London: Hogarth Press, 1929, p. 193.

61. Metraux, Alfred, *Voodoo*. New York: Alfred Knopf, 1959.

62. Dawson, John, "Urbanization and Mental Health in a West African Community," *Magic, Faith, and Healing: Studies in Primitive Psychiatry Today*, edited by Ari Kiev, New York, Free Press, 1964.

63. Calley, Malcolm, "Pentecostal Sects Among West Indian Migrants," *Race* 3:55–64, 1962.

64. Cerny, Jan, "Psychiatry in China," *Czeskoslovenska Psychiatrie* 59:4, 273–82, 1963.

65. Kline, N. S., "Psychiatry in Kuwait," *British Journal of Psychiatry* 109:766–774, 1963.

66. Hallaji, Ja'Fai, "Hypnotherapeutic Techniques in a Central Asian Community," *International Journal of Clinical and Experimental Hypnosis* 10:271–274, 1962.

67. Ames, Michael, M., "Buddha and the Dancing Goblins: A Theory of Magic and Religion," *American Anthropologist* Vol 66: No 1, February, 1964.

68. Gaitonde, M. R., "Hindu Philosophy and Analytic Psychotherapy," *Comprehensive Psychiatry* Vol II: 299–303, 1961.

69. Doi, Takeo L., "Morita Therapy and Psychoanalysis," *Psychologia,* Vol. V, No. 3, September, 1962.

70. Freud, S., "On Psychotherapy," *Collected Papers* Vol I. New York, London, Vienna: International Psychoanalytic Press, 1924, p. 250.

71. Fenichel, Otto, "Brief Psychotherapy" in Fenichel, *Collected Papers,* Second Series. London: Routledge and Kegan Paul, Ltd., 1955, pp. 243–59.

72. Devereux, G., "Normal and Abnormal: The Key Problem of Psychiatric Anthropology" in Casagrande, J. B. and Gladwin, T. (eds.), *Some Uses of Anthropology: Theoretical and Applied.* Washington: Anthropological Society of Washington, 1956, pp. 23–48.

73. Frank, J., *Persuasion and Healing: A Comprehensive Study of Psychotherapy.* Baltimore: Johns Hopkins University Press, 1961.

74. Sargant, William, *Battle for the Mind: A Physiology of Conversion and Brainwashing.* London: William Heinemann, 1957.

75. Frank: see ref. 73.

76. Kiev, A., "SUBUD and Mental Illness," *American Journal of Psychotherapy,* 18: No. 1, January 1964, pp. 66–78.

77. La Barre, W., *They Shall Take Up Serpents.* Minneapolis: University of Minnesota Press, 1962.

Chapter 6

1. Esquirol, J. E. D., "Remarques Sur la Statistique des Aliens et Sur le Rapport du Nombre d'Aliens à la Population. Analyse de la Statistique des Aliens de la Norvège," in *Ann. D'Hyg. Publ. et De Med. Leg.* 4:332–359, 1830.

2. Georget, E. J., "De la Folie. Causes Morales et Physiques de la Folie," in *Dictionnaire De Médicine* Vol. 25. Paris, 1820.

3. Kraeplin, E., *Psychiatrie,* Vol. I, 8th Ed., 1909. Leipzig: Barth.

4. Faris, B. R., "The Nature of Human Nature," New York, 1937, Cited in G. M. Carstairs, "Some Problems of Psychiatry in Patients from Alien Cultures," *The Lancet* 12–17–1220, June 1958.

5. Laubscher, B., *Sex, Custom and Psychopathology.* London: Routledge and Kegan Paul, 1937.

6. Tooth, G., *Studies in Mental Illness in the Gold Coast,* Colonial Research Publication No. 6. London: H. M. Stationary Office, 1950.

7. Carothers, J. C., "A Study of Mental Derangement in Africans, and an Attempt to Explain its Peculiarities, More Especially in Relation to the African Attitude to Life," *Journal of Mental Science* 93:549–97, 1947.

8. Field, M. J., *Search for Security: An Ethnopsychiatric Study of Rural Ghana.* Evanston, Ill: Northwestern University Press, 1960.

9. Boroffka, A. and Marinho, A. A., Psychoneurotic Syndromes in Urbanized Nigerians. Lagos, Nigeria. Typescript 35 pp.

10. Leighton, A., Lambo, T. A., Hughes, C. C., Leighton, D. C., Murphy, J. M. and Macklin, D. G., *Psychiatric Disorder Among the Yoruba.* Ithaca: Cornell University Press, 1963.

11. Uchimura, Y., "The Syndrome of Imu in the Ainu Race," *The American Journal of Psychiatry* 94:1467–1469, 1938.

12. Lin, Tsung-Yi, "A Study of the Incidence of Mental Disorder in Chinese and Other Cultures," *Psychiatry* 16:313–336, November 1953.

13. Faris, R. E. L., and Dunham, H. W., *Mental Disorder in Urban Areas.* Chicago: University of Chicago Press, 1939.

14. Dhunjibhoy, J. E., "A Brief Resume of the Types of Insanity Commonly Met With in India, with a Full Description of Indian Hemp Insanity Peculiar to the Country," *Journal of Mental Science* 76:254–264, 1930.

15. Lopez, C., "Ethnographiche Betrachtungen Uber Schizophrenie Ztscht. Gesamte Neurol.", Psychiat. 142:706–711, 1932. Referred to in Benedict, P. K. and Jacks, I., "Mental Illness in Primitive Societies," *Psychiatry* 17:377–389, 1954.

16. Beaglehole, E., "Culture and Psychosis in New Zealand," *Journal of Polynesian Soc.* 48: 144–155, 1939.

17. Kallman, F. J., *Heredity in Health and Mental Disorder.* New York: W. W. Norton, 1953.

18. Myerson, A., and Boyle, R. D., "Incidence of Manic-Depressive Psychosis in Certain Socially Important Families: Preliminary Report," *American Journal of Psychiatry* 98:11–21, 1941.

19. Carothers, J. C., "The African Mind in Health and Disease, A Study in Ethnopsychiatry," *WHO,* Monograph Series, Geneva, 1953.

20. Mahoney, J. C., and Biddle, C. R., "Psychiatric Observations in Okinawa Shima; Psychology of Okinawans in Psychiatric Hospitals in Military Government," *Psychiatry* 8:391–401, 1945.

21. Gans, A., "Ein Beitrag Zur Raccine Psychiatrie Beobachtugenan Geisteskranken Javanern," *Munchener Medizinische Wochenschrift* 69:1503–1506, October 1922.

22. Murphy, H. B. M., "Culture, Society, and Mental Disorder," *Journal of Abnormal and Social Psychology* 29:1–9, 1934.

23. Seligman, C. G., "Temperament Conflict and Psychosis in a Stone-Age Population," *British Journal of Medical Psychology,* November, 1929, 9:187–202.

24. Hallowell, A. I., "Culture and Mental Disorder," *Journal of Abnormal and Social Psychology* 29:1–9, 1934.

25. Weinberg, A. A., Psychosociology of the Immigrant: An Investigation Into the Problems of Adjustment of Jewish Immigrants into Palestine, Social Studies 2, Jerusalem, The Israel Institute of Folklore and Ethnology, 1949.

26. Murphy, H. B. M., Culture, Society and Mental Disorder in South East Asia. Manuscript, referred to in Reference 22 above.

27. Jaco, E. G., "Mental Health of the Spanish-American in Texas" in Opler, Marvin K. (ed.), *Culture and Mental Health.* New York: Macmillan, 1959.

28. Lamont, A. N., "Affective Types of Psychotic Reactions in Cape Colored Persons," *South African Medical Journal,* 1941, pp. 25–40.

29. Laubscher, B., *Sex, Custom and Psychopathology.* London: Routledge and Kegan Paul, 1937.

30. Carothers, J. C., "A Study of Mental Derangement in Africans, and An Attempt to Explain Its Peculiarities, More Especially in Relation to African Attitude to Life," *Journal of Mental Science* 93:549–97, 1947.

31. Tooth, G., "Studies in Mental Illness in the Gold Coast," *Colonial Research Publication No. 6.* London: His Majesty's Stationary Office, 1950.

32. Beaglehole: see ref. 16.

33. Winston, E., "The Alleged Lack of Mental Disease Among Primitive Groups," *American Anthropologist* 36:234–238, 1934.

34. Joseph, A., and Murray, V. F., *Chamorros and Carolinians of Saipan: Personality Studies.* Cambridge: Harvard University Press, 1951.

35. Dohrenwend, Bruce P., "Social Status and Psychological Disorder: An Issue of Substance and an Issue of Method," *American Sociological Review* 31: 14–34, 1966.

36. Tooth, G., "Studies in Mental Illness in the Gold Coast," *Colonial Research Publication No. 6.* London: H. M. Stationary Office, 1950.

37. Lin, Tsung-Yi, and Standly, C. C., *The Scope of Epidemiology in Psychiatry,* Public Health Papers, World Health Organization, Geneva, 1962.

38. Lin, H., and Lin, Tsung-Yi, "Mental Illness Among Formosan Aborigines as Compared with the Chinese in Taiwan," *Journal of Mental Science* 108: 134–146, 1962.

39. Leighton, A., Lambo, T. A., Hughes, C. C., Leighton, D. C., Murphy, J. M. and Macklin, D. G., *Psychiatric Disorder Among the Yoruba.* Ithaca: Cornell University Press, 1963.

40. Leighton, A. H., *My Name Is Legion: The Stirling County Study of Psychiatric Disorder and Sociocultural Environment.* New York: Basic Books, 1959, p. 425.

41. Bowlby, John, "Maternal Care and Mental Health," Geneva, *WHO,* Monograph Series No. 2, 1951.

42. Pasamanick, B., and Lilienfeld, A. M. "Maternal and Fetal Factors in Development of Epilepsy: Relating to Some Clinical Features of Epilepsy," *Neurology* 5:1259–1264, 1958.

43. Gruenberg, E. M., "Epidemiology of Mental Disorder," *Milbank Memorial Fund Quarterly* 35:107–126, 1927.

44. Murphy, H. B. M., Wittkower, E. D., Chance, N A. et al., "Cross-Cultural Inquiry into the Symptomatology of Depression: A Preliminary Report and Critical Evaluations, *International Journal of Psychiatry* 3:1–22, 1967.

45. Meadow, Arnold and Stoker, David, "Symptomatic Behavior of Hospitalized Patients. A Study of Mexican-American and Anglo-American Patients," *Archives of General Psychiatry* 12:267–277, March 1965.

46. Mead, M. and Bateson, G.: Character Formation in Different Cultures. (6) Films. New York, New York: New York University Film Library, 1951–1953.

47. Chapple, Eliot and Arensberg, C. M., "Measuring Human Relations: An Introduction to the Study of the Interaction of Individuals." *Genetic Psychology Monograph,* Vol. 22, pp. 3–147, 1940.

48. Wallace, Anthony and Ackerman, Robert, "An Interdisciplinary Approach to Mental Disorder Among Polar Eskimos of Northwest Greenland," *Anthropologica* Vol. II, No. 2, 1960.

49. Zubin, J. and Fleiss, J., "On the Methods and Theory of Clustering," *Journal of Multivariable Behavioral Research* Vol. 4, 1969, pp. 235–250.

50. Zubin, Joseph, and Kietzman, Mitchell," A Cross-Cultural Approach to Classification in Schizophrenia and Other Mental Disorders," *Psychopathology of Schizophrenia.* Grune & Stratton, Inc., 1966.

51. Lazarsfeld, Paul and Henry Neil, *Latent Structure Analysis,* Boston, Houghton Mifflin Co., 1968.

52. Zubin, Joseph, and Kietzman, Mitchell, "A Cross-Cultural Approach to Classification in Schizophrenia and Other Mental Disorders," *Psychopathology of Schizophrenia.* Grune & Stratton, Inc., 1966.

53. Burdock, E. I., and Zubin, J., "A Rationale for the Classification of Experimental Techniques in Abnormal Psychology," *Journal of General Psychology* 55:35–49, 1956.

54. Zubin, Joseph, and Kietzman, Mitchell, "A Cross-Cultural Approach to Classification in Schizophrenia and Other Mental Disorders," *Psychopathology of Schizophrenia.* Grune & Stratton, Inc., 1966.

55. Venables, P. H., "Periodicity in Reaction Time," *British Journal of Psychology* 51:37–48, 1960.

56. King, H. E., "Anticipatory Behavior: Temporal Matching by Normal and Psychiatric Subjects," *Journal of Psychology* 53:425–440, 1962.

57. Johnassen, G., Dureman, I. and Salde, H.: Motion Perception and personality. *I Nord. Psykologi* 3:113–120, 1955.

58. Fesanaro, G., "Studi sulla rapidita della percezione visiva. Nota II. Rapidità di percezione visiva di immaginin in movimento in alcune offezion neuropsichiatriche." *Acta. Neurol.* Napoli 7:323–331, 1952.

59. Kaswan, J. W., "Tachistoscopic exposure time and spatial proximity in the organization of visual perception. *Brit. Journal of Psychology.* 49:131–138, 1958.

60. Shagass, C., and Schwartz, M., "Excitability of the cerebral cortex in Psychiatric Disorders" in Roessler, R., and Greenfield, N. S. (eds.), *Physiological Correlates of Psychological Disorder.* Madison, Wisc.: University of Wisc. Press, 1962, pp. 45–60.

61. Zubin, Joseph, and Kietzman, Mitchell, "A Cross-Cultural Approach to Classification in Schizophrenia and Other Mental Disorders," *Psychopathology of Schizophrenia.* Grune & Stratton, Inc., 1966.

Chapter 7

1. McDermott, Walsh, "Medical Institutions and Modification of Disease Patterns," *American Journal of Psychiatry* Vol. 122:1398–1406, June, 1966.

2. Read, Margaret, *Culture, Health and Disease.* London: Tavistock Publications Ltd., 1966, p. 92.

3. Foster, G. M., "Problems in Intercultural Health Programmes," Pamphlet No. 12, *Social Science Research Council.* New York, 1958.

4. Margetts, Edward, "The Future For Psychiatry in East Africa," *East African Medical Journal* Vol. 37: No. 6, June 1960.

5. Gluckman, Max, *Custom and Conflict in Africa.* Oxford: Blackwell, 1955.

6. Burton-Bradley, B. C., "Some Implications of Betal Chewing Papua and New Guinea Transcultural Psychiatry," *Medical Journal of Australia* Vol. 2, 744–746, 1966.

7. Dubos, Rene, *The Mirage of Health: Utopias, Progress and Biological Change.* Garden City, New York: Doubleday and Co., Inc., 1961.

8. Millikan, Max, "Problems of Underdevelopment: An Economist's View," *American Journal of Psychiatry,* 1966, p. 1393.

9. Seventh Report of Expert Committee, *WHO,* pp. 5–20.

10. Bordeaux, M. and Kline, N. S., "Experiences in Developing Psychiatric Services in Haiti," *World Mental Health,* XIV, November 1962, pp. 1–13.

11. Douyon, Lamarque, *Bulletin de Statistiques Medicales.* Annee 1968–69.

12. Denber, H. C. B., and Bente, D., "Clinical Response to Pharmacotherapy in Different Settings," Proceedings of the Vth International Congress

of the Collegium Internationale Neuropsychopharmacologicum, *Excerpta Medica International Congress Series No. 129,* March 1966, pp. 28–31.

13. Wintrob, R. M., "Psychiatric Training and Treatment in Liberia," Paper Presented at Roundtable Conference on Psychiatry in Underdeveloped Countries, held in New York in 1967, Eastern Regional Meeting, American Psychiatric Association.

14. Jayasundera, M. G., "Mental Health Survey in Ceylon" in Caudhill, William, and Lin, Tsung-Yi (eds.), *Mental Health Research in Asia and the Pacific.* Honolulu: East-West Center Press, 1969, pp. 54–65.

15. Lin, Tsung-Yi, "A Study of the Incidence of Mental Disorder in Chinese and Other Cultures," *Psychiatry* 16:313–336, Nov. 1953.

16. Kohlmeyer, W. A. and Fernandez, Vellore, Psychiatry In India: Family Approach in the Treatment of Mental Disorders. Third World Congress of Psychiatry. Montreal, 1961. Typescript 2 pp.

17. Lambo, T. A., "Neuro-Psychiatric Observations in the Western Region of Nigeria," *British Medical Journal* II, 1385, December 1956; Lambo, "A Form of Social Psychiatry in Africa," *World Mental Health,* XIII 190–203, Nov. 1961.

18. 1967 Annual Report of the International Committee Against Mental Illness, New York.

19. Singer, Philip, Araneta, Enrique and Aarons, Louis, Integration of Indigenous Healing Practices of the Kali Cult with Western Psychiatric Modalities in British Guiana. Presented at the Tenth Interamerican Congress of Psychology, Lima, Peru, April 1966.

20. Gelfand, Michael, "Psychiatric Disorders As Recognized by the Shona," in Kiev, A. (ed.), *Magic, Faith, and Healing: Studies in Primitive Psychiatry Today.* New York: The Free Press, 1964, pp. 156–173.

21. Prince, R. H., and Wittkower, E. D., "The Care of the Mentally Ill in a Changing Culture (Nigeria)," *American Journal of Psychotherapy* XVIII: No. 4, 644–648, Oct. 1964.

22. Field, M. J., *Search for Security: An Ethnopsychiatric Study of Rural Ghana.* Evanston, Ill.: Northwestern University Press, 1960.

23. Spens, T., Social Aspects of a Health Education Programme in Trans-Volta Togoland. Paper to Seminar on Social and Technological Change, Institute of Commonwealth Studies. London (unpublished).

24. Amara, I. B., "Psychiatric Problems—Observations in Sierra Leone and Liberia," Paper presented at Roundtable Conference on Psychiatry in Underdeveloped Countries, held in New York in 1967, Eastern Regional Meeting, American Psychiatric Association.

25. Beaubrun, M. "Psychiatry in the Caribbean," Paper presented at Roundtable Conference in Psychiatry in Underdeveloped Countries, held in New York in 1967, Eastern Regional Meeting, American Psychiatric Association

26. Argandona, Mario and Kiev, Ari, "Social Psychiatry in Latin America: Report on the Cali Project," to be published.

Index

INDEX

213

218 Index